Networks of Collective Action

A Perspective on Community Influence Systems

This is a volume of

Quantitative Studies in Social Relations

Consulting Editor: Peter H. Rossi, University of Massachusetts, Amherst, Massachusetts

Networks of Collective Action

A Perspective on Community Influence Systems

Edward O. Laumann
Department of Sociology
University of Chicago
Chicago, Illinois

Franz U. Pappi
Zentrum für Umfragen, Methoden und Analysen (ZUMA)
Hilfseinrichtung der Deutschen Forschungsgemeinschaft
Mannheim, Germany

ACADEMIC PRESS   New York   San Francisco   London

A Subsidiary of Harcourt Brace Jovanovich, Publishers

COPYRIGHT © 1976, BY ACADEMIC PRESS, INC.
ALL RIGHTS RESERVED.
NO PART OF THIS PUBLICATION MAY BE REPRODUCED OR
TRANSMITTED IN ANY FORM OR BY ANY MEANS, ELECTRONIC
OR MECHANICAL, INCLUDING PHOTOCOPY, RECORDING, OR ANY
INFORMATION STORAGE AND RETRIEVAL SYSTEM, WITHOUT
PERMISSION IN WRITING FROM THE PUBLISHER.

ACADEMIC PRESS, INC.
111 Fifth Avenue, New York, New York 10003

United Kingdom Edition published by
ACADEMIC PRESS, INC. (LONDON) LTD.
24/28 Oval Road, London NW1

Library of Congress Cataloging in Publication Data

Laumann, Edward O
    Networks of collective action.

    (Quantitative studies in social relations series)
    Bibliography: p.
    Includes indexes.
    1.   Social surveys—Germany, West.   2.   Community
leadership—Case studies.   I.   Pappi, Franz Urban,
joint author,   II.   Title.
HN450.L37   309.1'43   75-36649
ISBN 0—12—437850—1

PRINTED IN THE UNITED STATES OF AMERICA

To Eric, Lisa, and Urban

Contents

PART 2 THE COMMUNITY INFLUENCE SYSTEM

PART 3 THE INTERFACE BETWEEN COMMUNITY AND ELITE

List of Figures

List of Tables

Preface

For some time, we have been fascinated with the problem of explaining how social groupings of any complexity come to make collective decisions that are more or less acceptable to their diverse membership. Of the many approaches to this problem that have been proposed, we were particularly struck by the promising possibilities of tackling it from the perspective of network analysis. By examining the myriad networks of relations linking a collectivity's members to one another in continually forming and realigning coalitions in support or opposition to particular courses of collective action, we hopefully will be able to identify a set of principles organizing both the structures of and the underlying processes in these networks. Currently enjoying a burgeoning of scholarly interest, this perspective had already provided us a mode of attack for studying the complex interrelationships among social groupings in a large metropolitan system (Laumann, 1973). The methodological tactics devised in this earlier work provided a useful starting point for studying the intricacies of the widely ramifying linkages among community influentials and their "subject" population. At the outset, we should stress, however, that despite the considerable attention given in this book to methodological matters and illustrative data analysis, we conceive our central task to be that of building a theoretically informed research framework for the structural analysis of social systems.

To this end, we pay special attention to two fundamental issues in structural analysis: First, how does one most usefully define or identify the elementary units, be they individuals, corporate actors, or population subgroups, that comprise a given social system, and in what ways should these elementary units be characterized or differentiated from one another? And, second, what are the relational modalities by which these actors are linked to one another in ways that are relevant to understanding how their individual preferences and behavior are coordinated or integrated with one another for purposes of collective action (i.e., to achieve collective goals)? In the course of examining these and related theoretical questions, we are forced to explore a number of other intriguing substantive questions about the structure and functioning of community elite decision-making systems, the nature and role of different types of influence resources in such systems, leadership strategies, typologies of community controversies, value and issue preferences of elite members and population groups, the types of coalitions and their stability, the aggregational biases of integrative subsystems in articulating the collective demands of the rank-and-file members subject to their control, the causal model for the formation of a community affairs influence structure, and many more. Each of these derivative questions clearly deserves more attention than we shall give it. Our brevity of treatment is justified only insofar as our tentative answers clothe our more ambitious theoretical speculations with sufficient substance to demonstrate their empirical implications and plausibility. We surely do not intend the particular community case study we discuss in such detail to serve as validation of our general propositions—but merely as a convenient empirical illustration of our overall theoretical and methodological strategy.

This book is the result of a seemingly fortuitous concatenation of events and circumstances. With hindsight, perhaps we could argue that our collaboration was inevitable, especially if we take seriously the perspective adopted in this book with respect to the density and interconnectedness of social networks grounded on particular substantive concerns. But our experience with the "small world" phenomenon, so often remarked upon at academic cocktail parties, still amazes us. Certainly when the senior author arrived in Cologne in the late summer of 1970 to begin his sabbatical from the University of Michigan, primed to put the finishing touches on his book about social relations among white men in Detroit, little did he suspect that he would soon become deeply involved in an extended and personally rewarding collaborative effort with a German researcher of whom he had not yet heard.

To be sure, the choice of Cologne to spend the sabbatical year was not entirely accidental. Long interested in facilitating greater interchange between German and American sociologists, Erwin K. Scheuch, one of the principal professors of sociology at the Universität Köln and Co-Director of the Zentralarchiv für empirische Sozialforschung and the Institut für vergleichende Sozialforschung, had been one of Edward Laumann's graduate teachers at Harvard and had expended considerable effort in arranging his coming to Cologne. Ironically, Franz Pappi, then a research associate at the Zentralarchiv, was in Ann Arbor at the time of Laumann's arrival in Cologne for his second summer of participation in the program of the Inter-University Consortium for Political Research. Upon his return from Ann Arbor in late August, Pappi received notification that his grant application to fund a replication of Laumann's earlier work on subjective social distance and the social class structure had been approved. In applying for the grant, Pappi was quite unaware of Laumann's plans for coming to Cologne. It was during the course of our early discussions on how best to mount the replication study in a German community that the more ambitious conception of the research reported here began to take shape.

In sum, we were members of at least three common networks. We were both in Scheuch's personal network; we shared a number of mutual acquaintances and friends in Ann Arbor, all of whom were professionally active in areas of research related to ours and likely to call each of us to the other's attention; and, finally, we belonged to a much larger "invisible college" of researchers interested in studying the community from the vantage point of social stratification and political sociology. In addition, we shared a number of personal characteristics, including being almost of identical age and at similar stages in our professional careers, as well as sharing a common admiration for the work of Talcott Parsons and an enthusiasm for quantitative methods of sociological inquiry. Finally, Edward was of German ethnic extraction and knew a moderate amount of German, while Franz was of a cohort heavily exposed to things American in his youth as a result of the American Occupation and was especially fluent in English. It is thus not so difficult to construct a most plausible post hoc account implying the inevitability of our meeting and collaboration.

Acknowledgments

So many colleagues and graduate students, both in Germany and in the United States, have played diverse and, at times, critical roles in contributing to the successful completion of this broadly conceived project that it is difficult to know where to begin in acknowledging our intellectual and other debts. Throughout the project, our German colleagues, especially Professor Erwin Scheuch, Drs. Hans-Dieter Klingemann and Max Kaase, have in their different ways provided an appreciative and supportive audience with timely and useful intellectual advice and technical facilitation. Our German research assistants, Dipl. Soz. Regina Perner and Dr. Karl-Heinz Reuband, and research associate, Erwin Rose of the Zentralarchiv, contributed much to the successful design and implementation of the data-collection procedures, as did the Arbeitsgemeinschaft für System- und Konzeptforschung (Köln) (and especially the field work supervisors, Drs. Karl-Heinz Diekershoff and Gustav Kliemt), which did all the interviewing for us. Our "feeling" for Altneustadt was greatly enhanced by the astute and perceptive observations of Mrs. Perner, who enjoyed an intimate familiarity with the community, having lived there for four to five years before the study began. During the data-analysis phase of the project, two different teams of graduate assistants in the United States provided invaluable assistance, including Richard Senter, Lois Verbrugge, John Blair, Dan Ayres, William Roy, and Bruce Fireman at the University of Michigan, and Peter Marsden, Joseph Galaskiewicz, and Margaret Troha at the University of Chicago.

While at the University of Michigan, we greatly benefited from the professional criticisms of our faculty colleagues on different phases of our argument, including Professors Paul Siegel, Werner S. Landecker, James C. Lingoes, Michael Flynn, and Otis Dudley Duncan (now at the University of Arizona). In coming to the University of Chicago in the middle of the project period, the senior author was exposed to an even wider range of perspectives, critical as well as supportive of what we were trying to do. We are especially grateful to the following faculty colleagues for their stimulating intellectual and technical criticism: Professors Morris Janowitz, David McFarland, Shelby Haberman, Terry Clark, James S. Coleman, William Wilson, and Harrison C. White (Harvard). As is customary in such things, we absolve them all of any responsibility for the mistakes we made in attempting to take advantage of their suggestions.

Finally, we gratefully acknowledge the financial support from the following organizations: Landesamt für Forschung im Ministerium für Wissenschaft und Forschung des Landes Nordrhein-Westfalen (providing funds for the data collection in 1971), the Deutsche Forschungsgemeinschaft and the Heinrich-Hertz-Stiftung (for travel grants to the United States for the junior author), the Ford Foundation's Behavioral Science Postdoctoral Fellowship (held by the senior author in 1970–1971), and the National Science Foundation (GS-32002 and Soc. 75-13113) (for data-analysis operations in the United States and travel expenses to Mannheim, Germany, to complete the manuscript in the spring of 1975). We are especially appreciative of the physical and computational facilities provided by the Zentralarchiv für empirische Sozialforschung (Köln), the Center for Research on Social Organization at the University of Michigan, and the Zentrum für Umfragen, Methoden und Analysen (Mannheim). Technical illustrations were prepared by Eugene Leppanen at the University of Michigan, Technical Illustration Department of the Office of Research Administration, and by Dwight Osborne at the University of Chicago's Audio–Visual Department. Mr. James Bone and Mrs. Earline Franklin provided exemplary secretarial assistance in preparing the manuscript for publication. Margaret Troha deserves a special note of appreciation for her painstaking editorial services and the preparation of the subject and author indexes.

Perhaps a closing word on the availability of our data for secondary analysis. Some scholars have already used our data for secondary analyses, including Ronald L. Breiger (Harvard University), Ronald S. Burt (University of Chicago), and Michael O. Zängle (Regensburg)— thus, our book will not be the only report on our community. Scholars interested in secondary analysis of our data should know that the study can be retrieved from the data files stored at the Zentralarchiv für empirische Sozialforschung (Universität Köln). For identification of the data source, one may use either the pseudonym given the community in our English publications based on the elite data or the actual name of the community given in the German publications analyzing the cross-section survey data.

1

Introduction: A Theoretical and Methodological Overview

The central task of this monograph is to propose a theoretical and methodological strategy for studying the differentiation and integration of large-scale, complex social systems. Stated without further preamble, such a task is clearly far too ambitious, indeed downright presumptuous, because it raises nearly all the central issues animating the sociological tradition (cf. Parsons, 1937). In the limited compass of a single book, no one could hope to exploit the many, often fundamentally contradictory suggestions to be found in this rich heritage. We do, in fact, have a more modest goal: reporting in detail a case study of how a community in West Germany made a series of collective decisions about what it should do about some controversial issues. We hope, however, to do more than describe just another, possibly interesting case study. The case study was designed and executed explicitly to provide a vehicle for making more concrete and convincing a set of theoretical and research strategies of much broader applicability. These strategies, we believe, will prove useful, not only in studying community decision making more generally, but also in investigating other complex social systems that are confronted with finding an answer to the central integrative question: How does a social system as a whole establish priorities among competing sets of ends (or goals) requiring the expenditure of its scarce resources (means), given the existence of competing standards for evaluating these alternatives among its component actors?

1

As an initial orienting framework for answering this and related questions, we have found very useful a freely interpreted application of the action scheme developed by Talcott Parsons and his students over the past 25 years.[1] Especially helpful have been elaborations of the action scheme in the past 15 years with respect to the structural and functional differentiation of societies according to the AGIL paradigm and the treatment of money, power, influence, and commitment as integrative mechanisms in complex societies (cf. Parsons, 1951, 1960, 1966, 1969; Parsons and Smelser, 1956). We should emphasize here the phrase "freely interpreted" since we have not always rigorously followed Parsons' dicta either because they seemed unnecessarily restrictive and simply wrong on substantive grounds or because they eluded our best efforts to operationalize them.

Although we shall assume the reader's familiarity with at least the broad outlines of Parsons' approach, it still may be helpful to highlight those features of special relevance to us. First, we wholeheartedly endorse his assumption that social systems must be treated as open-ended rather than closed systems. That is, social systems are analytically distinguishable from their environments which consist primarily of other social systems and with which they maintain continuing and essential transactions of needed resources (or inputs) and system-produced "outputs." These transactions are dually consequential in that they may serve either to maintain the internal arrangements among the focal system's components (that is, its structure) or to change them. Changes in these internal arrangements may also be caused by a variety of intra-system processes. Second, Parsons asserts that structural differentiation of a social system tends, over time, to lead to subsystems performing more functionally specialized roles for the larger system. Moreover, the interchanges among the component subsystems (which may, for certain purposes, be treated as systems in their own right) serve to regulate the levels of activities of the subsystems with regard to one another.

Parsons does emphasize the fact that his scheme is analytic and abstract by design and, consequently, that a given empirical phenomenon cannot be equated on a strict one-to-one basis to his analytic scheme. To do so is to be guilty of the fallacy of misplaced concreteness where one has reified one's analytic distinctions. In other words, a given empir-

---

[1] To be sure, Parsons' approach can be seen to be an important variant of an emerging "systems perspective" on social phenomena that has multiple roots in cybernetics, economics, and related social sciences as well as in the life and physical sciences (cf. Buckley, 1967, 1968; Katz and Kahn, 1966; Sztompka, 1974). We have chosen to follow Parsons' formulations primarily because they are the most self-consciously articulated with respect to the analysis of social systems.

ical phenomenon may be treated in radically different ways, depending on the investigator's analytic purposes in following a Parsonsian approach. To maintain this distinction between the analytic and the real, however, is very difficult in practice, especially since Parsons has provided so few operational rules to guide the empirical investigator in avoiding these very pitfalls. It is precisely this difficulty of building operational bridges from Parsons' highly abstract formulations to the real world that has led so many empirically oriented investigators simply to abandon attempts to do anything with the scheme, despite its obvious attractions as one of the few systematically coherent, comprehensive approaches to the study of system differentiation and integration. We do not for a moment claim that we have succeeded in operationalizing Parsons' scheme when so many others have failed. Rather, we propose only to use the scheme as a sensitizing framework that alerts us to problems that we and others might otherwise overlook. It is on these grounds that we rest our plea for the right to make a "free translation" of Parsons' intent.

Of course, many others have found more serious difficulties in Parsons' scheme than that of rendering adequate empirical translations (cf. Black, 1961; Buckley, 1967; Gouldner, 1970). We woud like to note a few. Perhaps unfairly, in our view, Parsons has often been criticized for making overly restrictive assumptions about the conditions for maintaining system stability or order (that is, pattern maintenance) in the face of ubiquitous forces for social change both from within the system and from without (cf. Dahrendorf, 1959, 1968). Parsons' emphasis on the mechanisms for maintaining social order has been a special point of attack for his critics (e.g., Wrong, 1961). Especially problematic has been their exaggeration of the generality of Parsons' assumption of an overarching value consensus shared by all, or at least most, members of the social system, be it a society, community, complex organization, or small group, as a result of their socialization to the system's core values and other mechanisms of social control. Theorists stressing the role of coercion and the differential power of system members in maintaining social order and determining collective decisions have also faulted Parsons' apparent reluctance to discuss the ubiquity of social conflict (cf. Lenski, 1966; Dahrendorf, 1968; Gouldner, 1970). While these concerns may have some validity, we find nothing inherent per se in Parsons' treatment of integrative mechanisms that precludes the analysis of conflictual processes. Indeed, given Parsons' early training as an economist and his resultant fascination with the institutionalization of the market, it is not at all surprising that he has long recognized the central significance of competitive processes, usually ultimately organized around some set of more inclusive system rules, as key integrative mechanisms in highly differentiated systems (cf. Parsons and Smelser, 1956).

It is also true, however, that Parsons has tended to downplay the discussion of social conflict in the development of his theoretical apparatus. Therefore, we have found it useful to turn to theorists who are much more explicit in dealing with the sources of structural differentiation in conflicts of interests arising from the division of labor and the unequal distribution of power and authority (cf. Dahrendorf, 1968; Ossowski, 1963; Lenski, 1966; Giddens, 1973; Sztompka, 1974). Although we are greatly oversimplifying the matter, we might say that Parsons directs our attention to social values as channeling social behavior toward certain ends and to the possibility that these values themselves may ultimately be in conflict with one another. The so-called "conflict" theorists, on the other hand, remind us of the importance of real differences of interest resting on the division of labor (that is, the class structure in the Marxian sense) and differential power and influence in accounting for recurrent conflicts in large-scale complex social systems.

In other words, we shall argue that large-scale systems are usually differentiated around at least two axes or dimensions of potential cleavage and/or social differentiation. The first, which we shall call the *adaptive axis*, refers to the extent and character of the division of labor in the system resulting in a number of population subgroups who differ significantly from one another in their characteristic round of daily work activities and in the corresponding rewards and privileges associated with these occupational activities. For societal social systems, this roughly corresponds to Weber's treatment of the economic class structure. As we shall see, it is here that discussions of objective interest differentiation have special relevance.

The second, which we shall call the *pattern-maintenance axis*, refers to the differentiation of the population into subgroups holding distinctive social values regarding the desirable or ideal states of the social system of which they are members. The bases for differentiation of value commitments in a population are quite varied and may ultimately depend on the degree to which given population subgroups form distinctive groupings that prefer to confine intimate social interaction among themselves (cf. Laumann, 1973; Pappi, 1973b, 1974). Two bases are, however, especially noteworthy. The first relates to membership in what Weber called *status groups* that have various ascriptive criteria for membership, such as age, religion, ethnicity, place of residence, and race. The second relates to membership in distinctive population subgroups determined by the division of labor that may at times develop distinctive value preferences, such as a working class subculture.

PRINCIPLES OF STRUCTURAL ANALYSIS

In relating this abstract discussion more directly to our current concerns, we shall argue that the first theoretical and methodological task in studying system differentiation and integration is to devise a way that can be replicated and falsified of answering the following question: How is a given social system differentiated? Logically this question comes before the integrative question of the opening paragraph. Unfortunately, there can be no unique answer to the question of system differentiation because, according to Parsons, a system may be differentiated in any number of ways, depending on the questions the analyst is interested in answering. It is, of course, also true that certain bases of social differentiation are likely, in any given empirical case, to be of special salience and significance (cf. Blau, 1974). The evident importance of certain bases of structural differentiation in a social system—evident, that is, both to the members and to the observer—reduces the apparent arbitrariness of the analysis.

This, then, is, above all, a monograph on social structural analysis. Structure and various descriptive terms related to structure, such as hierarchy, dominance, structural differentiation, structural change, power or class structure, and so on, are probably the most popular concepts in the sociological lexicon. Despite the many differences in nuance that various authors associate with the term "structure," the root meaning refers to a persisting order or pattern of relationships among some units of sociological analysis, be they individual actors, classes of actors, or even behavioral patterns (cf. Nadel, 1957: 1–19; Mayhew, 1971; Blau, 1974, 1975). The apparent consensus in the usage of the term masks the unfortunate fact that there is little agreement on the concepts in terms of which, and the methodology whereby, one measures, or perhaps more modestly, describes given "social structures." Unless, however, one can develop some means of adequately describing the structure of a system, one can hardly turn to what is perhaps a more fascinating problem of describing structural change in that system.

Elements of Social Structures

Many of the results to be reported in this book will be based on new procedures for describing social structures and their principles of organization. Armed with strategies that can be replicated and falsified for describing such structures, we can then make some preliminary attempts to describe how one structure is related to another and how given social structures may be used to account for particular collective decision-making processes and outcomes. In analyzing a social system, we must first identify the individual *actor* (be it an actual person, a corporate actor, or a set of actors) *in* a particular kind of *social position* in that social system (cf. Parsons, 1951). It is important to bear in mind the distinction between *incumbent* and *social position,* inasmuch as an incumbent of a given social position may in fact simultaneously occupy many other positions. An earlier formulation of these distinctions further argued:

> At this stage of theoretical development it is impossible to relate a given individual's set of unique social positions in society (with respect to his manifold role relations with specific other family members, neighbors, work partners in a particular firm, and so on) to another individual's set of unique positions. We are forced for analytic purposes to categorize social positions into aggregates that hopefully share a sufficiently common core of performance requirements so that the positions may be treated as more or less equivalent. Consequently, since we will be discussing a complex urban social system, the individual's set of social positions will be characterized categorically, that is, in terms of his group memberships and social attributes, such as religious affiliation (including denomination), ethnic origin, occupation, and the like. In short, a person's social position locates him with respect to others in the community within some socially defined and differentiated domain [Laumann, 1973:3].

A *social structure* will be defined as a persisting pattern of social relationships among social positions (see Laumann, 1966). A *social relationship* is any direct or indirect linkage between incumbents of different social positions that involves mutual, but not necessarily symmetric, orientations of a positive, neutral, or negative affectual character and/or may involve the exchange of goods, services, commands, or information (see Homans, 1951; Parsons, 1951; Blau, 1964). The unit of structural analysis is, then, the specific relationship obtaining between any pair of actors, as defined earlier. The absence of the specified relationship between a pair is as theoretically important as its presence. Note that an important theoretical and methodological problem in analyzing any structure of social relations is the determination of its symmetric or asymmetric character—that is, whether the relationship typically involves relative parity between the participants with respect to the exchange of goods, affect, or services, or whether there is an unequal exchange of services or resources, such as in an authority relationship in which one participant gives commands and the other obeys.

Postulates of Structural Analysis

Our current work permits us to go considerably beyond the arguments concerning social structure advanced in Laumann (1973), whose analysis was confined only to interpersonal ties of intimacy. To achieve this generalization of approach, we have had to adopt three postulates.

Postulate I (relationship-specific structures) asserts that there exists a multiplicity of social structures in any complex social system that arises out of the many possible types of social relationships linking positions to one another.

Social positions are arranged with respect to one another as a function of the pattern of social relationships directly and indirectly linking them. Positions that are close together because they have close links with respect to a given type of social relationship (e.g., friendship, business ties, neighborhood, or information exchanges on community affairs) can be "far apart" when a different relationship, in which the positions do not enjoy either direct or indirect links, is considered. In short, relationship-specific structures arrange positions in quite different patterns of association, and there is no inherent theoretical reason to suppose that these different patterns are to be regarded as more or less adequate approximations of *the* "true" underlying social structure. On the contrary, each structure may be thought of as reflecting its own logic of social and functional constraint. In other words, a social structure of intimate association among social positions has no logically necessary implication for determining the social structure of political dominance relationships, although one might anticipate some empirical correspondence between the two. Note that this postulate does not preclude the formulation of a theory of structural priority, which would hold, as in certain Marxian formulations, that certain types of relationship structures are more fundamental (in the sense of being formative) than others.

Postulate II (distance-generating mechanism) asserts that, for any given relationship-specific structure, there exists a principle of systematic bias in channeling the formation of (or making more likely the) relationships between certain kinds of positions and the avoidance of such relationships between others.

In other words, we assume that relationships among social positions are usually not formed on a strictly random or chance basis, but rather in accord with some principle of the differentiation among positions. When discussing the distance-generating mechanism for social structures of intimate association, for example, Laumann (1973:5) argued that: "Similarities in status, attitudes, beliefs, and behavior facilitate the formation of intimate (or consensual) relationships among incumbents of social positions." And, conversely, that: "The more dissimilar two positions are in status, attitudes, beliefs, and behavior of their incumbents, the less likely the formation of intimate (or consensual) relationships and, consequently, the 'farther away' they are from one another in the structure." He was then able to interpret the relative proximities among various ethnoreligious groups by pointing to their differentiation in relative social prestige, socioeconomic status, and commitment to religiously linked activities.

By Postulate II, we are merely asserting that there exists some distance-generating mechanism aranging the relative proximities of positions for every social relationship. The nature of this mechanism will, of course, differ from one type of relationship to another. For instance, the distance-generating mechanism for a structure involving actors' work contacts outside his immediate circle of co-workers would not appeal to shared social values, as in the case of the intimacy structure, but to instrumentally required contacts for the execution of their work responsibilities. That actors thus connected would also be concerned with mutual personal attractiveness to the same degree as they are in establishing a friendship relationship is quite unlikely, especially in very large systems. Whatever the distance-generating mechanism, it is what will be meant by the *principle of organization* of the social structure under analysis.

Finally, *Postulate III* (structural contradictions) holds that, given a plurality of relationship-specific structures predicated on different principles of organization, structural contradictions are possible features of any complex social system.

A structural contradiction exists when the relative proximities of social positions in a given relationship-specific social structure are negatively correlated with those of another structure. In other words, positions that are in close proximity in one structure are far apart in another. To the extent that several functionally significant social structures result in similar. arrangements of positions (that is, to the extent that proximities of positions in various social structures are positively correlated), then one may speak of the social system in question as being *structurally crystallized.*

Structural crystallization may have serious *negative* implications for the overall functional integration of the system, insofar as all the various relationship structures tend to place the same positions either close together or far apart. One result would be that disparate positions (that is, positions that are some distance from one another) would have very few links between them by which to communicate and coordinate (mediate) their respective needs or claims on the system as a whole. In short, a structurally crystallized system tends to be characterized by groupings of similarly circumstanced positions with respect to their patterns of forming various relationships, with the groupings themselves located at some distance from one another. The reader will readily see how the postulate of structural contradictions may be linked to the classic discussions in political sociology of crosscutting versus reinforcing societal cleavages and cross pressures on voting decisions (cf. Lazarsfeld *et al.*, 1944; Lipset, 1963a,b).

Summarizing our discussion thus far, we shall argue that the structural differentiation of large-scale complex social systems has two fundamental implications for the integrative problems that such systems confront. First, structural differentiation is the basis of the objective differentiation of interests—that is, it is the base for the differentiation of claims for scarce goods, services, and facilities that component actors make on the larger social system and for the differentiation of means (or relative power) by which they assert these claims with greater or lesser effect. Second, structural differentiation is also likely to lead to the differentiation of evaluative standards (values) that are used by various system elements to specify and establish the priorities among competing ends or goals that the system should collectively seek to achieve. With these implications in mind, we are at last in a position to discuss the integrative question posed at the outset.

MODELS OF INTEGRATION

The history of modern social science, as we have already suggested, can almost be written in terms of the efforts to provide answers to this question. The question in its most general form, of course, admits of many answers, whose validity depends on what one is prepared to assume and on one's purpose. It is perhaps foolhardy to suppose that one could identify any simple way of codifying these answers that would do justice to their variety and subtlety. For our limited purposes, however, we find it useful to distinguish between three broad varieties of answers, within which one may identify many subvarieties and many intermediate positions as one moves from one variety to the next.

At one extreme, there are those models of the utilitarian tradition that take a radically individualistic or atomized stance in which the component units are assumed to be many, with quite varied wants and capacities, and none of which can decisively influence the outcome by its own behavior. The exemplar of such an approach is, of course, the classical economists' model of the perfect market which functions as an integrative or collective decision-making mechanism in the sense that, through the competitive interaction of many buyers and sellers, an equilibrium price and level of production and consumption is achieved that is not intentionally imposed by any single component actor. Integration is achieved by impersonal market forces, and the evaluative standard maximized is some essentially arbitrary standard of economic efficiency and rationality.

The second variety of models includes what can be termed social choice models that are distinguished from the first primarily in *(1)* their assumption of greater intentionality on the part of the component actors with respect to their efforts to influence collective (system-level) decisions, *(2)* their recognition that component actors may have greater or lesser impact on the determination of the outcome of particular collective decisions, and *(3)* their willingness to admit the possibility of a number of component actors acting in concert to influence such decisions through bargaining and other political procedures. Much of western political theory, especially democratic political theory, is concerned with specifying models that describe, both ideally and empirically, the linkages that obtain between the preferences of component members of a social system and its collective decision-making procedures and outcomes and that provide evaluative standards for judging the relative efficacy of given procedures -in maximizing some integrative standard (e.g., "the greatest good for the greatest number"). While the first variety of models excludes, by definition, the possibility of an elite or specialized subset of system members who have special functional responsibility for making collective decisions, social choice models are quite likely to distinguish between leaders and followers and typically see the nature of their interrelationships as being of critical importance.

Finally, coercive or administered models of integration assume, usually on grounds of "functional necessity," that some specialized subset of actors in a complex system must assume the responsibility of coordinating the diverse, functionally differentiated activities of its component parts in order to achieve system goals. Thus, a high level of centralized intentionality or planning with regard to integrative issues is assumed. Because of the extreme specialization of the parts, it is not meaningful or possible for the component units to participate in the resolution of integrative issues. At the societal level of analysis, theorists of the totalitarian state have minimized the role subordinate units may play in affecting integrative of collective decisions, while many organizational theorists (e.g., Weber, 1947; Thompson, 1967; Perrow, 1970) of administration have also tended to minimize the formative role of subordinates in influencing general organizational policy, at least in certain types of organizations.

Each type of model implies, of course, radically different research questions. The first denies the relevance of the elite–population distinction or even the utility of examining very closely the preferences and behavior of individual unit actors, while the third focuses most attention on the study of the elite, relegating the population under control to a negligible role. Only the second variety of social choice models recognizes, at least in principle, the coordinate importance of both population and elite and the significance of examining the interface (interrelationships) between them in accounting for the integrative process. Even within this broad type, one observes great variation between those subvarieties that lay greater stress on more impersonal market mechanisms for accomplishing integrative tasks (e.g., those radical democratic and pluralist models that treat elections as critical political markets that cause minor adjustments around equilibrium states [e.g., Parsons, 1960: 199–225]) and those that stress the greater and perduring influence of the elite over its population in resolving integrative issues, subject only to very broad and episodic checks on its behavior by the population at large (e.g., Cnudde and Neubauer, 1969; Lipset, 1959, 1963).

We have chosen to work within the broad framework of "social choice" models because they offer, in our view, the richest range of research questions both with regard to the differentiation of the population and its elite and with regard to their interrelationships. We recognize that, in doing so, we pay the price of having to work with a very complex model that requires specification of two subsystems, the population and its elite, as well as their interrelationships.

WHY COMMUNITY DECISION MAKING?

We have completed our general overview of the theoretical issues that form the basis of our research enterprise. Given this agenda, the question naturally arises: How can we best explore these issues empirically? Research on community decision making struck us as an especially attractive empirical base for at least four reasons. First, as will become apparent later, there are obvious analogues between our theoretical concerns and the types of issues that have centered considerable research attention on community decision making. Thus, we are able to build on a solid base of past research. Second, if it is suitably chosen, the research site can be of sufficient complexity and scale to provide a substantial empirical confrontation to our theoretical distinctions regarding structural differentiation and integration. Third, and closely related to the second consideration, we can select a site that will not generate a data base exceeding our current analytic capacities. As we shall show in the methodological discussion later, many of the procedures for structural analysis that we and others have proposed are still in the developmental stages. These procedures have rather fixed upper limits with respect to the number of cases that can be handled. Moreover, they require care in their application and cross checking of results with different procedures to enhance credibility, as well as to permit further refinement. Finally, the community and its elite is an especially accessible research site in the quite practical sense of being readily studied by a small research staff with limited budget and time. Empirical studies of whole societies using our theoretical vantage point and its implied data requirements are simply impractical at our present stage of development.

Some of these advantages are, of course, shared by other research traditions as well. For example, a classic issue in the literature on complex organizations (cf. March and Simon, 1958; Etzioni, 1961; Parsons, 1956; March, 1965; Thompson, 1967; Perrow, 1970; Lawrence and Lorsch, 1967) has been the problems of organizational decision making in the face of environmental uncertainty and internally differentiated levels of authority and functional responsibilities. There have been attempts to develop theories of the ways in which organizations should be structurally and functionally differentiated, given a general organizational goal. While this literature has indeed been of considerable help to us in formulating our ideas about differentiation and integration, it seemed to us at the time when we were designing our study that the community decision-making literature was somewhat more developed empirically and included a broader range of contributions from various theoretical vantage points. In any event, our decision to use community decision making as the research vehicle in no way precludes our turning to organizational studies for inspiration. We are, in fact, currently conducting a large-scale study of a 12,000-member professional organization and its associated professional community in a large American city, employing the procedures first developed in this study.

A HEURISTIC MODEL FOR STUDYING COMMUNITY SOCIAL SYSTEMS

Since we shall discuss the pertinent theoretical and research literature in the course of the analytic chapters themselves, it may be more useful to direct these introductory remarks to the highlighting of some key themes in this literature as markers to assist the reader in making his way through the complex argument. Even a cursory review of recent literature on community decision-making systems (cf. Clark, 1968a, 1973; Aiken and Mott, 1970; Bonjean *et al.*, 1971) impresses the reader with the number of promising developments in the field. After years of rancorous conflict over the "best" way to study the subject (cf. Walton, 1966a,b) and the relative merits of ruling elite and pluralist models of the elite subsystem (e.g., Polsby, 1963), investigators have begun to assess alternative assumptions and strategies in designing new studies. The emphasis of the 1950s and early 1960s on qualitative case studies, following the classic leads of Hunter (1953) and Dahl (1961), has shifted to comparative and quantitative questions in which investigators try to study as many communities as possible, using a wide range of quantitative data.

The contemporary emphasis tends at times to be excessively empirical and pays insufficient attention to the sort of theoretical issues we have been talking about. Nevertheless, a fairly explicit theoretical model that is quite compatible with ours underlies current efforts—namely, an open-ended system or input–throughput–output–feedback model of community decision making (cf. Clark, 1968b,c,d, 1973). Schematized in Figure 1.1, this model posits, first, that certain features of communities, including their population size and stability, regional location, age of community, industrial and economic base (wealth), and occupational and ethnoreligious heterogeneity, act as "inputs" in the sense of generally facilitating and constraining the resources of the community as a whole in collective enterprises and as sources of the various bases of structural differentiation of the community's population. Together with attributes of the communities' political institutions, these "inputs" are, in turn, associated with or determine certain features of their decision-making apparatus, such as the degree of centralization or diffusion of decision making (i.e., "throughput" or, in our terms, the internal organization of the elite subsystem). Finally, these determine how and which issues will be brought to decision and with what outcomes (i.e., policy "outputs" of the elite subsystem), which may, of course, have "feedback" effects sustaining or modifying the structures of the community and the elite subsystems and their interface. (In addition, Figure 1.1 will also serve as a synoptic view of the overall organization of the monograph and will be discussed at greater length in the concluding section of this chapter.)

Since "hard" data on inputs and outputs are more readily available and seemingly less ambiguous than information regarding the nature of the decision-making apparatus itself, the tendency has been to treat the throughput or "elite decision-making core"—the focus of earlier case studies—as a relatively unobservable "black box" about which only inferences or approximations can be made. For us, of course, examining this black box in some detail will be one of our central tasks. (We should note in passing that even interpretations of the so-called "hard" data on inputs are more ambiguous than is usually realized. These data are normally derived from published governmental statistics gathered for unrelated purposes. One result is that quite tenuous inferences about the meaning of the correlations, such as, for example, between community characteristics and the bases of structural differentiation in the com-

14

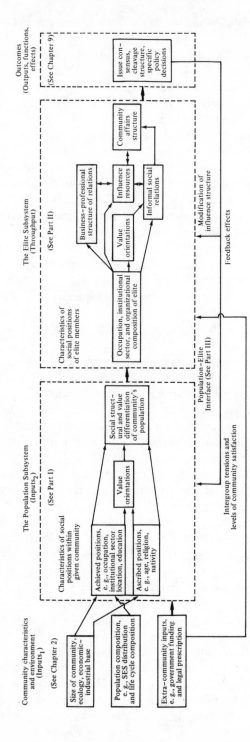

Figure 1.1 An input–throughput–output–feedback model for the analysis of community decision-making systems.

munity, must be made. In Part I, we shall propose a more rigorous exam-ination of the bases of population differentiation than has been cus-tomary.)

Perhaps the most active area of recent research has been concerned with policy outcomes and the assessment of their impacts (cf. Clark, 1973). Granting the obvious importance of these concerns, we shall not say much about them primarily because our theoretical objectives were already sufficiently ambitious, and we could not realistically incorporate any further complications into an already overburdened study design.

Given these current research interests, how can we justify our decision to undertake yet another intensive case study of a small city? It is to this question that we now turn.

ALTNEUSTADT: A CASE OF THE DROSOPHILA FRUIT FLY?

In the 11 data-analysis chapters to come, we shall devote a great deal of attention to an obscure city in the Rhineland. For the American reader, this may well tax his patience and credulity even more than did his reading at interminable length about Newburyport, Massa-chusetts, or Morris, Illinois (better known by their pseudonyms, Yankee City and Jonesville, respectively), which at least had the virtue of being small American communities. Some enthusiasts of community studies even claimed that they were microcosms of small-town America, if not of American society more generally. No such claims can or will be made for Altneustadt (a pseudonym). On the contrary, Chapter 2 will take some pains to show the specific ways in which Altneustadt is *atypical* of German cities of similar size in the same region. But then how do we lay claim to the reader's indulgence and patience?

We shall argue that Altneustadt is going to serve for us much the same role that *Drosophila* fruit flies have served for geneticists. Ad-vances in the theory and practice of genetics were greatly facilitated by the fact that certain simpler organisms, whether molds or fruit flies, could be closely observed, using rather crude methods, under highly con-trolled conditions. They had the further virtue of producing a large number of organisms in each of a number of generations, each genera-tion being of relatively short duration. The relative simplicity of their genetic material enabled investigators to discover some of the rules of genetic inheritance that appear to be useful in understanding the genetic makeup of higher organisms as well. It is most unlikely that a direct frontal attack on human genetics would have been successful at the very outset of serious study. Only with the experience and insights gleaned from studying less complex organisms could recent advances in population genetics have been possible (cf. Dobzhansky, 1962).

Now we are fully cognizant of the many pitfalls of using biological analogies to serve as models for sociological research. We have only recently begun to shake off the legacy of the nineteenth century organismic analogy to society in our theorizing, and we certainly are not interested in repeating such mistakes again, perhaps in a more sophisticated form. We do think, however, that some lessons may be profitably drawn from the history of genetics. Just as the geneticists were "really" interested in understanding the genetic improvement of domesticated plants and animals, human genetics, and the role of genetics in the evolutionary process, we are really interested in understanding how power and influence processes operate in large-scale, highly differentiated societies. Our ambition, however, just as theirs, far exceeds the grasp of the observational techniques currently available to us, not to mention the lack of theoretical and methodological procedures capable of reducing these observations into forms that are meaningful, coherent, and faithful at some level to the "real world." Studying complex metropolitan and societal-level decision-making systems simply because we need urgently to know how they work so that we can more effectively intervene to improve their undesirable characteristics—that is, because they have high social relevance for us as citizens—may not be the best strategy to adopt if it is our purpose to devise a scientific theory of system differentiation and integration.

In other words, we can know a town like Altneustadt with a comprehensiveness and intimacy and with multiple means of observing and validating our observations in a manner that is presently impossible to achieve for large metropolitan regions containing hundreds of thousands of inhabitants. We believe that coalition formation, resource mobilization, differential activation of persons and corporate groups in different decision-making situations, modes of network formation and degeneration are processes that occur in all differentiated systems in the course of integration, regardless of system scale. By closely observing these processes (or the results of these processes) in a particular system and devising techniques for doing so that can be replicated and falsified, we can gain insight into how they operate more generally and thereby fashion tools of broader applicability. Moreover, by trying to specify as clearly as possible the ways in which our particular case differs from others, we are explicitly stating some of the limitations of our generalizations. There are no doubt important differences among social systems as they increase in scale and complexity (cf. Coleman, 1973). We have tentatively assumed, however, that these differences are matters of degree and not of kind.

SOME GENERAL METHODOLOGICAL
OBSERVATIONS

The methodological discussion in this chapter is primarily intended to orient the reader to the various procedures we adopted in collecting and analyzing our data and to provide a general rationale for our broad methodological approach. Specific procedures and their rationales will be discussed in subsequent chapters as they become relevant to a particular problem. We assume that the reader has some background in statistics and will consult the cited technical references when he needs further clarification of our procedures. Even the novice to statistical analysis, however, should be able to follow most of our arguments without much difficulty. The heavy reliance on pictures and diagrams in the following chapters should provide good intuitive means for grasping the quantitative analysis.

To do structural analysis of the sort we have been discussing requires combining disparate techniques, some of which have only recently become available. Here we want to stress how certain techniques can be integrated into a broader research strategy that has sociological and not merely statistical justification. When considering what we needed to engage in social structural analysis, it became apparent that we would have to depart from some of the assumptions customarily made in research paradigms derived from conventional survey research that center upon atomistically conceived individuals (that is, the individual respondent as the unit of analysis, randomly chosen from a larger population universe). The social survey has been the principal technique for studying large population aggregates, and it clearly had to be used if we hoped to characterize certain distributional features of the population subsystem. Our central concern, however, was with the way in which unit actors are connected with or related to one another (remember the unit of structural analysis is the relationship between pairs of unit actors). Some real dilemmas were raised in fashioning an analysis that would permit shifts from the individual to the relational level of analysis. Laumann (1973) had already proposed some ways of doing this in his analysis of a Detroit sample survey. These procedures were readily applicable to our German community and provide the overall strategy adopted in Part I of this monograph.

Network Analysis

Currently receiving a good deal of rather uncritical theoretical and research attention, network analysis immediately recommends itself as the obvious strategy for dealing with our theoretical interests in social structures. What really makes up this approach? As so often happens with something seemingly new, closer examination reveals that network analysis consists of, at least in part, some rather old ideas that have been refurbished and made more attractive by being combined with sophisticated mathematical and quantitative tools (that is, sophisticated for sociology and anthropology). Moreover, it seems to refer to a veritable multitude of apparently diverse substantive and procedural applications. Starting with advances of this approach in the anthropological literature in the past 10 years (see Mitchell [1969b, 1974] for excellent reviews of these developments), rapidly growing interest in network analysis has been apparent in sociology as well (cf. Wellman and Whitaker, 1971; Kadushin and Rose, 1974).

A loose, metaphorical notion of networks has always been present in the social science literature; the novelty of the contemporary interest lies in its efforts to apply the concept in a more rigorous fashion. Mitchell (1974: 280) credits the anthropologist, J. A. Barnes, in his 1954 paper, for having raised "the notion of social network . . . from a metaphorical to a conceptual statement about social relationships in social situations." While possibly true in anthropology, it would appear that these ideas were very much in the air of other disciplines during the late 1940s and early 1950s as well (consider the work of Anatol Rapoport, Leon Festinger, and Charles Loomis, to mention only a few). Only more recently have disciplinary walls been breached sufficiently to reveal rather parallel concerns and developments.

Mitchell (1969b: 2) has proposed a useful working definition of a *social network* with which to start: "a specific set of linkages among a defined set of persons, with the additional property that the characteristics of these linkages as a whole may be used to interpret the social behavior of the persons involved." Unfortunately, if we were to limit ourselves strictly to this definition, we would not be able to do a network analysis of a social system whose component members exceeded a relatively small number. In other words, we would not be able to analyze large-scale, differentiated social systems. Consider, for example, that the number of possible pairwise relations for a city with about 20,000 inhabitants is almost 400 million, an unimaginably large number even for a large computer. To extract ourselves from this dilemma, we propose to define a social network in its most general form as a set of *nodes* (e.g., persons) linked by a set of *social relationships* (i.e., Mitchell's linkages) of a specified *type*. In addition, we propose to relax Mitchell's definition in two critical respects.

The first relaxation concerns the definition of the nodes. Specifically, we shall permit entities other than Mitchell's "real" persons—for example, corporate actors, such as business firms, or aggregates of persons sharing a particular attribute, such as ethnic or class groups—to act as nodes. This permits us to collect a number of persons into a given node and, thus, to reduce the number of nodes to a manageable number, even for very large populations of persons.

The second relaxation of Mitchell's definition concerns the treatment of a social relationship or linkage. What he quite clearly has in mind is a very concrete and observable transaction or exchange between two persons. We must weaken and relativize this notion if we hope to deal with large, complex systems. Earlier sociometric studies (e.g., Moreno, 1953; Davis, 1970; Newcomb, 1961) ascertained the presence of links between persons by asking them to choose, usually from a specified population, those others whom they regarded as friends, desirable co-workers, roommates or what have you. Well aware that even these choices differed among themselves with respect to intensity of affect, mutuality of choice, and frequency of interaction, to mention but a few characteristics that may differentiate social relations, the analytic procedures employed typically required an investigator to disregard all these facts and to code only the presence or absence of a choice. The more qualitatively oriented anthropologists (e.g., Epstein, 1969; Kapferer, 1969) usually make their own observations of specific behaviors occurring between two persons, rather than rely on simple self-report, in order to infer the presence or absence of a link or bond between two persons. Whether determined by observation or by self-report, one can, in this approach to network analysis, always ultimately reduce such information to a simple code of presence or absence.

How is one to infer the presence of links between nodes that are comprised of complex, nonobservable entities like ethnic or class groups? One solution is to relax the notion of a concrete social relationship, such as friendship, work partners, or marriage, into a stochastic relationship. That is, one can consider the "relationship" between two nodes consisting of complex entities as being indicated by the differential likelihood that their constituent elements have the relationship in question with one another. For example, members of the Protestant working class (PWC) node may be more likely to marry members of the Protestant middle class (PMC) node than members of the Catholic working class (CWC) node. Other things being equal, we might want to argue that the PWC node is more closely related to the PMC node than to the CWC node. Once the concept of social relationship in a network is broadened in such a fashion, there are any number of ways of measuring the relative presence or absence of relationships between nodes.

By adopting these two expedients, we are also in the position to broaden the concept of a "relationship" to include types of relations not normally considered in Mitchell's person-defined social nets. For example, transactions among corporate actors, such as the sharing of leadership personnel (e.g., interlocking directorships, cf. Levine, 1972; Zeitlin, 1974), flows of money, organizational information, and other forms of organizational support may become the basis for a network analysis (cf. Turk, 1973).

The hallmark of a network analysis, as noted in Mitchell's definition, is to explain, at least in part, the behavior of network elements (i.e., the nodes) and of the system as a whole by appealing to specific features of the interconnections among the elements. That is, network analysis assumes that the ways in which elements are connected to one another, both directly and indirectly, facilitate as well as constrain the element's roles. Nodes that are connected to others in such a way that they can "reach" most of the actors in the system who, in turn, must usually work through them to reach other actors are more favorably circumstanced to perform mediating and coordinating activities for the system of actors as a whole than are nodes who are linked to only a few other actors who are themselves poorly connected (cf. Bavelas, 1950).

Graph Theory and Blockmodeling Approaches to Network Analysis

Attractive as all these ideas may be, the critical question to ask at this point is whether or not one can devise means of systematically describing the structure of networks of any size and complexity. This is really what all the recent excitement about network analysis is about. Substantial inroads have, in fact, been recently made in the affirmative answering of this question. Indeed, one might almost say that we are embarrassed by our riches, since we seem to have more technical solutions than we have theoretical guidelines to choose among them. Let us postpone to the analysis of later chapters consideration of the practical problems of deciding how to define nodes and relationships empirically and confine our attention here to the more general methodological issues.

Broadly speaking, there have been at least two broad strategies for devising technical solutions for the analysis of network structure. The first, and by far the most developed and most frequently used, rests upon the mathematical theory of graphs and digraphs (cf. Harary *et al.*, 1965), while the second, blockmodeling, only recently developed by Harrison White and his associates (1976), rests on the strategic assumption of structural equivalence (cf. Lorraine and White, 1971).

The mathematical theory of digraphs is concerned with postulates and theorems relating to "abstract configurations called digraphs, which consist of 'points' and 'directed lines'" (Harary *et al.*, 1965: v). A graph consists of a set of points (i.e., our nodes) and connecting lines (i.e., our relationships) in which the direction of the lines is disregarded. Several graph theoretic ideas will be discussed to illustrate the basic approach, which is especially concerned with the nature of a graph's connectedness.

Consider the following sociometric (adjacency) matrix in which the rows and columns represent three persons, v_1, v_2, and v_3, and the entries in the cells are either "1" or "0" indicating whether or not v_i (in rows) chooses (is in relation with) v_j (in columns).

MATRIX 1.1
An Adjacency Matrix

	Chosen		
	v_1	v_2	v_3
Chooser v_1	0	1	0
v_2	0	0	1
v_3	0	0	0

This matrix may be diagrammed, as in Figure 1.2, where points represent persons and directed lines (arcs) between two points represent a relationship.

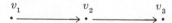

Figure 1.2 Graphic representation of Matrix 1.1.

A point v_j can be reached from point v_i if there is a path from v_i to v_j. In our illustration, v_1 can reach v_2 in a path of length "1" and v_3 in a path of length "2," and v_2 can reach v_3 in a path of length "1," but v_2 and v_3 cannot reach v_1. The reachable set $R(v)$ of a point v is the collection of points that can be reached from v. The *path distance* between two points in a digraph is the *minimum* number of directed lines that must be traversed in order to reach the second point from the first. (The path distance between two points in a graph is the *minimum* number of lines, disregarding direction [i.e., the adjacency matrix is symmetric], that must be traversed in order to reach the second point from the first.) A major technical advance has been the appearance of computer routines that permit the calculation of key graph theoretic quantities for much larger matrices than was heretofore possible. Even so, the upper limit seems to be about 1000 points (cf. Gleason, 1969; Farace, 1972; Richards, 1974).

Blockmodeling, in contrast to the graph theoretic approach, de-emphasizes the connectivity of structures and is more concerned with blocking groups of points on the basis of their structural equivalence; that is, individuals are treated as being in structurally equivalent locations (i.e., a block) when they have similar patterns of links with members of other blocks. A further advantage of the approach (in contrast to the graph theoretic approach which considers only one relationship at a time) is that an explicit machinery is provided for examining a number of relationships simultaneously. Thus, we may have in hand tools for developing a theory of relations. Unfortunately, blockmodeling was developed with appropriate computer programs only after the bulk of our data analysis using the graph theoretic approach was complete. Fortunately, very preliminary analysis of our data using blockmodeling by Ronald Breiger (personal communication) reveals results that are fairly consistent with those obtained using our procedures. It is still too early to assess the ways in which this new approach will enrich our theoretical understanding of social structure.

Data-Reduction Problems

To be sure, both approaches are presently limited to rather small numbers of nodes. Even a path distance matrix for 50 points is singularly complex, and it is difficult to comprehend its essential structure by inspection alone. It is obvious that some data-reduction procedures are needed to assist the analyst in describing such a network's structure. Again, we can distinguish two general strategies for this task: cluster analysis and multidimensional scaling. In cluster analysis (cf. Bailey, 1974), the end result is a set of discrete clusters of nodes, such as cliques; while in multidimensional scaling (cf. McFarland and Brown, 1973; Shephard *et al.*, 1972), the end result is a spatial solution where the points are mapped as a function of their proximities into a space, usually Euclidean, with a minimum number of dimensions. The advantage of multidimensional scaling over cluster analysis is that the relative locations of all points with respect to one another can be visualized, provided the solution requires no more than three dimensions. We find the spatial portrayal of social structure quite appealing, which is after all, according to Ossowski (1963: 19–25), implicit in most conceptualizations of structure. That the spatial solutions can be interpreted intuitively may not seem to be a great advantage from a rigorous theoretical standpoint, but we are convinced that, in the present state of social science research characterized by a dramatic lack of nontrivial formal theories, theory building can profit from this detour into *Gestalt* sociology.

The nub of the problem in multidimensional scaling is, of course, to devise plausible estimates of the proximities of pairs of points. There are usually a number of different ways to estimate these proximities, even when one's distance-generating mechanism is well-defined. Unfortunately, there is usually little theory or practical experience to help one in choosing the best ones. At times, we have had to proceed fairly arbitrarily on such issues. Fortunately for us, however, it turns out that various ways of calculating proximity estimates for a given structural problem seem to come up with similar spatial solutions—that is, the solutions are fairly robust (see Alba [1975] for a comparison of our results with several alternative estimates of the proximities in our elite social structures).

Perhaps our most radical innovations are concerned with the research strategy we devised for examining the relationships of various structures to one another and the causal model we proposed to account for the formation of structures. We have already noted in passing that one of the limitations of the graph theoretic approach to network analysis is its inability to handle more than one type of relation among a set of points at a time. Given our set of postulates for structural analysis, especially Postulate III on structural contradictions, however, we were confronted with the theoretical necessity of specifying methodological procedures for comparing and predicting structural arrangements. The obvious candidate for the unit of structural comparison is the relationship between a pair of points. Since, for a given social system, one can specify the set of member actors and this number implies a determinant set of possible pairwise relationships (in fact, $n[n-1]$ if asymmetric relations are permitted and $n[n-1]/2$ if only symmetric relations are permitted), and since the elements of nodes and possible links are invariant across relationship-specific structures, the possibility of comparing structures of a given social system is guaranteed by our approach. The problem is merely one of measuring the characteristics of these pairwise relationships. The tactic we adopted, and we believe with considerable success, was to use the interpoint distances of our multidimensional scaling solutions as structure-specific estimators of these characteristics. Finally, by appropriate modifications of even these assumptions, we have been successful in devising a strategy for mapping the pattern of relationships in a social system comprised of different types of nodes (e.g., specific persons and population subgroups).

PLAN OF THE BOOK

As the reader will recall, a synoptic overview of the monograph is presented in the open-ended system model schematized in Figure 1.1, which depicts the sequential development of our analysis of community structural differentiation and integration. The book is organized into three main parts. The first two parts take up the analysis of the sets of variables labeled the "population subsystem" and the "elite subsystem," respectively, in the figure (delineated by the dotted lines). The third part directs attention to the interrelationships between these analytically defined subsystems of the community social system.

More specifically, in Part I, we first describe the research site and its environmental context and then make a structural analysis of the internal social and value differentiation of the population subsystem. The results of this analysis will provide the central points of reference in studying the collective decision-making subsystem that has emerged in Altneustadt over the past 15 years. In Part II, attention is focused on the elite subsystem, the "throughput" structure in our model, and on its role in resolving specific community controversies. Finally, in Part III, we turn to a topic often neglected in studying democratically legitimized influence systems: the systematic theoretical and empirical characterization of the relationships between the elite and the population subsystems in the community. The only aspect of the model shown in Figure 1.1 for which we are unable to provide any empirical discussion is the consequences of the operations of these subsystems in sustaining or modifying their structures over time. With this broad overview of the organization of the book in mind, we can now describe in some greater detail the contents of specific chapters.

Chapter 2 describes the community in terms of its historical and environmental context as well as its contemporary demographic and socioeconomic composition. Using census-type data, we compare Altneustadt to all the other communities of comparable size in the region in terms of the descriptive schemes developed in factorial ecology. The results alert us to the specific features of our community that are typical and atypical of communities of similar size in the Rhineland and suggest some of the limitations of generalizations of our results.

Chapter 3 describes in considerable detail the procedures and results of our structural analysis of the social differentiation of the population subsystem. Following the leads of previous research, we identify generalized social positions in terms of occupation and membership in religious groups, the two most important bases of social differentiation in the community. Suitable manipulation of the information on the patterning of intimate social relationships among groups of incumbents of these positions yields measures of the social distances among the positions. The principles underlying the distance-generating mechanisms are then identified and tested for their explanatory power. Using the inferred social distances among the generalized positions in a cluster analysis, we construct a set of discrete, relatively bounded population groups that will be used as the analytic unit components of the population subsystem in the subsequent analysis.

Chapter 4 turns to the value differentiation of the population subsystem. After constructing a set of value scales to measure an individual's positions with respect to a variety of general social values regarding the economy, polity, social stratification, family, and religion, we characterize the population groups identified in Chapter 3 in terms of their value profiles and propose a procedure for representing the relative proximities of groups in terms of similarities in their value profiles (or value homophyly). Group proximities in terms of choices of social intimates and of value homophyly are shown to be similar, but by no means identical. The results are discussed with respect to the light they shed on the interest differentiation of the community population subsystem, which must somehow be taken into account by the community decision-making subsystem, to which we now turn.

The community decision-making elite is defined as the set of incumbents of theoretically identified categories of leadership positions in the various institutional sectors of community life. Two features of individual elite members are briefly noted in Chapter 5: *(1)* their primary and secondary locations in functionally defined institutional sectors, and *(2)* their relative influence status.

In Chapter 6, we turn to a wide-ranging, more qualitative account of these people and their informal relations with one another. Using a graph theoretic approach, we first identify a number of informal cliques and social isolates, at least with respect to informal participation in elite circles. The two most important cliques, the dominant CDU coalition and its arch rival, the SPD coalition, are described with regard to their personal and social composition, resource bases of influence, and general sociometric organization. Paralleling Part I, we then study the value similarities of the elite members, the set of value scales being comparable to those we used to characterize the population groups. We conclude the chapter with a description of differences between the coalitional groups with respect to strategies for performing leadership roles and preferences on specific issue outcomes. One of the purposes in providing such a detailed description of the elite members and their coalitions is to give the reader a good empirical basis for evaluating the results of the more formal and abstract analyses of the following chapters.

In addition to the informal network of the elite, we ascertained the business–professional relationships and the contacts regarding community affairs among elite members. In Chapter 7, we propose a general methodology for generating a theoretically meaningful description of relation-specific social structures and present our results in graphic form.

Instead of confining our interpretation of these structures to a looser, qualitative account, as we did in Chapter 6, we use the more rigorous causal modeling of path analysis in Chapter 8 to account for our target structure, the community affairs structure, in terms of the business–professional and informal social structures and other theoretically relevant characteristics of relationships between elite members. This causal model is our theory about the structural formation of the throughput subsystem.

These three chapters on the structure and functioning of the decision-making system set the stage for a discussion of the conflict structure of the community influence subsystem in Chapter 9. It is difficult to imagine a community comprised of a socially and economically heterogeneous population that does not disagree on the allocation of scarce community resources. More formally, a central premise of our analysis is that conflict is an endemic, necessary feature of *any* decision-making apparatus, which poses the fundamental functional problem of establishing binding priorities among competing goals. Consequently, using a theoretically grounded strategy for identifying community issues and tracing their impact on the formation of opposing factions and coalitions, we describe the way in which conflict or cleavage patterns are superimposed on the elite structure.

Up to this point, investigation of the elite system is based solely on individual actors in particular kinds of social positions and their interrelationships. In Chapter 10, we expand this narrow concept of an elite and include corporate actors as well. We propose some hypotheses about the systematic differences revealed in the cleavage structures for individual and corporate actors.

Compared to previous research on community influence, a novel feature of our study is that we propose some new tactics for systematically exploring the interface between the elite and the population subsystems. We begin with a study of the influence resource bases of the community leaders in Chapter 11. This problem is related to the interface question because at least some of the influence resources are ultimately rooted in the popular trust in and esteem for specific leaders that population groups have. First, we develop an analytic scheme for classifying the variety of influence resources. We then introduce a hypothetical model of the process of resource conversion into binding collective decisions. The model asserts that resources generated outside the elite subsystem must first be converted into intra-elite resources before they can have any impact on the implementative resource of authority and on the final decision itself. Following a more descriptive section on the distribution of influence resources among institutional sectors and oppositional cliques, we study the relationship between the types of resources that an elite member controls and the trust he gets from the population at large. In the last section of the chapter, we report some illustrative empirical evidence for our basic model of resource conversion.

Chapter 12 is more centrally focused on the population–elite interface. In order to construct this interface, we had to solve some perplexing methodological problems not previously encountered in the literature. These problems arise from the fact that we wanted to analyze a network consisting of two quite disparate kinds of nodes, namely, individual actors and population subgroups. In addition, the relationships themselves are essentially asymmetrical in character, being orientations of trust expressed by population groups toward specific elite members. The data to construct this "trust" space come from our cross-section survey of the population. (See Appendix A for a detailed description of the cross-section sample design.) Because we assume that the attributes of the elite members determine the trust that they instill in the population at large, we use these characteristics to predict the trust distances generated from the cross-section data. On the other hand, the same data device provides a means for answering the question regarding the types of influence resources to which given population groups have access.

Instead of summarizing the main arguments of the book, the concluding chapter formulates some general theoretical propositions about system differentiation and integration. These are intended to put back into focus the central theoretical agenda of the monograph that may have been obscured by our detailed empirical analysis. On the more speculative side, the propositions suggest some promising avenues to explore in future work.

PART 1

The Community: Context and Internal Structure of its Population Subsystem

2

Introducing the Community: The Research Site for an Illustrative Case Study

THE COMMUNITY CONTEXT

The site for our illustrative case study, Altneustadt (a pseudonym), is a German town of 20,000 inhabitants located not far from the Dutch–German border and some 20 miles from the nearest large city. Its labor force finds employment almost exclusively in the city or in its immediate vicinity. The town is located in rich farming country and functions as a service center for its primarily agricultural hinterland. At the time of the field work for our study, it still was a district (county) capital with a variety of governmental agencies and a correspondingly large number of public officials and bureaucrats. Having recently lost its district capital functions to a somewhat larger city in the region when two districts merged, it still retains some of its public service functions for the new district.

Historically, these public service functions have always been important to the city. During the Middle Ages, it served as the capital of a dukedom and later became a district capital and a garrison town. As a result of these governmental functions, the occupational composition of its population has always been heavily middle class. In the latter half of the nineteenth century, the garrison was removed, but another government-run operation was finally set up in the town after World War I:

a large repair shop for the state-owned railway system, which encouraged the immigration of some working-class people. The central or state government appears to have always felt a certain obligation for the economic and social well-being of the town—perhaps because of its strategic border location. From this, and perhaps only from this, standpoint, it was logical for Altneustadt to become a candidate for the location of a Natural Science Research Center that the state government wanted to establish in the late 1950s. This decision was finally made in favor of Altneustadt. At the time, it was already known that the railway repair shop was to be phased out of operation by 1959.

Today this Natural Science Research Center is the employer of about twice as many people as all local industry combined. About one-fifth of the center's employees are scientists, the overwhelming majority of whom live in Altneustadt. Compared to the research center and the public administrative sector, local industry is of relatively minor, but not negligible, importance. The town does have a number of small and intermediate light manufacturing plants owned by local businessmen. Compared to other towns of the same size in the state, a low percentage of Altneustadt's labor force is employed in the manufacturing (secondary) sector of the economy. The tertiary or service sector, the most important one for the town, is comparable in its proportion of the labor force only to larger cities in the region. At the time of the field work, the number of farmers living within the city limits was negligible. More recently, a number of neighboring villages were incorporated into a larger city administrative unit, resulting in a small increase in the proportion of farmers residing within the city limits.

The outstanding difference between Altneustadt and other towns in the region is the high percentage of *Akademiker* (people with university degrees) living there. Of the adults in Altneustadt, 7.3% are university-educated, compared to a mean of 2.7 for all towns of comparable size in the state. Altneustadt is, in fact, more than three standard deviations above this mean. This high figure is due to the major in-migration caused by the founding of the research center. Now almost 50% of the inhabitants are *Neubürger* who arrived after 1957, the founding date of the research center.

The majority of these *Neubürger* thus have distinctive status characteristics that are considerably different from those of the *Altbürger* (i.e., the native born). Coming for the most part from the universities and engineering or technical schools, they are highly paid salaried workers with urban backgrounds and have strong cosmopolitan and urban values and perspectives. In addition, they even tend to have different religious backgrounds, compared to the dominant Catholicism of the *Altbürger*.

Of the inhabitants living in the town since birth, 92% are Catholic, compared to 57% of those who arrived after 1957. Among the natural scientists, the percentage of Catholics is even smaller, being only 26%. This arises from the fact that Protestants and those without any religious preference are heavily overrepresented in natural science and technical occupations in Germany. The two major religious groups are evenly balanced in the population of the Federal Republic, the percentage of Catholics being 47%. Among people in the labor force with university degrees, however, the percentage of Catholics was only 39 in 1961, and this figure decreases to 31% among natural scientists (cf. Nellessen–Schumacher, 1969: 98). Thus, the scientists moving to Altneustadt appear to reflect fairly well the religious composition of their population universe.

Altneustadt differs from other cities not only with regard to the social composition of its population, but with respect to its growth rate as well. The population increase from 1961 to 1970, the two latest census years in Germany, was one-third (based on the 1961 figure), which is much higher than that of most other German cities. Altneustadt was almost completely destroyed at the end of World War II. Consequently, the inmigration did not start in 1957 with the establishment of the research center, but much earlier when the city was gradually reconstructed in the immediate postwar period. Although the "newcomers" in the early 1950s were predominantly former inhabitants, a small number were refugees from the eastern provinces of the former German Reich. The overall consequence of these postwar events is that the percentage of people who have resided in the city since their birth is quite low. Even if one disregards the population movements immediately caused by the extensive war damage, 23% of the adult population are residents since their birth, which is only half as large as that for German communities in general.

A SYSTEMATIC COMPARISON OF ALTNEUSTADT
WITH OTHER GERMAN CITIES

In recent years, a growing amount of research effort has been devoted to quantitative analyses of community decision-making systems. One objective of this research has been to detect general relationships between certain features of community-based decision-making systems, such as their degree of centralization, and community characteristics, including demographic, economic, legal–political and cultural attributes (cf. Clark, 1973: 13–26). Until the mid-1960s "researchers seldom allocated much attention to community characteristics differentiating their research sites from others." (Clark, 1973: 13) Even if a systematic comparison was attempted in a case study, as in Dahl's classic study of New Haven (1961), it was only to show that the community under study was sufficiently similar to other cities to guarantee meaningful generalizations.

Comparative community research (cf. Clark, 1973: 33–34; Gilbert, 1968; Walton, 1970; Aiken, 1970), however, has established some empirical regularities concerning the relationships between community characteristics and selected features of the community power structure. It is, therefore, incumbent on the investigator reporting a case study in detail to attempt to delineate, in as systematic fashion as possible, the ways in which his case is similar to and different from other communities in the relevant population universe. None of the empirical regularities uncovered to date is, of course, definitive in the sense that there are no exceptions to it. By highlighting particularities and similarities of the case to the relevant population of communities, however, one can at least assess some of the probable limitations and contingencies that should be kept in mind in evaluating generalizations drawn from an intensive case study. We have already noted some ways in which Altneustadt deviates in certain essential respects from other communities of comparable size in the region. We shall briefly summarize here the results of a more detailed examination of these comparative questions (see Pappi, 1973b, for a more extended treatment).

Factor analysis has often been used as a procedure for classifying census-type variables of local communities and constructing community profiles via the resulting factor scores. The results of these analyses have been very promising because there appears to be a stable set of dimensions differentiating communities, not only in the United States, but in other countries as well (cf. Berry, 1972). The three most important factors identified by Berry (1972) in his analysis of 1762 urban places in the United States are (1) the functional size of cities, (2) their socioeconomic status composition, and (3) the characteristic stage in the family life cycle of city residents. The latter two factors have been found to be the most important dimensions of social differentiation among residents of cities and of counties by other researchers as well (cf. Bonjean, 1971).

To obtain a comparative picture of the demographic and social structural characteristics of Altneustadt and those of other German cities, we also turned to a factor analysis of census variables. We restricted our universe to cities ranging in size from 10,000 to 32,000 inhabitants that are located in the same German province as Altneustadt, thereby eliminating the relevance of Berry's size factor in comparing communities. We then factor analyzed a set of 15 variables drawn from the 1970 German census and computed factor scores for our population of communities. Among the variables included were the percentages of blue-collar workers, salaried employees, and self-employed people, respectively, the percentages of the labor force in the secondary and tertiary sectors of the economy, respectively, certain features of the population distribution according to educational attainment, and demographic variables, such as mean age of the population, mean size of households, and marital status. The first two factors were used as a basis for comparison because they explained 72% of the total variance.

The percentage of people working in the tertiary sector of the economy had the highest positive loading on the first factor, with a corresponding high negative loading for percentage of labor force engaged in manufacturing. Closely linked with these variables were percentage of salaried workers on the positive end of the factor and percentages of blue-collar workers and people with only primary school education *(Volksschule)* on the negative end. Since percentage white collar and median school years also had high loadings on Berry's socioeconomic status dimension, we adopted his interpretation for our first factor. A high positive score on our first factor thus indicates that a community is heavily middle class in composition, while a high negative score indicates that a community is heavily working class in composition.

The second factor had high positive loadings for mean age of the population and the percentage of widowed people and high negative loadings for size of household and percentage unmarried, which justifies interpreting this factor as tapping the characteristic stage in the life cycle of community residents. In other words, a high positive factor score for this second dimension indicates a high mean age of the residents of a community, while a negative score indicates low mean age and younger families with children. A typical difference on this dimension would be one between a city with a lot of retired people and a city with many young families with children, a demographic characteristic, for example, of most newly built suburbs.

Altneustadt occupies the extreme position on the positive side of the first dimension and an intermediate position on the negative side of the second dimension. In other words, of all cities of comparable size in the region, it has the strongest middle class bias, whereas, with regard to family life cycle, it leans only slightly toward the negative extreme of the dimension characterized by a low mean age of the population and a relatively higher incidence of younger families with children.

Only 35% of Altneustadt's labor force are blue-collar workers, compared to a mean of 49% in all the small cities studied. The middle-class bias of Altneustadt is revealed even more clearly when we use self-identified class as an indicator. Only one-fifth of the adult population identifies itself with the working class, two-thirds with the middle class, and 10% with the upper middle class. The comparable figures from a cross-section of the adult population of West Germany are 38% working class, 51% middle class, and 8% upper middle class (cf. Pappi, 1973b).

As we already noted, Altneustadt has always had a middle-class bias in its social composition. After a long period with a stable class structure dominated by a partly self-employed and partly salaried middle class, there was a slight disturbance of this stability due to the working-class in-migration caused by the establishment of the railway repair shop in the 1920s. Together with the influx of refugees after World War II, this led to a small Protestant working class in the city. Both these movements, however, never had the profound impact on the social system of the local community as that of the in-migration caused by the establishment of the Natural Science Research Center. The differences in world views and life styles between the *Altbürger* and the predominantly Protestant upper middle-class *Neubürger* have almost inevitably led to many conflicts and tensions in accommodating (if not assimilating) the newcomers. These conflicts have generated a dynamic political situation with clearly delineated and perceived coalitions and interest structures. This provides a setting for studying a conflict structure very much concerned with what Lipset and others have called "status politics" rather than "class politics" (cf. Lipset, 1963) since most major groups share roughly similar "middle-class" socioeconomic status positions but differ fundamentally in their conceptions of appropriate status behavior and life styles (cf. Laumann and Senter, 1976; Reuband, 1974). These extensive social and value cleavages within the middle class, in fact, form the basis of our expectation that the central axis of structural cleavage in Altneustadt will be in the pattern-maintenance sector rather than in the economic or adaptive sector, which appears to be much more modestly differentiated into factions with more muted, negotiable conflicts of interest.

Of particular interest in this connection is the fact that the SPD (German Social Democratic Party), historically a party rooted in a working-class and predominantly Marxist world view, has been co-opted by the *Neubürger* as the vehicle for expressing their urban, secular and middle-class demands for social change in Altneustadt. Natural scientists and engineers have not been traditional recruits for the SPD. The Christian Democratic Union (CDU), on the other hand, has proved to be a reliable vehicle of control for the *Altbürger*. They manage to remain the dominant political coalition, especially since part of the agrarian hinterland became incorporated into the city (this is discussed later), albeit their hegemony, as we shall learn, has been successfully challenged on occasion.

One can hardly expect a single case to provide opportunities to explore in depth the full range of decision-making issues that have confronted communities even of comparable size in a given region. And Altneustadt is no exception. While more or less typical of communities in the region with respect to a number of compositional attributes, it still departs in important ways from other communities. The fact, for example, that it was almost totally rebuilt within the last 30 years has fundamental implications for the nature of urban renewal and the transportation policy options that it must face. These factors set it apart from other historical towns that did not suffer extensive war damage. Having one of only two natural science research center facilities in West Germany also creates an almost unique constellation of economic and social forces that have an impact on the political structure of the community. To our mind, however, it is precisely these obvious differences that provide the key reference points for getting a good conceptual grasp on the community's social and political structure because they are likely to throw into high relief the formative elements of these structures. We must, therefore, be most circumspect in our effort to generalize our particular empirical findings about collective decision-making systems to other communities. If our enterprise, however, is actually to devise theoretical and methodological procedures that can be validated in fine detail in an empirical situation readily grasped and understood on other, more intuitive grounds, this circumspection is a price we are quite willing to pay.

In the next two chapters, we shall explore in greater detail the major axes around which the community's population is socially differentiated and, correspondingly, differentiated in terms of commitments to certain social values with relevance for community affairs.

3

The Internal Social
Structural Differentiation
of the Community*

The theoretical scheme portrayed in Figure 1.1 of the introductory chapter and discussed at some length clearly indicates that one of our principal tasks is to make the scheme operational and testable in empirical research. As the first installment of this task objective, this chapter proposes a systematic, replicatable strategy for describing the social structure of Altneustadt's population subsystem that reflects the population's bases of social differentiation in its patterns of social relationships. Earlier we discussed the futility of attempting to enumerate all the linkages among a large population of individuals (i.e., the so-called total network of relationships). Such a task boggles the minds of even our most intrepid quantifiers and "computer jockeys." Another approach is obviously needed. This chapter, then, is devoted to a detailed consideration of this other approach and its empirical results when applied to Altneustadt.

* Although this chapter draws heavily from Pappi (1973b), we have made no effort to provide a literal translation of the German article. On the contrary, this chapter was entirely rewritten with the central themes of the monograph and the probable interests of an English-speaking readership in mind. Discussions, tables, and references primarily directed to the German context have been eliminated in the interests of brevity and relevance. The reader should consult the original article if he is interested in pursuing such matters in greater detail.

The elements of our strategy for recovering the social structure(s) of large populations, first advanced in Laumann (1973), are threefold and quickly summarized. First, we must take seriously the distinction between social positions and their incumbents and aggregate persons occupying similar social positions into a single "generalized" social position to be treated in contradistinction to other such positions. Obviously the persons occupying a single generalized social position (for example, a population subgroup sharing a common ethnic identity or occupation) can be most diverse with respect to their incumbencies in other types of social positions. Second, we must recognize that our postulate regarding relation-specific social structures implies that a multiplicity of social structures can be identified in a given population subsystem. Their internal arrangements or patterns (order) will vary as a function of the types of relationships that are considered in linking positions to one another. One's theoretical purposes must, therefore, guide the selection of the type of relationship to be studied. Finally, we must broaden the notion of "relationship between social positions" in network analysis to permit positions to be more or less closely linked to one another by the differential likelihood (or some similar stochastic concept) of incumbents of given generalized positions forming specified relationships with incumbents of other generalized positions.

Two critical questions immediately confront us. First, of the many ways that one can distinguish social positions from one another, what are the bases of differentiation of social positions that should particularly concern us? Second, of the many sorts of social relationships that can be identified, which ones are especially relevant to our theoretical objectives?

In answering the first question, we note once again that social theorists have long recognized that social positions can be distinguished from one another in two fundamental respects: namely, *(1)* the bundles of tasks or role performances characteristically associated with them and *(2)* the characteristic bundles of rewards, privileges, and disabilities associated with a position as well as its social evaluation in comparison to other positions (cf. Merton, 1957; Nadel, 1957). That is, social positions tend to be unequally rewarded, whether because of social valuation of their different contributions to the social system as a whole (e.g., Davis and Moore, 1945) or because of their differential power to coerce and extort more or less favorable rewards in comparison to other positions (cf. Dahrendorf, 1968; Lenski, 1966; Laumann and Senter, 1976).

To answer the second question, we recall that theorists have typically distinguished between two broad types of social relationships. On the one hand, instrumental relationships are seen as involving the exchanges of necessary facilities, such as information, commands, goods, services, or more generalized media of exchange like money, between incumbents of positions that are required in performing the task responsibilities associated with their respective positions. On the other hand, expressive relationships are seen as involving exchanges of more diffuse, affectively toned, directly consummatory facilities, such as positive expressions of love, esteem, trust, and social approval or negative expressions of hatred, dislike, and disapproval (cf. Parsons, 1951; Homans, 1961; Blau, 1964; Ekeh, 1974).

Unfortunately, a rigorous translation of these broad theoretical distinctions into concrete empirical operational procedures that remain faithful to them is no simple matter. In fact, we must be the first to admit the critical role our "informed" intuition has played in devising the expedients we finally adopted in characterizing meaningful social positions and relationships in Altneustadt. We, of course, also got many useful suggestions from a close reading of the rich ethnographic literature on communities, including, to name but a few, studies by the Lynds (1937), Warner and his associates (1960, 1963), Davis *et al.* (1941), and Vidich and Bensman (1960).

Occupation is the obvious candidate for identifying social positions in terms of their differentiated roles in the division of labor and, to be sure, has been the strategy most frequently used to do so. Even occupation, however, is inadequate to the task of mapping the complexity of the division of labor in modern communities. There are, for example, many social positions, such as those of housewife and student, which many adult members of a community occupy, that are not easily related to occupational differentiation as it is usually treated in the sociological literature.

Of course, there are many other practical difficulties in using occupation as a base for distinguishing among social positions. First and foremost is the fact that there are literally thousands of occupations to be found in developed societies—far too many for each to be taken into account in a study of a local community. How is one to classify this multitude of occupations into a smaller set of categories that are relatively homogeneous internally and yet capture the myriad intrinsic and extrinsic differences among them? One customary strategy has been to assume that a unidimensional measure of prestige differences among occupations (i.e., the differential attribution of social honor and respect accorded a nominal classification of occupations [cf. Hatt, 1950; Reiss, 1961; Hodge, Siegel, and Rossi, 1963; Treiman, in press]) will suffice to distinguish among occupations for many analytic purposes. Other strategies for coding occupations, however, (e.g., the famous Alba Edwards' [1943] Scale and the occupational classification by situs proposed by Morris and Murphy, 1959) recognize other important differences among occupations that surely must be considered in any satisfactory study of occupational structures (cf. Laumann, 1966, 1973).

The problem, then, is to devise a scheme of occupational coding that is sensitive to socioeconomic differences among occupations as well as other differences regarding the nature of the work and the organizational context of work (e.g., between employees of large factories or government bureaus and self-employed professionals) at the same time that it yields a manageable number of categories to sustain analysis. Consideration must also be given to the irreducible arbitrariness of any coding scheme such that differences among occupations that are ignored in the coding rules must necessarily drop out of the analysis. That is, they are not retrievable as axes of differentiation among occupational positions. We think, however, that no useful purpose would be served here by engaging in a long technical excursus on how such a coding scheme can best be constructed to meet our analytic objectives (the reader is referred to Pappi [1973b] for an extended discussion of these matters). With these general caveats very much in mind, we shall briefly describe in the following section the coding scheme we finally devised to meet our specific needs.

We still have not entirely solved our problem of ascertaining the bases of social differentiation in our population. Community sociology also teaches us that there are likely to be other important sources of differences in a population, especially having to do with ascriptive membership groups, that crosscut occupational distinctions and have important implications for channeling the formation of social relationships in a community. Unfortunately, there is no systematic, theoretically grounded inventory of the possible sources of ascriptive solidarities. At best, we have lists of examples, such as ethnic, linguistic, religious, racial, and age groups, that have been found to be important in one or another community context. In addition, we must recognize that communities themselves vary greatly in the specific types of ascriptively based subcommunities that make up their population. Some communities are thoroughly riddled with deeply felt ethnic differences among their inhabitants, while others lack entirely such a basis of differentiation. Consequently, we can only propose an ad hoc solution for each community studied. Our reading of Altneustadt's history and current situation suggests that religious and social differences between Protestants and Catholics, which happens also to be closely associated to the question of whether people are native born (i.e., *Altbürger*) or newcomers to the community, are likely to provide a significant basis for distinguishing among incumbents of social positions.

One final theoretical issue remains before we can apply our empirical procedures to study Altneustadt's population subsystem. What social relationships should we consider in connecting social positions to one another? Both theorists and empirically oriented students of the community seem to agree that intimate (expressive) relationships, such as marriage and friendship, are especially responsive to intrinsic differences among social positions. That is, intimate relationships tend to form between social positions most similar in social standing and other pertinent social characteristics and to be absent between highly disparate positions (cf. Laumann [1966, 1973] and Verbrugge [1974] for extensive reviews of the relevant theoretical and empirical literature).[1]

We know considerably less about the principles by which instrumental relationships are formed. Community studies simply have not examined them in any systematic detail. Instrumental relationships would seem to be, by their very nature, more ad hoc and transitory, often bringing incumbents of highly disparate positions together for delimited or specific purposes. Clearly these relationships are very important in the social life of a community and deserve intensive study. Limitations of time, however, necessitated our neglecting them, at least in analyzing Altneustadt's population subsystem. We shall, in fact, pay considerable attention to them in the analysis of its elite subsystem in Part II.

In confining our attention to the better studied expressive relationships, we at least have the advantage of using the strategies and rationales developed by the senior author in his study of friendship ties in Detroit, Michigan. More specifically, we shall adopt his formulation of the distance-generating mechanism (also see our discussion of Postulate II in Chapter 1) that underlies the structural differentiation of friendship ties and permits us to interpret its underlying dimensionality. This crucial postulate or assumption (Laumann, 1973: 5) asserts: "Similarities in status, attitudes, beliefs, and behavior facilitate the formation of intimate (or consensual) relationships among incumbents of social posi-

---

[1] In fact, a useful generalization of this proposition is to regard social classes as bounded, ordered, and mutually exclusive interaction groups (cf. Hodge and Siegel, 1968: 316). Social classes, in other words, exist in a community to the extent to which persons occupying similar positions in the division of labor confine intimate access to one another. In more formal terms, a social class is a set of individuals and families of equal social standing having high informal contact densities with each other and limited intimate contacts with individuals of unequal status (cf. Weber, 1953; Davis *et al.*, 1941; Warner *et al.*, 1960; Laumann, 1966; Pappi, 1975).

tions." The corollary to this postulate is: "The more dissimilar two positions are in status, attitudes, beliefs, and behavior of their incumbents, the less likely the formation of intimate (or consensual) relationships and, consequently, the 'farther away' they are from one another in the structure."

In sum, our preliminary hunches about the probable bases of social differentiation in this community have guided the construction of our coding scheme for social positions. The procedures we shall employ, however, in analyzing social *structural* differentiation by no means require us to recover these bases of differentiation if they do not, in fact, serve as the principles intentionally or unintentionally used by the population in selecting intimate interaction partners. Our occupational code, for example, is a nominal scale, without a "natural" order among the categories. The dimensional analysis of the similarities of friendship choices between occupational groups will show whether or not a unidimensional status dimension serves by itself as the distance-generating mechanism for the social structure under examination. If it is, and if we can distinguish different clusters of occupations as falling at clearly separated points on a status gradient, then we shall have empirically delineated a local stratification system with relatively discrete social classes (see footnote 1).

On the other hand, we could observe that occupations of roughly equivalent social standing (i.e., falling roughly at the same place on the prestige dimension) are located at some distance from one another on another axis that reflects an important basis of dissimilarity among them (e.g., whether people in the occupations are usually self-employed or employees of large organizations). To put the matter another way, then, it is impossible to recover a dimension in the structural analysis that was not logically implied by the distinctions drawn in the coding scheme. A logical distinction made in the coding scheme, however, may prove to be empirically irrelevant in structuring interaction choices.

ALTNEUSTADT'S BASES OF SOCIAL DIFFERENTIATION

Devising an Occupational Code

With these preliminaries completed, we may now turn to a consideration of the empirical results obtained in Altneustadt. First, we must consider more carefully the occupational differences that we want to be able to recognize in Altneustadt. This task obviously poses a more general set of issues. When occupations are the units of analysis, we have already argued that many properties of these occupations can be meaningfully distinguished. As Siegel (1971: 148) remarks in his outstanding work on occupational prestige, "there is no single quantity which captures the 'essence' of (or 'measures') occupation." Given the myriad possibilities for distinguishing among occupations, it is small wonder that, despite the voluminous work on occupations, there is no single occupational code agreed upon by most workers in the field. Siegel does provide a useful orienting perspective on occupation:

> The production of goods and services in human society requires work. In a sociological discussion we can distinguish the particular goods and services produced (industrial distinctions) from two important aspects of work itself—the specific kind of work a person does, and the social situation in which he does it. A given individual performs a specific kind of work in a particular social setting, and this is his job. His occupation refers to characteristics of his job that are transferable among employers, and to some extent, among situations. . . . The analytical distinction between kinds of work and work situation suggests that occupation ought to be defined solely in terms of the former [p. 149].

Comparing this explication with the standard occupational code used by German survey researchers (viz., wage earners, salaried employees, civil servants, and self-employed), it is readily apparent that this code is not so much a classification of occupations as of "classes of workers," which rests on characteristics of the work situation. When American researchers use the manual–nonmanual or blue-collar–white-collar distinction as the broadest categorization of kind of work, this distinction is almost identical to the classification of wage earner versus salaried employee *(Arbeiter* versus *Angestellte)* in the German context.

In a more refined coding scheme, German survey researchers typically subdivide the self-employed by size of firm. Salaried employees are subdivided, in part, according to their hierarchical position in the work organization (i.e., management versus nonmanagement positions) and, in part, according to the educational qualifications needed for the kind of work (i.e., qualified versus nonqualified salaried employees). This latter criterion is the only one used for civil servants because the association between general educational prerequisites for entry into particular work positions in the civil service and qualifications explicitly required for entry to these positions is closest for them. A comparison of this standard German code with the 10 Major Occupational Groups used by the U.S. Bureau of the Census shows that the American code is a classification of the kinds of work to a higher degree than the German code.

Our objective was to improve the German standard code so that the resulting subgroups contained more information on the kind of work than the original code, without giving up the broad principles of categorization of the original code. In addition, the 71 categories with which we started could be matched with the International Standard Classification of Occupations (International Labor Office, 1969). A by-product was that we could then utilize Treiman's (forthcoming) Standard International Occupational Prestige Scale, which provides prestige rankings for the occupational codes of the International Labor Office.

Even 71 occupations, however, were simply too many to sustain analysis, given the limited number of cases available in our community survey. Thus, we had to devise a more compressed code. In doing so, we tried to preserve the peculiarities of occupational composition of Altneustadt's local labor market rather than to construct an optimal general code. The resulting 19 occupational groups are presented in Table 3.1, together with pertinent information on their socioeconomic standing, internal variation, and religious composition. (See Appendix A, Part I, for a description of our cross-section survey of Altneustadt's population.)

Among the 10 major occupational groups distinguished in the U.S. Census code, the category "professional, technical, and kindred workers" is the most heterogeneous in composition (Siegel, 1971: 164). This would be even more true in Germany where the school system is more specialized than in the United States. Thus, even in our collapsed code, we thought it desirable to distinguish among at least five categories of professional, technical, and kindred workers because they play such a potentially important role in our community. The natural science research laboratory, the largest employer in Altneustadt, employs a large number from this group. In fact, we can nicely indicate the degree to which a given occupational group depends on the laboratory for employment by the percentage of the labor force in nonprofit (excluding governmental) organizations, an economic sector which, in our community, is roughly equivalent to employment at the laboratory, reported in Column 5 of Table 3.1.

As can readily be seen from Table 3.1, two of the five professional groups, the scientists and the engineers, are overwhelmingly employed by the natural science laboratory, as well as slightly over 50% of two other groups, the technicians and engineers' aides. The free professionals, who are coded together with the small number of local entrepreneurs, and the teachers and other salaried professionals, however, have nothing to do with the new community focused around the research laboratory. They are at the core of the *Altstadt* sector of Altneustadt, as are the independent small businessmen and artisans, the three groups of civil servants, and the salaried service and sales workers. The occupations coded as "lowest ranking civil servants" are mainly policemen. The minor civil servants are overwhelmingly employed by the state-owned railways and the postal service in such occupations as locomotive drivers, postmasters, and post office clerks.

Craftsmen and foremen and operatives and laborers are strictly comparable to the equivalent groups in the American census code, with the exception of master craftsmen, a well-defined category in Germany, who have been coded separately. Service and sales workers have been separated into two groups, depending on whether they are salaried employees or hourly wage earners. Barbers, waiters, janitors, and watchmen are typical of the occupations included in the latter category.

Columns 1–4 of Table 3.1 provide information on the average educational attainment and income of the 19 occupational categories, together with their coefficients of variation. These latter coefficients are intended to measure the internal heterogeneity of each category with respect to the two socioeconomic characteristics. These variables were selected because they have long been regarded as the best summary measures of the more important prerequisites for entry into given occupations and one of the most important rewards to be derived from occupational activity. The 19 groups have been roughly ordered in the table by the means of the two socioeconomic variables.

The coefficients of variation indicate that the most homogeneous groups in socioeconomic composition are the scientists and engineers, the three groups of civil servants, and craftsmen and foremen. The independent small businessmen and artisans and the laborers and hourly wage earners in the service sector are very heterogeneous, especially with regard to income, just as we might have expected. Low variation in income can be taken as an indicator of similar conditions of employment, which, in our community, usually means that the majority of the group is employed by the same employer.

The labor market of small cities is, of course, less diversified than the national labor market. A consequence of this greater homogeneity is that our occupational classification explains much more of the variance in education and income within the community (see the squared eta coefficients in the bottom row of Table 3.1) than do the 10 major occupational categories or even the 323 detailed occupational categories for the United States (cf. Hodge and Siegel, 1968: 322; Siegel, 1971: 239). Comparable figures for Germany as a whole are, unfortunately, unavailable.

Measuring Social Distance between Occupational Groups

As discussed in our introductory remarks to this chapter, we are interested in inferring the character of Altneustadt's class structure from the patterning of social distances between occupations. We propose to estimate the relative proximities among occupational groups (that is,

TABLE 3.1

Education, Income, Branch of Economy, and Religious Composition of Altneustadt's Occupational Groups[a]

Occupational group	School years completed[b]		Net monthly income in DM[c]		Percentage of labor force in nonprofit organizations (excl. government service)[a]	Percentage Catholic[c]
	Mean (1)	Coef. of Variation (2)	Mean (3)	Coef. of Variation (4)	(5)	(6)
1. Free professionals and entrepreneurs	16.3	17.8	2334	26.0	6.7	74.1
2. Natural scientists	18.0	0	2315	18.3	75.7	26.4
3. Teachers and other salaried profs.	16.3	15.3	2084	27.3	13.0	78.8
4. Engineers	14.4	8.3	1764	28.1	68.4	55.3
5. Managers	13.1	19.1	1786	32.5	25.0	70.0
6. Independent small businessmen and artisans	11.4	18.4	1526	58.7	—	90.2
7. Government inspectors	13.0	8.5	1700	17.1	6.7	73.1
8. Minor civil servants	11.5	7.8	1338	31.7	—	85.1

9. Lowest ranking civil servants	10.7	8.4	1031	18.0	—	72.2
10. Clerical workers	12.4	11.3	1181	39.4	18.2	71.4
11. Clerical aides	11.7	12.8	996	36.2	39.1	81.4
12. Technicians	12.7	11.8	1436	32.3	52.9	63.8
13. Engineering aides	11.7	17.9	1150	20.7	57.1	66.7
14. Salaried service and sales workers	10.7	15.9	1166	36.7	9.1	70.6
15. Master craftsmen	11.2	6.3	1245	33.8	25.0	68.0
16. Craftsmen and foremen	11.0	6.4	1067	28.7	17.7	72.3
17. Operatives	9.7	15.5	1110	33.0	14.3	73.5
18. Laborers	9.5	16.8	820	43.8	19.0	65.6
19. Wage earners in service sector	10.5	19.0	908	41.2	30.8	61.1
	$\eta^2 = .65$			$\eta^2 = .50$		

[a] Sources: Pappi, 1973: 42, 63, Tables 4 and 10. (See Appendix A, Part I, for a description of our cross-section survey of Altneustadt.)

[b] Based on all respondents who were in the labor force or retired at the time of the interview.

[c] Based on occupation of head of household.

[d] Based only on people active in the labor force at the time of interviewing.

their social distances from one another) in terms of their differential rates of forming informal social relationships with one another, as indicated by the patterning of friendship choices among occupational groups. In the simplest case, we could assume that the lower the probability of a friendship choice between incumbents of two occupational categories, the higher the social distance and, correspondingly, the lower the social similarity between them. Unfortunately, as we shall see, the highly unequal proportions of the population found in different occupations and other sources of statistical artifact make the adoption of this simple expedient of estimating occupational proximities unacceptable. Once we do obtain satisfactory estimates of the proximities, however, we can then employ smallest space analysis to map the matrix of proximities into an Euclidean (metric) space having the fewest number of dimensions consistent with an acceptable goodness of fit (or coefficient of alienation) between the original proximity estimates and the derived (or fitted) Euclidean distances (see McFarland and Brown [1973] for an extended discussion of the rationale for smallest space analysis). The theoretical task then becomes one of making substantive interpretations of these dimensions.

This strategy has already been successfully used in analyzing friendship data limited to men active in the labor force (cf. Laumann, 1966, 1973). When one wants to consider, as we do, the entire adult population of a community, the question of what to do with the people outside the labor force cannot be ignored. Unfortunately, there is no general solution to this problem; it always depends on the intended analysis. In the sociology of stratification, it has usually been assumed that the family or household, classified according to the occupation of the head of household, can reasonably be used as the smallest unit of analysis. Even accepting the meaningfulness of this procedure with regard to assessing the household's general socioeconomic resources and standing in the community, however, it by no means follows that the household is still the optimal unit for analyzing the patterning of friendship choices. Friendship selection of adult children still living with their parents, for example, is likely to be misrepresented by such a procedure, as is that of widows classified according to the occupational groups of their late husbands, who may have died many years ago. In view of these problems, we decided to classify only married women by the occupational groups of their husbands. As a matter of fact, we have evidence (not reported here) that married women usually report the same friends as their husbands. In all other cases, we used the occupation of the respondent. For retired persons or their spouses, we used their last full-time occupation. For those persons who never were gainfully employed, we added the following groups to our 19 occupational categories: housewives (spouses absent), students, and apprentices.

In addition to asking for the occupation of the respondent or of her husband, we asked the respondents to tell us the occupations of their three closest friends (in the case of married female friends, the occupation of their husbands).[2] The basic table for the following analysis is a cross-tabulation of the occupations of the respondents as the row variable and the occupations of the three friends as the column variable, with rowwise percentages. To construct it, we added the corresponding cell entries of the three tables cross-tabulating the occupation of each friend reported by the occupation of the respondent. This basic table has the same structure as a mobility table with the occupations of fathers in the rows and the occupations of their sons in the columns. In our case, the marginal distribution of the row variable is weighted by the number of friends reported (note that not every respondent reported three friends); in a mobility table, it is weighted implicitly by the number of sons. The unweighted and weighted marginal distributions for the occupations of the respondents are given in Columns 1 and 2 of Table 3.2. The second column is identical with the row totals of our basic table; the third column gives the column totals.

Occupational Self-Selection

Before turning to an analysis of the overall patterning of friendship choices across occupations, it is of critical importance that we first examine most carefully occupational self-selection (also called endophily), that is, the tendency to choose friends disproportionately from one's own occupational group. In fact, the existence of self-selection by a generalized social position may be taken as a precondition for justifying many of the theoretical postulates and assumptions of our entire approach. If there were no evidence of endophily (that is, if persons in a given category manifested no significant tendency to overselect friends from their own group or, in the more extreme case, even a tendency to avoid people in their own group), we would be in a most embarrassing position theoretically because the lack of endophily would suggest that the coding of generalized social positions was not tapping any distinctive basis of social differentiation among people that served to channel their choices of partners for intimate relationships. Random association within and

---

[2] The questions used to elicit the identification of the three friends and information about them were German translations of those used in the Detroit study (cf. Laumann, 1973: 264–269).

TABLE 3.2
Percentage Distributions for the Occupations of Respondents and Friends and Measures of Occupation Self-Selection[a]

Occupational group	Percentage of respondents unweighted[b] (1)	Percentage of respondents weighted[b] (2)	Percentage of friends[e] (3)	Percentage of occupation self-selection[d] (4)	Index of Association[e] (5)	Inbreeding bias[f] (6)
1. Free professionals and entrepreneurs	3.3	3.6	4.1	29.1	8.8	.261
2. Natural scientists	6.5	6.8	6.0	48.0	7.4	.447
3. Teachers and other salaried profs.	4.0	4.4	6.3	28.1	7.0	.233
4. Engineers	4.6	4.6	3.7	16.8	3.7	.136
5. Managers	3.7	3.7	3.4	7.3	1.9	.040
6. Independent small businessmen and artisans	6.2	5.3	9.5	29.9	4.8	.225
7. Government inspectors	3.2	3.2	3.1	11.4	3.5	.086
8. Minor civil servants	5.7	5.9	5.9	23.3	4.1	.185
9. Lowest ranking civil servants	2.2	2.4	1.1	5.7	2.5	.047
10. Clerical workers	3.4	3.3	3.1	9.7	2.9	.068
11. Clerical aides	5.2	5.0	7.5	14.5	2.8	.076
12. Technicians	5.7	5.8	2.0	8.7	1.5	.068
13. Engineering aides	2.2	2.4	1.9	11.3	5.1	.096
14. Salaried service and sales workers	2.1	2.1	2.5	13.3	6.3	.111
15. Master craftsmen	3.0	3.4	2.3	12.2	4.1	.101

16. Craftsmen and foremen	14.5	15.0	13.3	31.3	2.1	.208
17. Operatives	8.3	8.0	5.4	20.0	2.4	.154
18. Laborers	3.9	3.0	2.7	26.2	6.7	.241
19. Wage earners in service sector	2.2	2.0	2.3	13.9	6.3	.119
20. Housewives	3.5	3.2	4.7	18.3	5.2	.143
21. Students	3.7	4.1	5.3	60.7	16.4	.585
22. Apprentices	1.3	1.5	1.0	27.3	21.0	.266
23. No information	1.5	1.2	2.9	7.4	4.9	.046
	$N = 820$	$N = 2187$	$N = 2187$	$N = 2187$		

[a] Source: Pappi, 1973: 47, Table 6.

[b] Percentage of respondents unweighted $= \dfrac{N_i}{N} \, (100)$.

[b] Percentage of respondents weighted $= \dfrac{A_{i.}}{A_{..}} \, (100)$.

[c] Percentage of friends $= \dfrac{A_{.j}}{A_{..}} \, (100)$.

[d] Percentage occupational self-selections, $\delta_i = \dfrac{A_{ii}}{A_{i.}} \, (100)$.

[e] Index of association $= \dfrac{\delta_i}{(N_i/N) \, (100)}$.

[f] Inbreeding bias, $\tau_i = \dfrac{(\delta_i/100) - A_{.j}/A_{..}}{1 - A_{.j}/A_{..}}$.

across social positions implies that our postulated distance-generating mechanism, which presumes to specify the systematic biases underlying a given social structural arrangement—that is, the bases of structural differentiation, is inoperative and, consequently, that further analysis would be unwarranted.

Relatively low levels of endophily present an ambiguous situation to interpret. On the one hand, it may mean that the categories used for distinguishing among social positions are comprised of such heterogeneous groupings of positions that the conflicting attractions and repulsions they pose for their incumbents to form relationships among themselves tend, on balance, to cancel one another out. On the other hand, they may merely mean that the bases of social differentiation reflected in the coding of positions exert a very modest influence on the formation of social relations among them.

Because of its importance to the subsequent analysis, we think it worthwhile to consider several alternative indicators of occupational self-selection—none of which is wholly satisfactory by itselves due to one or another feature of its calculation. The problem is that each measure highlights an interesting aspect of self-selection often at the expense of another of equal interest. There is no single indicator optimal for all the purposes the analyst might have in mind.

First, we can look at the least satisfactory measure: the proportion of friends chosen from one's own group (actual endophily, see Column 4 in Table 3.2). These percentages considered by themselves are unsatisfactory because they are directly dependent on the relative sizes of the groups in the population as a whole. That is, the larger the group in the population, the higher is the probability of choosing a member from this group, even under the assumption of random mixing. Of course, the size effect reflected in this measure is not without considerable substantive interest. To ignore it completely would lead to a serious misrepresentation of the opportunity structure confronting people in finding suitable partners for intimate interaction (cf. McFarland and Brown, 1973: 238–40).

Our second measure is the index of association—the so-called "Rogoff mobility ratio of observed to chance selection" (see Column 5 in Table 3.2)—that was originally proposed by students of occupational mobility to remedy the drawbacks inherent in the simple percentages of self-selection. Values over "1" indicate how much the actual endophily exceeds the endophily expected by chance, while values under "1" indicate the extent to which people are avoiding the choice of persons in their own group. Unfortunately, as Duncan (Blau and Duncan, 1967) has shown, this index is also ultimately dependent on the marginal distributions.

Finally, we calculated the inbreeding bias (see Column 6 in Table 3.2), a measure proposed by Fararo and Sunshine (1964) that goes some way toward eliminating the deficiencies of the other measures at least with respect to depressing the impact of size effects. Our basic table corresponds to a "who-selected-whom" matrix with which Fararo and Sunshine started when developing their measures. This table can, in turn, be thought to consist of 23 fourfold tables when P_1 stands for a given occupational group and P_2 for all other groups. If a member of P_1 selects another member of P_1, this is called endophily. The entries for these tables are not respondents, but rather friendship pairs, with the total number of pairs $A_{..} = 2187$. The actual inbreeding proportion is defined as A_{11}/A_1, that is, the number of pairs in which both friends are members of occupation P_1 divided by the number of pairs in which only the main respondent is a member of P_1. Fararo and Sunshine divide the actual self-selection into two components: the random inbreeding expectation and the inbreeding bias. The random inbreeding expectation corresponds to the proportion of an occupational group in the entire population. This figure is based on individuals and not on pairs (see Column 1 of Table 3.2).

There is one precondition of this simple definition of the random inbreeding expectation that is not strictly met in our case, that is, that the friends are to be chosen from within a prespecified group. In our case, this would presumably mean that the friends were to be selected from the population of Altneustadt. Our respondents, in fact, chose almost 40% of their friends from people who were not residents of Altneustadt. The vast majority of these, of course, lived in the immediate vicinity of the city. It seemed unrealistic to exclude these people on the grounds of their living outside an essentially arbitrary geographic boundary. (In fact, subsequent to our survey period, much of the environs of Altneustadt, were incorporated into the city. See our discussion of the community controversy over incorporation in Chapters 6 and 9.) Thus, we decided to take the marginal distribution of the friends (Column 3 of Table 3.2, $A_{.j}/A_{..}$) as the best estimator of the inbreeding proportion under the assumption of random mixing.

After computing empirical measures of the actual and the random inbreeding proportions, an occupation-specific bias component in friendship selection can be defined. Fararo and Sunshine (1964: 73) give the following rationale for postulating an event on which friendship selection is said to be dependent:

If the event occurs, then the contact is certain to target on its 'own kind'. If the event does not occur, then the contact selects its 'own kind' in proportion to the existence of this kind in the population, i.e., at random.

We will not specify what this event is. It remains a hypothetical construction. Instead, we introduce a probability parameter, such that with probability τ_i a contact from Subpopulation P_i selects its own kind by virtue of the occurrence of the hypothetical event. Thus, with the complementary probability $1 - \tau_i$ the event does not occur, so that the contact finds its own kind with probability N_i/N. The first component of inbreeding is here called the biased component—that which is associated with certain selection of the own kind—and the second is called the random component.

Thus, the actual endophily can be expressed as a sum of two probabilities:

$$\delta_i = \tau_i + (1 - \tau_i)\frac{N_i}{N}.$$

We have used this formula, with the alteration of estimating N_i/N with $A_{.j}/A_{..}$, to compute the inbreeding bias or systematic endophily. These results are given in the last column of Table 3.2. Comparing these numbers with the indices of association, it can be seen that there is some agreement on the relative levels of self-selection of different occupational groups, but the correlation between the values of these two columns is only .67. Considering the fact that these two measures are supposed to be indicators of the same concept, however, this is a rather low correlation.

All three indicators of self-selection, whatever their individual strengths and weaknesses, provide consistent support for the view that the occupational groups we identified all manifest some systematic bias toward selecting friends from within their own groups, but that there is also considerable variability in the strength of this tendency from group to group. In general, groups that are most homogeneous in composition with respect to other social attributes of their incumbents, such as their age, place of work, socioeconomic status, and/or native-born–newcomer status (for example, the students and the natural scientists), show the strongest tendencies toward self-selection. As other studies have found (e.g., Laumann, 1966, 1973; Curtis, 1963), occupational self-selection appears to be highest at the upper and lower ends of the occupational prestige continuum and relatively low in occupational groups of middling status. "Edge effects" (that is, persons at the top [or bottom] of a hierarchy simply cannot choose persons of higher [or lower] status than themselves while persons in the middle have the option of choosing those who are of higher or lower status as well as those of comparable status) may partially explain this pattern.

Laumann (1973) reported for his Detroit sample an especially high self-selection among the free professionals, self-employed sales workers, craftsmen, and operatives in manufacturing. The roughly comparable groups in Altneustadt, viz., the free professionals and entrepreneurs, the independent small businessmen and artisans, and operatives and laborers, also reveal high levels of occupational self-selection. The fact that the patterning of endophily across different occupational categories is so similar in such diverse communities strongly suggests that the social distance-generating mechanism may be well-established in the occupational and class structure of industrialized societies (cf. Laumann and Senter, 1976).

The Similarity of Friendship Choices between Occupations

Having established that our occupational groups do manifest definite, albeit varying, tendencies toward self-selection, it should come as no great surprise that we also find a relatively high (product–moment) correlation of .54 between the occupational prestige of the respondent's group and that of his friends.[3] This correlation, however, is not entirely explained by group self-selection alone. When choosing friends outside their own group, people definitely prefer to find them in occupational groups of roughly comparable socioeconomic standing to their own group. This tendency to forming friendships among people of comparable social status has been consistently found in all studies with which we are familiar (e.g., Duncan and Artis, 1951; Riecken and Homans, 1954; Ellis, 1957; King, 1961; Curtis, 1964; Warner *et al.*, 1960; Laumann, 1966, 1973; Reuband, 1974). Thus, prestige or socioeconomic differences among occupations provide one of the key organizing principles in establishing attractions and repulsions for the purposes of forming intimate ties among their incumbents.

There are, of course, many other possible grounds for these attractions and repulsions in forming such ties. For example, persons in two different occupational categories might often share common work places and/or reside in neighborhoods close to these work sites and, thus, would have more opportunities to meet one another than persons in occupations lacking these commonalities. (In other words, the physical propinquity of groups might be expected to enhance their mutual choices, all other things being equal.) They might engage in types of work tasks that require similar sorts of skills, attitudes, and interests (e.g., consider the classic distinctions between people-oriented, symbol-oriented, and thing-oriented occupations, or between bureaucratic and entrepreneurial occu-

[3] A correlation of approximately equal strength (viz., .50) was also observed for our Detroit sample of white male friendship pairs (cf. Laumann, 1973: 41).

pations) (cf. Mortimer, 1972). Or they might hold similar realtionships to the ownership of property or to the exercise of authority over others. Finally, they might even recruit preferentially from the same status groups (e.g., religious, age, place of birth, racial, or ethnic). Each similarity (or its absence) might provide yet another basis of mutual attraction (or repulsion) between groups that would raise or depress the likelihood of intimate bonds being formed between their incumbents. In a microstructural analysis of intimate social relationships, in which the individual is the focal analytic unit, it is possible to do a more refined analysis of the possible roles that different bases of similarity among occupations may play in the process of selecting friends (cf. Laumann, 1973: 83–130). For a macrostructural analysis such as ours, however, which is focused on the patterning of links among grosser categories of social positions, coarser distinctions among aggregated characteristics of these positions must be used. The resulting interpretations of the macrostructural bases of similarities must, of necessity, be more tentative because of certain intrinsic ambiguities in the data and the coding schemes employed.

For our purposes, we shall describe the macrostructure of our community's population subsystem "in terms of the differential likelihood of the formation of specified relationships [in this case, friendship] among social positions [Laumann, 1973: 43]." We shall further assume that the degree of similarity between two occupational groups with regard to their friendship choices across all possible groups is some monotonic function of the underlying similarities and differences among occupations with respect to their bearing on attractions and repulsions in the formation of intimate ties among their incumbents. Since these bases of similarity are potentially of the most varied character, we can anticipate that the structural differentiation of social positions is likely to take a multidimensional rather than a strictly unidimensional form.

Practically speaking, we propose to estimate the relative proximities of the occupational groups in terms of the pairwise similarities of their profiles of friendship choices across all the occupational categories. While there are a number of alternative ways of estimating these proximities, each possessing some advantages and disadvantages, our experience to date with many such strategies (cf. Laumann, 1966, 1973) indicates that they all yield roughly comparable results. For purposes of this analysis, therefore, we shall only consider the index of dissimilarity (cf. Duncan and Duncan, 1955), as our proximity estimator. The index of dissimilarity (specifically, the sum of the positive percentage differences between two percentage distributions) contrasts the percentage distribution of a given occupational group's friends across the set of occupational categories with that of another specified group. It tells us the proportion of persons in one group *or* the other that would have to be redistributed such that the two percentage distributions being compared would be identical. Maximum similarity (i.e., an index of "0") between two occupations (and, therefore, the closest proximity) is reached when they recruit their friends in exactly the same proportions from among the 19 categories of occupations. The groups of housewives, students, and apprentices were omitted from the following analysis for reasons explained later. In the next section, we shall add a further refinement of our occupational coding scheme by distinguishing religious differences—an essentially ascriptive attribute in Germany—among the incumbents of a particular occupational category.

The indices of dissimilarity between the 19 groups range between .26 and .93. (This matrix is printed in its entirety in Pappi [1973b: 54].) As one might have expected, the largest index, .93, is found between the scientists and laborers, the most dissimilar groups on a number of comparative grounds. The coefficients between craftsmen and operatives and between the different middle class occupations are generally toward the lower end of the range. Since the classification of occupations from 1 to 19 in Table 3.1 essentially orders them by their socioeconomic characteristics, the importance of this factor is readily deduced from the fact that the indices regularly become larger the farther they are from the main diagonal. It is very difficult, however, to observe other regularities in the matrix of dissimilarity coefficients by simple inspection. The detection of such regularities, if any are indeed present, require the assistance of further data reduction techniques.

Smallest space analysis was especially designed to aid the investigator in recovering the underlying structure of such a complex matrix as we have here, with its 171 entries and 14,535 possible paired comparisons of these entries. As we have already noted, the matrix of dissimilarity coefficients will be used as our estimates of the proximities of the occupational categories to one another. It is the input matrix for the smallest space analysis. The task of the computer routine is to find the fewest possible dimensions in an Euclidean space that will permit the graphic representation of the original proximity matrix in a metric space in which the derived Euclidean distances distort the original proximities only to a degree prespecified as acceptable, according to an objective criterion. What counts in an Euclidean space are the distances between the points and the fact that these distances remain unchanged under rotation of the axes. It is this latter characteristic of Euclidean spaces that has an important consequence: The coordinates of the space are completely arbitrary and normally will have no interpretable meaning. For most purposes of interpretation, a solution with up to three dimensions is optimal. When interpreting such structures, it is meaningful to look not only for unidimensional arrangements of points along some axis, but also for other configurations of points, such as their arrangements into circles, sectors, or clusters.

An acceptable two-dimensional solution is presented in Figure 3.1. Both the original axes and the axes that make most sense for interpretation (solid lines) are drawn on the picture. The axis extending from the bottom left side to the top right side (labeled "prestige") can be interpreted as the dimension of prestige or socioeconomic status differences among occupations. The correlations of the values of the 19 groups on this axis are .95, with occupational prestige, .90, with the average educational attainment of these groups, and .91, with their average income (see Table 3.1). The interpretation of this axis as the prestige dimension would thus appear to be justified. This result is also fully in agreement with comparable American studies (cf. Laumann, 1966: 89–104; 1973: 73–89). Blau and Duncan (1967: 67–75) report a similar result in their analysis of intergenerational occupational mobility in the United States.

While there seems to be little ambiguity in identifying the prestige dimension in the patterning of friendship choices, there is somewhat

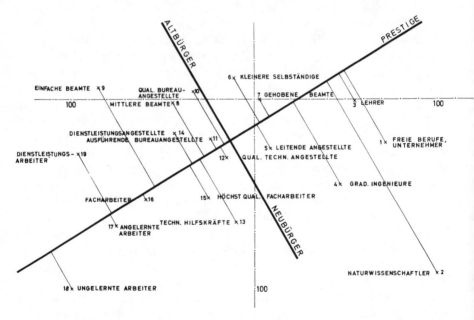

Figure 3.1 The social distance among occupational groups. (Two-dimensional solution for similarities of friendship choices, Guttman-Lingoes coefficient of alienation = .133. The corresponding numbered rows in Table 3.1 translate the German occupational titles in this figure.)

more difficulty in interpreting the second dimension. The only point of agreement among the available studies is that prestige differences are insufficient by themselves in accounting for the patterning of friendship choices in a community—that is, at least a second dimension is always required to portray adequately (that is, without unacceptable levels of distortion) the original proximity matrix of friendship choices. The substantive interpretations of the second or the second and third dimensions that Blau and Duncan and Laumann offer are very tentative, and they are not very conclusive empirically. Blau and Duncan discuss principles of labor organization and of the acquisition of the necessary occupational abilities as accounting for their second axis. Laumann suggests that differences in occupational situses as well as differences between bureaucratic and entrepreneurial occupations account for the ordering of the second or third axis. In his second study, Laumann found some independent confirmation for the latter interpretation.

When we used his indicator of bureaucratic versus entrepreneurial orientation in an occupational category, however, we found no support for this interpretation in our Altneustadt solution. Occupations with opposite orientations toward bureaucratic and entreprenurial work activities were found in the same region of the spatial solution, while those with similar orientations were sometimes located far apart from one another.

What did seem to account for the ordering of occupations on the second axis in Altneustadt was the relative proportion of persons in the occupational category who were native-born *(Altbürger)* or newcomers *(Neubürger)* to the community. The correlation of the percentage *Altbürger* in an occupational group and the location of that group on the second axis, which is orthogonal to the prestige axis, is .73. (Incidentally, the correlation of this axis with the average level of the groups' general satisfaction with the community [see Appendix B, Part II] is even higher [.84]—possibly another indication of the relative social assimilation of various occupational groups into this bifurcated community social system. The *Altbürger*, in general, express higher levels of satisfaction with living in Altneustadt than do the newcomers.) We should also note the fact that the percentage of people in an occupational category who are employed in a nonprofit organization (which amounts, in Altneustadt, to working at the natural science research facility) is highly correlated with the second axis. Since this percentage is also highly associated with the *Altbürger–Neubürger* split, one is not entirely certain whether to interpret the second axis as reflecting a principle of structuring friendship choices in terms of commonalities of work place and type of work or in terms of nativity.

Length of residence in a community is not an abstract categorization of people in quite the same sense as some of the other interpretations of the second dimension that we have mentioned. That is, people are usually not consciously aware of other people's bureaucratic and entrepreneurial orientations or type of work activities in their daily informal interactions. The distinction between *Altbürger* and *Neubürger*, in contrast, is a socially perceived stimulus which is, at least in small communities, used consciously by the average citizen to "sort people out" (cf. Suttles, 1972), given the existence of at least some variance with regard to this criterion. The importance of this dimension can be inferred from the fact that such groups are frequently mentioned when respondents are asked in open-ended questions to identify the population groups that are important in community affairs. In asking such a question of our respondents, different versions of the *Altbürger–Neubürger* distinction were spontaneously mentioned even more frequently than social classes or religious groups were. In answering a close-ended question asking whether or not there were conflicts between *Altbürger* and *Neubürger*, over 44% of our sample said "yes," 33% said "no," and the rest "did not know." Thus, it seems quite plausible to treat length of residence as an important distance-generating mechanism in this community.

An interpretation of the axes of Figure 3.1 by no means exhausts the theoretically meaningful information to be derived from the spatial solution. The different clusters of occupations can also be examined, for example, to determine the presence or absence of "discrete" social classes. Clearly demarcated gaps on the prestige dimension are readily discerned between the working-class occupations at the lower end of the prestige continuum and the middle-class occupations, as well as between these groups and the free professionals, entrepreneurs, and the natural scientists. The engineers are located midway between the middle-class and upper middle-class "clusters." While the different middle-class groups are relatively tightly clustered, the working-class groups are farther apart from one another. It is also interesting to learn that the lowest ranking civil servants appear to belong more with the working-class than with the middle-class occupations—at least on the criterion of friendship choices—contrary to the conventional categorization of this group in German survey research. The master craftsmen also appear to be a part of the middle class. They are located near the engineers' aides and technicians, two occupations with very similar work activities.

Of all the occupations, the natural scientists are farthest from the center of gravity (centroid) of Figure 3.1.[4] As we noted in Chapter 2,

---

[4] The centroid is the center of the smallest space solution. A physical analogy gives an intuitive sense of its meaning: If all points in a two-dimensional smallest space

the scientists are very much in the role of social outsiders in this community and form a relatively self-conscious, internally oriented group in forming informal social ties. Generally speaking, the more distant a group is from the centroid, the higher is its occupational self-selection. The correlation between systematic endophily and distance from the centroid is .75. In fact, it was because of this high correlation that we could not include the students in the final dimensional analysis. In our first attempt at a smallest space solution, the students turned out to be so far away from all the other groups because of their extraordinarily high endophily that these other groups were tightly clustered as far as possible from the students. As a result, the structural pattern of these groups was not easily discernable. Since we also lacked information on several important interpretive variables for the students, as well as for housewives and apprentices, such as their relative prestige standings, we decided to exclude all three from the smallest space analysis.

In accord with other dimensional analyses of social distances among occupations, occupational prestige proved to be the most important mechanism in generating social distance in Altneustadt. Can we, however, get a more precise estimate of how important this factor is? One possibility is to test how much of the total variance of the interpoint (i.e., interoccupational) distances is accounted for by prestige differences alone. The resulting r^2 can be treated as a quantitative measure of the importance of the prestige dimension in generating the overall social distances among occupations. The analytic unit, then, is the distance between each pair of occupations (or $[^{19}_{2}]$ interpoint distances for our 19 occupational groups). We found that prestige differences explain 66.7% of the variance of the social distances overall.

The explained percentage of the total variance attributable to prestige differences does vary from one analysis to another in some most suggestive ways. When we compute a spatial solution only using data on male friendship pairs, the proportion of explained variance attributable to prestige differences drops to 54.3%. This decline suggests that the differences in occupational prestige may be a more important distance-generating mechanism for women than for men (cf. Laumann and Senter, 1976). This may have to do with the fact that women are less involved in the labor force and that prestige is the only characteristic of occupations about which there exists a strong consensus, regardless of whether or not one is in the labor force. Even if the correlation of the

---

solution were a set of equal weights resting on a weightless plane, the centroid would be the point on which the plane would balance. For a technical discussion, see Roskam and Lingoes (1971).

distances observed in the general solution (Figure 3.1) and that of the "males only" solution is very high (in our case, it is .88), so that the two main organizing principles are the same in both solutions, there are still some interesting differences in detail to be observed. Exigencies of the work organization can readily be detected in the "males only" solution. That is, occupational groups whose members tend to work in the same work places are closer together than in the general solution. This can be seen in the smaller distance between scientists and engineers as well as between the three groups of civil servants. This mechanism appears to work at some cost to the prestige dimension but results in only slight modifications of the overall picture.

The Social Distance between Catholic and Protestant Occupational Groups

The religious differentiation of a population has often been of considerable social and political consequence in a society. Whether or not it has specifically had consequences for friendship selection in a local community like Altneustadt shall be considered in this section. Religious group membership in Germany is very closely linked to another ascribed position, regional origin or even length of residence in a local community. The principle of *cujus regio, ejus religio,* laid down in various treaties shortly after the Reformation, had the consequence of a regional segmentation of the religious groups that has been essentially maintained up to the present day, despite the in-migration of large numbers of East German refugees after World War II into various parts of West Germany.

The dukedom of which Alneustadt was a part originally belonged to the Catholic territories, and it has remained predominantly Catholic ever since. According to recent census figures, somewhat more than 70% of Altneustadt's population are Catholic, about 25% are Protestant, and 3% belong to other denominations or have no religious preference. As we noted in Chapter 2, length of residence is highly correlated with religious preference. Of the adults born in Altneustadt, 92% are Catholic, while only 57% of the more recent immigrants are. In fact, the more recent a person's arrival in Altneustadt, the more likely he is to be Protestant. The strong correlation between length of residence and religion is, of course, found at the aggregative level of occupational groups $(r = .77)$ as well. Thus, an interpretation of the second axis of Figure 3.1 as the axis of religious differentiation in the labor force might also be quite defensible. We suspect, however, that the differentiation of the population according to its religious preferences is not so readily perceived by the average citizen as are the differences associated with length of residence.

Altbürger, in fact, speak (or at least know) a distinctive, readily identifiable German dialect, in contrast to the *Neubürger* who, given their heterogeneous origins, speak with a variety of accents that are not of the local region.

As you will recall, the percentage of Catholics in an occupational group is given in the last column of Table 3.1. In most cases, the deviation of an occupational group from the average for Altneustadt as a whole does not amount to more than five percentage points. The exceptions are, on the one hand, occupations whose members primarily work at the natural science research facility and, on the other hand, occupations that might have been typical of Altneustadt's social make-up before the foundation of the research laboratory, including independent small businessmen, artisans, minor civil servants, and clerical aides.

To determine the social distances between Catholic and Protestant occupational groups, we proceeded exactly as before, the only difference being that we now used the 703 indexes of dissimilarity for 38 groups (that is, 19 occupational categories for each religious group). People expressing no religious preference were included with the Protestants. The two-dimensional smallest space solution had an unacceptably high coefficient of alienation (.21), suggesting that there were too many violations of the monotone relationship between the input coefficients and the derived distances to warrant interpretation of the spatial solution. Figure 3.2, thus, portrays the three-dimensional solution, which did have a satisfactory coefficient of alienation (.15).

As in Figure 3.1, the prestige dimension (which happens, in this case, to follow quite closely the Y-axis) is the most important one in ordering the social distances among the occupational groups, irrespective of religious differences. It is striking that the Protestant groups (perforated lines) use the whole range of the Y-axis to express their prestige differences, whereas the Catholic groups tend to cluster toward the middle of the Y-axis—the single exception being the Catholic natural scientists (K 2). Above all, this clustering of the Catholic groups has the effect of making less marked the distinct gap between the working- and middle-class occupations observed in Figure 3.1. Catholic craftsmen and foremen, for example, are located nearer to the middle-class occupations than to the corresponding Protestant groups. A similar tendency can be seen for the upper middle-class groups, in which the Catholics tend to be located closer to the middle-class occupations than are the Protestants.

We were not able to come up with any straightforward interpretation of the second and third axes. Apparently the altitude of a group is linked to the religious cleavage. The Protestant groups are generally located higher on the Z-axis than the Catholic groups are. Since religion, how-

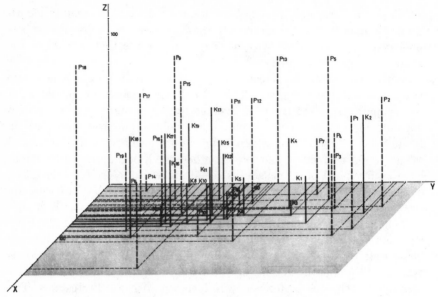

Figure 3.2 The social distance among Catholic and Protestant occupational groups. (Three-dimensional solution for similarities of friendship choices, Guttman-Lingoes coefficient of alienation = .152). P = Protestant; K = Catholic. For the number of occupational group, see Table 3.1.

ever, was measured as a dichotomy and, thus, there can be no intra-category variation, differences in altitude must be generated by some additional distance-generating mechanism. The X-axis is even more difficult to interpret. Particularly for middle-class occupations, one can observe a tendency for occupations that are more likely to be connected to the natural science research laboratory to be located toward the back of the space and occupations having no links to this organization to be located toward the front. More generally, one can construct an inclined plane oriented in the second and third dimensions and running from the back top to the front base in such a way that it almost perfectly divides *Neubürger* from *Altbürger* groups.

When we interpreted Figure 3.1, we stressed that the 19 occupations appeared to cluster in 3 broad groups: the working class, the middle class, and the upper middle class. Our interpretation of the social stratification of Altneustadt argued that its organization was in terms of social classes as hierarchically ordered, bounded groups and not as a prestige continuum. The question is whether or not this interpretation holds, when we are confronted with the somewhat more complex structure of the three-dimensional solution where distance-generating mechanisms associated with occupation, residence, and religion are simultaneously operative.

One can detect a certain clustering of the groups in Figure 3.2 with the naked eye. Can we find a more objective basis for delineating bounded social groups? We thought that a divisive hierarchical clustering technique might provide a satisfactory answer to this question. This procedure treats the groups as one big pool at the start which is successively separated in the following 37 steps into a larger and larger number of clusters until every group forms its own cluster of one (cf. Johnson, 1967). The researcher then chooses how many clusters he wants to identify, guided, of course, by objective information on meaningful cut-off points. The input data to the program are the 703 pairwise distances which are computed from the coordinates of the points in the three-dimensional space of Figure 3.2.

Our main interpretation of the group structure of Altneustadt is most convincingly supported by the results of this cluster analysis. In the first step, the occupations of the upper middle class are separated from the rest; and, in the second step, the remaining groups are divided into a working-class and a middle-class cluster. It is only in succeeding steps that the classes are subdivided according to religious criteria. With a few exceptions, the corresponding Protestant and Catholic occupational groups belong to the same social classes as we anticipated from the findings based on occupational distances alone.

When we interpret Figure 3.2 guided by the results of the cluster analysis, a very simple and convincing interpretation is possible. Each of the three broad classes has the structure of a circle. The three circles are located at different levels on the first axis (which, the reader will recall, is the axis of socioeconomic differentiation). The centroid of the upper middle-class circle is dominated by Protestant groups, while the centroids of the other two classes are dominated by Catholic groups.

In order to use certain statistical techniques on the cross-section sample, the results of which will be reported in subsequent chapters, it was apparent that we could not continue to use such detailed classifications of groups as we did in the two smallest space analyses because of the excessively small numbers falling into some of the categories. On the basis of the smallest space and cluster analysis results, we, therefore, constructed a classification of people into nine social categories that captured, in our judgment, the principal grounds of social differentiation in the community.

In this new coding scheme, two segments of the working class and six sections of the middle classes were identified. (Remember that, while we shall speak of members of specific occupations belonging to different class clusters, this is an elliptical expression for the entire family unit, whether represented in our sample data by the wage earner or by his non-working spouse.) The Protestant working class includes persons who had moved to Altneustadt before the research facility was built and who appear to occupy the lowest prestige position in Altneustadt at some distance from the other working-class groups. The *Altbürger* working class is predominantly comprised of Catholic manual workers plus a very small number of Protestant craftsmen, who socially belong to this group on the basis of their close proximity to the Catholic groups in terms of friendship choices. The third group is the *Altbürger* lower middle class, the overwhelming majority of whom are Catholic clerical workers employed in local industry and governmental agencies. The *Neubürger* lower middle class is comprised predominantly of technicians employed at the research center, who have a somewhat higher occupational prestige than do the *Altbürger* lower middle class. The *Altbürger* middle class includes the Catholic independent small businessmen and artisans, who are rather close in friendship preferences to the *Altbürger* lower middle class. The corresponding group in the Neustadt subcommunity, the *Neubürger* middle middle class, is comprised of engineers and Protestant government inspectors, both of whom enjoy much higher occupational prestige than their *Altbürger* class counterparts and came to town more recently than the *Neubürger* lower middle class. Protestant and Catholic scientists, recent arrivals to Altneustadt and almost exclusively employed at the research facility, have been combined to form the *Neubürger* upper middle class since they are very close to one another in their friendship preferences. The *Altbürger* upper middle class consists of Catholic entrepreneurs, free professionals, teachers, and other salaried professionals, all of whom tend to form a tight cluster of mutually chosen groups that avoid informal interaction with members of the *Neubürger* upper middle class. Finally, the students, because of their highly distinctive status and overwhelming tendency to form a socially exclusive group that makes it difficult to link them meaningfully to any other group, will be treated as a separate group, whenever possible.

CONCLUDING REMARKS

In what might appear at times to be an overly tortuous analysis, we have attempted to delineate an objective and replicable strategy for recovering the bases of social differentiation in a large population. The substantive results regarding the structural differentiation of Altneustadt's population will be of continuing significance throughout following chapters—providing critical reference points from which to evaluate the structuring of the elite decision-making subsystem and the interface between the elite and the community as a differentiated population subsystem with a distinctive organization of its own.

The results reported in this chapter closely conform with more impressionistic observations by long-term residents of the community who were either sophisticated in the ways of social science or were "naive" ordinary citizens who had participated in community affairs for a long time. The merit and justification of our approach must rest, therefore, not so much on recovering a structure that many "locals" already knew but on providing a set of tactics that yield quantifiable and falsifiable results that may, in turn, be replicated and used to build an increasingly precise and sophisticated model of a community's structural differentiation and to generate more precise estimates of its role in a theory of system integration. In the next chapter, we shall explore the ways in which the population's social differentiation is associated with its value differentiation as well.

4

Value Orientations: Their Structure and Social Differentiation*

A multiplicity of terms have been used to refer to the abstract evaluative standards that we have in mind when speaking of people's social value orientations. Attitudes, belief systems, ideologies, and opinions designate but a few of the partly overlapping concepts most frequently discussed in the literature (cf. Scott, 1968: 204–205, for a short list of related concepts). Given our already overly ambitious theoretical and empirical agenda, we have no interest in entering the voluminous and, at times, heated debates over the many complex theoretical and methodological issues raised in studying values and their empirically problematic role in serving as general normative guidelines constraining personal, social, and cultural choices (cf. Kluckhohn, 1951; Converse, 1964; Rokeach, 1968; 1973).

Our aims in this chapter must, of necessity, be more modest. First, we shall try to specify a reasonably circumscribed, but by no means rigorous, definition of our theoretical construct that will at least broadly

---

* Although this chapter again draws heavily from a previously published article in a German journal (cf. Pappi and Laumann, 1974), we have entirely rewritten it to provide a concise summary of our central argument and selected results especially pertinent to the issues raised in this monograph. The reader should consult the original article for a much more extended treatment of measurement strategies and discussions, tables, and references primarily directed to the German context.

indicate how we shall be using the term in the subsequent analysis. Second, we shall describe the research strategy we adopted in operationalizing specific instances of the concept. This strategy is by no means the optimal one we might have devised if the identification and measurement of social values were the central objective of our empirical study. On the contrary, our strategy reflects the many pragmatic compromises we had to make in exploiting a study design that served multiple and, at certain points, conflicting purposes. Finally, we hope to demonstrate the utility of the particular measures of social values and attitudes that we used in Altneustadt to help us interpret people's collective preferences as they relate to community affairs. We shall show how the social groupings identified in the preceding chapter are also differentiated from one another with respect to their basic value commitments. Of course, there may well be some overarching set of social values shared by almost all members of the community—so self-evident that no one thinks to articulate them or regard them as problematic—that provide the generally agreed upon framework within which collective decisions must be made. We are, however, more concerned with identifying those basic value orientations and attitudes that serve to differentiate individuals and groups from one another and, thus, to provide conflicting integrative standards, rooted in socially coherent entities, that provide the basis for persisting social controversies related to these standards.

Broadly following Parsons' (1951; Parsons and Shils, 1951) discussion of values, we can first distinguish between the types of objects (e.g., personality, societal, and cultural) toward which orientations are directed and the nature of the orientations themselves (e.g., cognitive, conative, and evaluative). In contrast to beliefs or attitudes with their strong cognitive or conative components, value orientations have an evaluative primacy that implies the application of certain normative standards in the selection of objects. As Parsons (1968: 136) himself observes: "The values which come to be constitutive of the structure of a societal system are, then, the conceptions of the desirable type of society held by the members of the society of reference and applied to the particular society of which they are members."

In complex societies, moreover, the desirable type of society can be further specified with reference to how arrangements and performances within particular societal subsystems should be evaluated. Thus, we can usefully distinguish among social values on the basis of how they specifically refer to functionally specialized social structures, such as the desirable forms of economic organization, political arrangements, social stratification system, and pattern-maintenance institutions, including the family and religious and educational subsystems. An exhaustive inventory of the relevant value conceptions in each institutional domain is certainly not feasible here, both because theory itself is undeveloped on these detailed points and because the data requirements exceed our available means. We can only make a crude first approximation of characterizing the more salient, and hopefully critical, value dimensions in each domain by culling from the diffuse literature on different institutional areas those values and attitudes that have attracted the most research attention and have been demonstrated to yield the most consistent differences between people located in different social structural positions. In short, the Parsonsian scheme is being used here primarily as a sensitizing framework alerting us to the broad range of values that should be systematically taken into account. It is really only a small first step beyond a completely ad hoc shopping list of potentially relevant value orientations.

Worth noting here also is the fact that we do not assume that there be any neat parallelisms between value orientations held in one institutional domain and those held by the same persons or groups in others. On the contrary, we assume that the patterning of correlations of values across institutional sectors is empirically problematic. As we shall see, values cohere in individuals and groups in quite distinctive patterns that may help us to explain certain dynamic features of the political process (cf. Converse, 1964). Having the society and its subsystems as the objects of orientation, our analysis differs from other investigations of value orientations that are focused on cultural values (e.g., Kluckhohn and Strodtbeck, 1961) or personal values (e.g., Allport *et al.*, 1960) or on standards for everyday life, without explicitly distinguishing between objects of orientation (e.g., Rokeach, 1971).

In the last chapter, we analyzed the social distances among generalized social positions and identified a set of population groups that could be regarded as bounded groups in the sense that their intragroup contact densities with regard to intimate relationships are relatively high compared to the between-group contact densities. According to the distance-generating mechanism postulated for the formation of intimate ties, the process of group formation may be seen as determined, at least in part, by the value similarities of prospective interaction partners. In this chapter, we turn our attention away from this "interaction" notion of social distance and determine distances among groups according to similarities of their value profiles (cf. McFarland and Brown [1973] for a discussion of these two types of distance concepts). We coined the expression "value distance," in contrast to social distance, in order to stress the point that, on this "cultural" level of analysis, distance is not generated by interaction rates between groups of people but is deduced from similarities with regard to an imposed value scheme. Even if we assume that the particular set of value orientations that we examined is a representative sample of the universe of value orientations influencing friendship formation, we should not expect the normative distances to be identical with the social distances among groups. There should, of course, be some correspondence between them, but by no means a perfect one. Apart from the random effect or "noise" hindering perfect agreement, social and cultural systems follow somewhat different organizing principles.

Interests are more obviously linked to specific social structural positions than values are, especially when they are more narrowly conceived in terms of who will pay the economic costs incurred by a particular policy and who will enjoy the economic benefits of that policy. Even if it is impossible to deduce the interests corresponding to given structural positions from general economic principles, there is usually a close empirical association between given structural positions and given interests, once these interests are articulated. Articulated interests or claims on the collective decision-making system, however, are generally evaluated in terms of legitimizing ideas, that is, in terms of appeals to broader, often shared values, so that it is most difficult to maintain the distinction between interests and values in empirical analysis. "Naked" interests are a limiting case for the integrative system in much the same sense that pure coercive force is for the political system. When we speak of the interest differentiation of Altneustadt's population subsystem in the following chapters, we assume that it derives, at least in part, from the differentiation of value preferences in the community (as well as from the instrumental logic of economic self-interest).

In the following sections of the chapter, first, we describe the procedures we employed in measuring specific social values in Altneustadt. We then examine the differential affinity of the population groups identified in the preceding chapter for these social values. Finally, we describe the relative proximities of these groups in terms of the similarities and dissimilarities in their respective value profiles. This value differentiation of the population subsystem is then linked to the structure of latent and manifest interests that the population subsystem poses for the community's integrative subsystem of collective decision making.

MEASURING SOCIAL VALUE ORIENTATIONS

In constructing the interview schedule for the cross-section survey, we included many questions designed to elicit people's evaluations of alternative ways of doing things on a wide-ranging variety of salient social, political, and economic topics. A number of questions were borrowed from other studies where they had already proven themselves to be effective discriminators of popular opinion. The questions were intentionally varied in style and format to militate against response sets and couched in terms meaningful to the average member of the community. For the most part, they were designed to address issues as concretely and specifically as possible, as well as to call for the clear expression of a preference between explicit or implicit alternatives or of approval or disapproval of a particular course of action. The 37 items finally selected for analysis met the criteria for satisfactory scale items, such as response distributions that were not badly skewed and low frequencies of nonresponse (e.g., "don't know"). (The items are listed in Appendix B, Part I. We shall use the identification numbers listed there to signify the position of the items in Figures 4.1 and 4.2.)

Although people were asked to make judgments on quite specific issues, we thought it not unreasonable to assume that we could infer the implicit operation of more general evaluative standards in accounting for the consistent patterning of people's judgments, if any, across a number of issue areas. Thus, as a preliminary to constructing unidimensional value scales, we examined the overall pattern of intercorrelations among the items, omitting those items that were uncorrelated with any of the other items. The 37-by-37 matrix of Pearsonian intercorrelations resulting after omitting unsatisfactory items was subjected to a smallest space analysis (cf. Lingoes, 1965a, 1973), which obtained a satisfactory two-dimensional solution (Kruskal's stress coefficient = .154; cf. Pappi and Laumann, 1975).

Items in close proximity in Figure 4.1, which portrays the smallest space solution, are relatively highly correlated with one another at the same time that they have similar patterns of correlations with items more distant from them. Figure 4.1 can thus be used to see, first, how the items clustered into various subsets that tapped different underlying value dimensions and, second, how the various subsets (clusters) were, in turn, interrelated to one another. Items in the same region of the spatial solution are positively correlated with one another, while those at greater distance from them are either uncorrelated or negatively correlated with them. To ease the inspection of Figure 4.1, we labeled the clusters with the names of the scales we subsequently constructed.

Turning to a substantive interpretation of the spatial solution, we observe a heavy concentration of items on the right side of the figure. Mostly related to integrative and pattern-maintenance functions, positive responses to these items reflect conservative values with respect to the importance of traditional religious beliefs and behaviors, traditional family values, justification or legitimacy of the existing levels of social

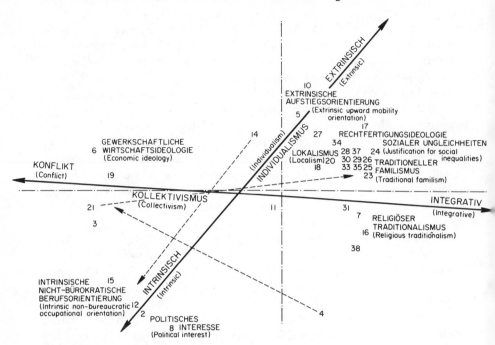

Figure 4.1   The structure of social value orientations, individual-level data. (Kruskal's stress coefficient = .154.) See Appendix B, Part I, for specific item content. [Source: Pappi and Laumann, 1974: 167, Figure 1.]

inequalities in Germany, and positive orientations toward the local community in preference to extracommunity and societal-level concerns. (This overrepresentation of conservative items has, of course, no substantive significance in itself, as it merely reflects the biases of our original item selection.) These items clearly suggest a positive commitment to an organic theory of society and the social order in which men are expected to accept their station in life and obey the dictates and guidance of traditional institutions. Items located to the left of the space are especially concerned with work, economic, and political values that presuppose a conception of society that is legitimately premised on political conflict among contending groups, particularly economic ones, and a rejection of the present levels of social inequalities (cf. Lenski, 1966; Duke, 1967). We have labeled this axis of value differentiation "conflict versus integrative collectivism."

Obliquely crosscutting this axis is a dimension that we have tentatively labeled "intrinsic versus extrinsic individualism," especially with respect to work values. Items in the lower left-hand quadrant tap orientations that positively evaluate jobs that provide opportunities for applying one's own capabilities, self-direction or work autonomy, and risk taking (what might be termed an "entrepreneurial" orientation; cf. Miller and Swanson, 1958, 1960; Kohn, 1969; Laumann, 1973: 73–82).[1] Items in the upper right-hand quadrant suggest a more extrinsic orientation to work situations in which opportunities for upward social mobility and good income are highly valued as well as such extrinsic work rewards as having good colleagues to work with and high job security (what has been called a "bureaucratic" work orientation; cf. Mortimer, 1972).

Because the conservative items were so heavily clustered in the space due to their relatively high positive intercorrelations among themselves and negative correlations with items on the left side of the space, we decided to examine their internal structure more closely by calculating the smallest space solution for the matrix of intercorrelations including only these items. (This purely technical procedure for "clarifying the structure" allows points to relocate themselves relative to one another by no longer subjecting them to the severe constraints imposed on their locations by the presence of a number of items that are strongly negatively related to them.) Figure 4.2 portrays the two-dimensional solution obtained (Kruskal's stress coefficient = .195).

A meaningful interpretation of the structure of conservative value orientations is readily apparent. The first axis arranges pattern-maintenance items in the upper half and economic values on the lower side. Crosscutting this axis is a second axis that locates collectivistic values toward the upper right side and more individualistic values toward the lower left side. The items clustered in the center tap integrative values with respect to social egalitarianism and localistic orientation. Their centrality in the space arises from their being correlated to, more or less, the same degree with all the items located toward the periphery of the space as well as their being modestly correlated with one another.

With these results in hand to guide us, we constructed seven unidimensional scales by combining the appropriate items into summary scores (see Appendix B, Part I, for which items were combined to form each scale). When constructing the scales, we did not strictly follow the information on the distances between the items. The results of the multidimensional scaling set constraints on our scale construction insofar as we chose only items clustered in the same region to form a scale. (This

---

[1] We ran several multidimensional analyses reflecting the signs of the coefficients of certain items to place them in their appropriate substantive cluster. Items that were used with reflected signs in the construction of the value scales can be identified in Figure 4.1 by the dotted arrows extended from them to the location that they "moved" to when their signs were reflected.

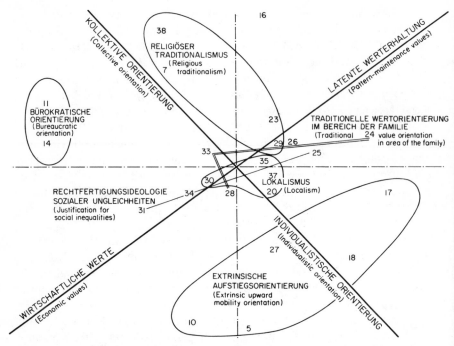

Figure 4.2 The structure of conservative value orientations. (Kruskal's stress coefficient = .195.) See Appendix B, Part I, for specific item content. [Source: Pappi and Laumann, 1974: 168, Figure 2.]

procedure is appropriate for Likert scaling. Note that, for Guttman scaling, the items should be located farther apart, provided they reveal a linear ordering.) The decision, however, of which specific items of a cluster to include in a scale was made on substantive considerations. Thus, we made a distinction between three aspects of the conservative "ideology" of integrative collectivism, depending on whether the object of orientation was the family (family traditionalism), the local community (localism), or religious institutions (religious traditionalism). The individualistic pole of the conservative subset of items is represented by two scales: upward mobility orientation and justification for existing social inequalities. The individualistic–collectivistic distinction pertains also to the nonconservative scales, with preference for work autonomy on the one side and an economic ideology favoring unions and the workers on the other. In addition to these seven scales based on multiple items, we thought it useful to include the single item on political interest as a scale of its own because of its substantive importance to our overall analysis. (See Pappi and Laumann, 1974, for further details on our scaling procedures, including a canonical correlation analysis of the items with standard demographic and social characteristics of the respondents.)

Table 4.1 presents the intercorrelation matrix for the eight measures. In summary form, it contains much the same information as Figure 4.1 but permits the reader to assess the relative strengths of association among the scales. All the scales on the conservative side are correlated positively with one another; the same is true for the three scales on the left side of Figure 4.1. The individual items comprising the two sets of scales are also consistently correlated negatively. In contrast to factor analytic procedures for scaling items that yield a set of individual factor scores that ideally have no correlation with one another, our procedure produces eight substantively different value scales that are theoretically distinct and yet empirically correlated with one another to varying degrees. We believe our approach provides a more meaningful depiction of the ways in which social value orientations empirically cohere in the same individual.

VALUE DIFFERENTIATION OF POPULATION GROUPS

Turning from this individual-level analysis of value preferences, we can now ask whether the population subgroups identified in the last chapter exhibit, on the aggregated level, any special affinities to particular constellations of social values (what we shall also call value profiles). If they do, we can then determine, in the next section, the groups' normative proximities to one another as a function of the simi-

TABLE 4.1

Matrix of Product–Moment Correlations of the Eight Scales of Value Orientations[a]

	Value scales							
Value scales	(1)	(2)	(3)	(4)	(5)	(6)	(7)	(8)
1. Political interest	—							
2. Economic ideology favoring unions	.066	—						
3. Preference for work autonomy	.276	.027	—					
4. Religious traditionalism	—.161	—.237	—.236	—				
5. Justification for social inequalities	—.261	—.256	—.291	.377	—			
6. Upward mobility orientation	—.323	—.113	—.398	.246	.406	—		
7. Localism	—.289	—.190	—.330	.499	.511	.472	—	
8. Family traditionalism	—.212	—.257	—.332	.483	.480	.425	.550	—

[a] Source: Pappi and Laumann, 1974: 170, Table 3.

larities in their constellations of preferred value positions. Since age proved to be one of the most powerful predictors of individual value preferences (cf. Pappi and Laumann, 1974: 171–177), we divided each of the 8 population groups into 2 subgroups consisting of people either younger or older than 35 years of age. This age seemed to be a meaningful cut-off point because people less than 35 years old received their decisive value and political socialization subsequent to World War II and the Nazi period and clearly manifested a generational shift toward less conservative value positions. In addition to these 16 groups, we treated the Catholic and Protestant students separately (all of the students were, of course, under 35). Additional information on housewives and apprentices was used to place them in one of the population groups. Thus, those respondents omitted from the social distance analysis in the last chapter are included here.

The means of the 8 value scales are given in Table 4.2 for the 18 population groups, together with information on their relative size and the Fararo–Sunshine measure on inbreeding bias (see Chapter 3, pp. 55–56). Although the groups do differ considerably in their tendencies to choose members of their own groups as friends, they all show some inbreeding bias so our assumption that we are dealing with self-selecting groups seems justified. These groups differ not only in their social distance from one another, but evidently in their normative distance as well. For every one of the eight value scales, the group means are significantly different. The percentage between-group variance of the total variance (η^2) ranges between 9 and 26.

Since the distinction between *Altbürger* and *Neubürger* is an organizing principle built into the classification of the groups, it may not be too surprising that the groups differ most with regard to localism: Of the variance of this scale, 26% is accounted for by between-group differences. What may be more surprising is that only 9% of the variance of economic ideology is explained by our classification of groups despite the fact that social class differences were the most important organizing principle in the social structural space. Here we should remind ourselves, however, that social classes, in the sense of prestige classes, are not identical with economic classes for which the self-employed–employee cleavage is an important constituent element. Class differentiation in Altneustadt appears to follow more closely this prestige principle than it does class interests strictly rooted in relations to the economic modes of production.

Interestingly enough, the most extreme attitudes with regard to economic ideology are found in the middle classes. The *Altbürger* middle classes, which are mainly what is called *alter Mittelstand* in Germany—

that is, self-employed people who are neither capitalists nor proletarians —are strongly anti-union. The *Neubürger* middle classes, on the other hand, the *neue Mittelstand,* are strongly pro-union. Elements of the working class—the actual object of these ideological concerns—fall somewhere in between the middle class groupings. The pro-union element in the middle class would seem to be based more on expressive than instrumental considerations.

From Table 4.2, it is almost impossible to gain any overview of the ways in which the groups might systematically differ from one another with respect to the eight value scales considered singly, let alone simultaneously. This difficulty can be overcome by submitting information on the groups' differing value orientations to a multidimensional scalogram analysis (MSA I, cf. Lingoes, 1973: 219–238; Laumann and House, 1970). The purpose of the analysis is to map the groups into an Euclidean space such that groups having similar profiles of value positions will be in close proximity (i.e., share a region of the space) and those having increasingly disparate constellations of value positions will be at ever greater distances from one another. In other words, the Euclidean distances will be assumed to be a monotonic function of an underlying, possibly multidimensional hypothetical construct, value distance, that separates or brings together groups on the basis of similarities in their constellations of social value orientations. (Remember that, in this procedure, as was true for smallest space analysis, the derived Euclidean distances are, of course, metric and fully at the interval level of measurement. We must initially assume, however, only ordinal-level measurement for the input matrix—that is, it is reasonable to rank input information about the relative proximities of groups, but we cannot say how far apart two ranked groups are from one another in comparison to two other ranked groups.)

To facilitate computation and avoid making unnecessary assumptions about the precision of our measurement instruments, we trichotomized each scale's group means into low, middle, and high categories, subject to the constraint that there be at least three groups in each category. Except for the scales concerning economic ideology and preference for work autonomy, the groups are distributed quite evenly across the three categories.

The input matrix thus consisted of the 18 population groups in the rows and 8 columns having entries of "1," "2," or "3," corresponding to the respective groups' value position on each scale. Figure 4.3 portrays the two-dimensional solution, which had a very satisfactory coefficient of contiguity of .979 (a perfect fit would be 1.00).

Three clusters of points can be distinguished in Figure 4.3. The older

TABLE 4.2

Population Proportions, Indices of Systematic Endophily and Means of the Eight Social Value Scales for the Eighteen Population Groups in Altneustadt[a]

Population groups in Altneustadt	Code[b]	Population proportion	Endophily[c]	Political interest	Economic ideology	Preference for work autonomy	Religious traditionalism	Justification for social inequality	Upward mobility orientation	Localism	Family traditionalism
Altbürger working class	AK1	19.3	.254	2.81	.38	−3.54	.90	−.17	2.94	2.49	1.60
	JK1	9.0	.295	2.47	.51	−2.29	−.74	−1.74	2.85	.65	−.65
Altbürger lower middle class	AK2	12.9	.037	3.01	−.06	−2.60	1.21	−1.92	1.38	1.98	.85
	JK2	7.7	.066	3.10	−.08	−1.74	−2.75	−2.67	.05	−3.37	−3.16
Altbürger middle middle class	AK3	9.8	.165	2.68	−1.56	−1.27	2.63	−.95	2.38	1.79	1.70
	JK3	3.3	.043	3.00	−.14	−.55	−.65	−2.37	.07	−2.07	−2.48
Altbürger upper middle class	AK4	5.2	.353	3.63	−2.89	.57	1.29	−1.67	−2.29	−2.12	−1.02
	JK4	1.1	.061	3.00	−1.17	−1.87	−1.50	−4.00	−.42	−3.44	−4.44

		%									
Catholic students	JK5	2.4	.399	3.50	1.22	3.76	−4.85	−5.50	−2.41	−7.40	−6.60
Protestant working class	AP1	5.7	.134	2.45	.46	−3.82	1.50	.19	4.09	3.28	2.55
	JP1	1.5	.164	2.50	1.25	−3.67	−1.73	−2.50	3.82	−2.17	−1.17
Protestant lower middle class	AP2	3.0	.033	3.04	−.88	−1.47	−.02	−1.48	1.05	.00	.40
middle class	JP2	2.4	.166	2.80	1.33	−3.66	−2.55	−3.50	1.33	−1.35	−2.70
Neubürger middle	AP3	3.0	.082	3.44	−.21	−.85	−1.02	−1.80	−1.67	−1.04	−1.20
middle class	JP3	2.6	.100	3.10	1.41	−2.29	−3.83	−2.91	−.53	−4.43	−3.14
Neubürger upper	AP4	4.9	.274	3.38	.16	2.37	−3.82	−3.90	−3.49	−5.48	−3.23
middle class	JP4	4.8	.347	3.44	2.77	1.50	−5.88	−3.64	−4.33	−6.41	−5.10
Protestant students	JP5	1.2	.380	3.50	2.50	2.12	−7.06	−4.90	−1.84	−8.20	−7.00
Total sample ($N = 819$)		100.0%		2.96	−.10	−1.67	−.42	−1.79	.93	−.38	−.59
F-test for group differences ($+ p < .01$)				5.84+	3.29+	9.80+	11.16+	6.14+	11.42+	16.20+	13.29+
η^2				.11	.09	.18	.20	.12	.20	.26	.22

[a] Source: Pappi and Laumann, 1974: 174–175, Table 5.

[b] The first letter indicates age: A = over 35 years, J = under 35; the second letter indicates religion: K = Catholic or *Altbürger*; P = Protestant or *Neubürger*; the number indicates social class or student group.

[c] Group self-selection calculated according to Fararo and Sunsine (1964: 72–74).

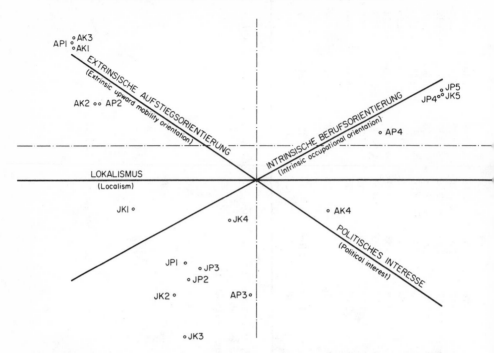

Figure 4.3 Value distances of population groups in Altneustadt: A multidimensional scalogram analysis. (Guttman–Lingoes coefficient of contiguity = .979.) See Column 1 of Table 4.2 for group code. [Source: Pappi and Laumann, 1974: 176 Figure 3.]

members of the working, lower middle, and middle middle classes are concentrated in the upper left-hand corner. Members of the two Protestant groups among them (i.e., the Protestant working and lower middle classes) typically moved to Altneustadt well before the research organization was founded. Thus, one could interpret this cluster as the Altstadt sector of Altneustadt. Opposite this cluster in the upper right-hand corner are the groups typical of the Neustadt sector of Altneustadt, namely, the *Neubürger* upper middle class and the student groups. As we shall learn in Parts II and III, these groups provide the principal support for the SPD opposition in the community influence system. A third cluster located toward the middle in the lower half of the figure contains almost exclusively the groups of younger people from all classes and nativity status. Only the students and the younger *Neubürger* upper middle class are not close to this cluster.

There is one population group that clearly does not belong to any cluster. This is the older *Altbürger* upper middle class (AK4), the principal group base of the dominant CDU coalition (see Part II). The younger members of this class are also located nearby.

In order to facilitate the substantive interpretation of these various group clusters in terms of shared value orientations, we have drawn axes for those value scales on which the groups can be arranged in a monotonic order. To determine a group's relative location on a value dimension, one simply drops a perpendicular line from that value scale's axis to the group in question. (One, of course, can refer to Table 4.2 for the group's actual mean score.)

The value orientation corresponding best to the left-to-right order of the three clusters is the localism scale. The older members of the working, lower middle, and *Altbürger* middle middle classes have the highest localistic orientation, while the natural scientists have the lowest. The younger people of Altneustadt are intermediate on this value. The differentiation of the groups according to religious traditionalism also parallels this ordering on localism, but with one important exception. The older members of the *Altbürger* upper middle class share the strong commitment to traditional religious values with the Altstadt cluster of groups in this community, in contrast to the less traditional orientations of the other groups located to the right of the space. Regarding other conservative values, however, this group typically occupies a moderate position, sometimes even close to the less conservative orientations of the older *Neubürger* upper middle class. These modest similarities in the value orientations of these rival sections of the upper middle class probably reflect their similarities in educational backgrounds (they are almost all university educated) and the fact that the majority in each group are in professional occupations, which tend to promote less traditional value orientations.

The biggest differences in occupational activities within a class is found between the older small businessmen and artisans in the *Altbürger* middle middle class and the engineers in the corresponding older *Neubürger* class. Perhaps, therefore, it is not so surprising that the largest value gap (distance) of all intraclass group comparisons is observed between these two groups.

The axis in Figure 4.3 representing preference for work autonomy essentially orders the groups according to their social class location. This finding is completely consistent with Kohn's (1969) cross-national study of class-based values in Italy and the United States. Values respecting political interest and upward mobility orientation appear to be less class linked because generational differences blur the influences of social class.

Group differences to be observed on some value scales do not follow a strict linear order in the spatial solution. This is above all true for economic ideology. All younger *Neubürger* groups, from the Protestant working class to the Protestant students, are among the supporters of an economic ideology favorable to unions, whereas all groups that include self-employed people are opponents of this ideology, irrespective of their age or socioeconomic composition. The most heterogeneous cluster with regard to economic ideology is the cluster of groups located in the lower middle region. The Altstadt cluster of groups contains both opponents and moderate supporters of unions, while the *Neubürger* cluster is composed mainly of supporters of an economic ideology favoring unions.

More generally, how do the organizing principles underlying the social structural differentiation of the groups compare to those structuring the value space? The answer seems to be that they are essentially similar in character. Apart from the apparent generational differences underlying group distances in the value space (these were simply not tapped in the social structural analysis because of our coding scheme that ignored age distinctions), both structures appear to use the *Altbürger–Neubürger* and class differences as the basic distance-generating mechanisms among groups. What is different in the two solutions is the relative salience of these two principles. The value profiles of the population subgroups have much more variation with regard to the *Altbürger–Neubürger* categorization than with regard to social class, whereas the reverse was true for the social structural space.

What, however, are the more general implications of this analysis of value differentiation among Altneustadt's population groups? Here we shall note only three broad sets of implications with respect to the social organization and political life of the community and its potential relevance to the analysis of the community integrative subsystem. More detailed consideration of the impact of these group-based value differences and corresponding group proximities will be deferred to succeeding chapters as they become relevant to our theoretical and empirical argument.

First, we should recall that the impact of multidimensional value proximities in facilitating the formation of intimate ties between members of different groups (see Chapter 3 and our discussion of value homophyly in Chapter 6, pp. 119) is a key element in our discussion of the distance-generating mechanism postulated for structuring intimate social relationships among generalized social positions. The results reported in this chapter clearly support the argument made in Chapter 3 that out-group choices of friends are by no means the result of a random process of selection but are likely to be directed, if at all possible, to the members of adjacent groups on the basis of similar values and attitudes. Since, for various reasons, we did not construct strictly comparable groups in the two analyses, we can only appeal, at this point, to an "eye-balling" of the two solutions that clearly suggests that roughly comparable groups tend to occupy similar regions of their respective spatial solutions. In other words, highly proximate groups in the value space are likely to be close together in the social structural space; and, conversely, highly distant groups in one space tend to be far apart in the other as well.

Second, we should note that the value space can help us make much more detailed substantive inferences about the probable preferences and behavior of the various constituent population elements in the community population subsystem with respect to the claims they are likely to make on the community integrative subsystem. For example, since the groups clearly differ systematically along class lines with respect to their levels of political interest and awareness—incidentally, this finding is consistent with most reported research (e.g., Verba and Nie, 1972); we might be able to infer differential rates of voting and other forms of political participation in community affairs (e.g., complaining to public officials about an unjust policy). By implication, differential likelihoods of groups' interests and demands being taken into account in community decision-making may not simply be functions of the groups' numerical strength in the voting population but may reflect their capacity for political mobilization as well. We shall also be able to use this information to predict how groups should line up with respect to specific community issues that activate one or another of their basic value commitments (see Chapters 9 and 12).

Third, we should be able to see now that there cannot be any simple mapping of political party support onto our group value space, nor should we expect to find an unproblematic, stable set of political coalitions of various groups acting together to advance and defend their value preferences on all community controversies. On the contrary, it should be obvious that the complex multidimensional value space could hardly be adequately mapped onto choices among two or three political parties without serious inconsistencies arising soon thereafter. The parties themselves represent highly complex, and often misperceived, stimuli for the voters and often advocate inherently contradictory programs in terms of various value standards. Indeed, examination of group party preference quickly reveals the three main clusters of groups in Figure 4.3 are far less homogeneous with regard to their party voting behavior than with regard to their value constellations (see Chapter 12). This is especially true for the cluster of the older generation of Altneustadt's working and middle classes. The *Altbürger* middle class is clearly a stronghold of the CDU. The older workers, however, close as they are to the independent small businessmen and artisans in the value space, give a majority of their votes to the SPD. For the middle classes, the association of value orientations and political behavior is more in line with the expectations one would have as an outside observer, given the programs of the parties, than it is for the working class groups (cf. Converse, 1964). The decisive effects of working class membership on party preference seem to be explained less in terms of the working class's constellation of value preferences than by its "traditional" affiliation with the SPD that, over the years, has been maintained even in the face of apparent discrepancies in the value postures of the party and its various constituencies on particular issues.

SOME GEDANKENEXPERIMENTE

Let us now become even more speculative and turn to a few *Gedankenexperimente* that are intended to stimulate thought on an old but critically important problem. Given a normatively democratic political system, how can one assess the biases of the collective decision-making subsystem charged with aggregating the demands for collective action or inaction of a population subsystem highly differentiated both in terms of basic value commitments and social organization?

Suppose, for the moment, that the arrangement of points in Figure 4.3 accurately represents the underlying "value topography" of the community's population elements (groups). Where a group stands in the space will very much determine the set of evaluative standards it brings to bear in judging specific policy proposals for the community. We must, of course, recognize that, as a matter of course, there are many proposals for community action that may well fall into the zone of political indifference (cf. Barnard, 1938). That is, such issues leave most groups' deeply held value commitments unactivated, and they are seen by most people as being purely instrumental questions, perhaps of special relevance to only particular groups (see Chapter 9 for a more extended discussion of a typology of issues). Assuming, however, that an issue does come to pose a basic value question for the population at large, we can see that the value topography depicted in Figure 4.3 immediately suggests the lines of value cleavage rooted in socially coherent population groups. Moreover, it tells us where certain inherent structural contradictions in the value positions of particular groups vis-a-vis other groups are located.

To illustrate this last point, note that working-class groups tend to be deeply conservative on certain social values, like religious traditionalism and localism, at the same time that they are quite liberal on others (e.g., economic ideology). Middle-class groups, on the other hand, appear to be more consistent—that is, they are either liberal on both economic and patter-maintenance value questions or relatively conservative on both. Since the elite decision-making personnel are recruited predominantly from the *Neubürger* and *Altbürger* upper middle class in Altneustadt (reflecting the class biases in elite recruitment observed time and again in community studies), there is no way of organizing this community's decision-making subsystem that will root it in a stable coalition of groups over time, given any reasonable mix of value-linked issues confronting the community. That is, one section of the upper middle class may form a successful alliance with the working-class groups on some issues, but not on others because of the constraints imposed by their differing value commitments.

The difficulties with Figure 4.3 as a topographical map are indeed many. First, it assumes that all value scales are potentially of equal significance in constructing the value-linked proximities of the groups. Second, it assumes that all population groups are of equal weight and salience in community deliberations about alternative courses of action. The first assumption is empirically problematic, to say the least, but there is literally nothing in theory or practice to guide us in devising a justifiable weighting scheme whereby the differing roles the various values may play in structuring group proximities can be taken into account. For the present, we are, therefore, forced to let the matter rest with treating all the values as equally important.

Devising reasonable modifications of the second assumption may not be quite so difficult. Given democratic political theory as a criterion model, we have a reason for systematically taking into account the relative sizes of the population groups. One obvious, if crude, strategy for doing this would be to weight each point in proportion to its share of the total population of inhabitants. It would then at least be possible to determine the "center of gravity" of the plane upon which the groups are scattered (i.e., technically speaking, its centroid) that would reflect the location of the general region of the value space where the population's value perspectives are, in some sense, typically found. This center of gravity might be taken as a first approximation of a measure of the location of the *unbiased* (i.e., unbiased in terms of normative democratic theory) aggregation of the groups' value stances that reflects a strictly democratic representation of the community's diverse points of view.

Offered purely as a basis for speculation, Figure 4.4 illustrates the results of applying this procedure to Figure 4.3. The areas delimited by circles around the various points are strictly proportional to the groups' numbers in the total population. The center of gravity clearly favors the sector of the value space in which the working-class groups are concentrated with their relatively conservative pattern-maintenance values and more liberal economic ideology.

This approach, of course, affords the opportunity to examine other models of biases in aggregating population groups. One interesting modification, for example, would take into account the fact that individuals vary greatly in their civic competence (cf. Almond and Verba, 1963). Suppose we were to "discount" a population group's representation in the value space as a function of its members' levels of civic competence. Using the items designed to measure civic competence by Almond and Verba, we found that they formed a satisfactory Guttman scale having six levels, from "0" to "5." Making the arbitrary assumption that people with scores of "0" should make no contribution to a group's effective political membership, those scoring a "1" should get only .2 of a vote, a "2," .4 of a vote, and so on, we "adjusted" the group sizes to reflect only the number of their effective political actors. The blank wedge-shaped sections in the circles of Figure 4.4 indicate the parts of the groups discounted on grounds of civic incompetence. Recalculating the center of gravity, we note that it shifts in Figure 4.4 toward the middle-class groups and in a slightly more liberal direction, reflecting the *aggregational bias* (cf. Almond and Coleman, 1960) of this particular model of representing the value perspectives of the "typical" inhabitant.

We do not intend these results to be taken seriously, as much remains to be done in refining the procedure to eliminate unwarranted assumptions. We do believe, however, that an elaboration of this approach may provide us with a means of assessing the aggregational biases in various models of community representation. If we can, in addition, determine the central tendencies in aggregation of the community elite's value preferences, we might then be in a position to assess the systematic discrepancies between these two system levels in representing preferred value outcomes.

CONCLUDING REMARKS

We have concluded, at least for the moment, our analysis of the social structural and value differentiation of Altneustadt's population sub-system. Despite its size, Altneustadt appears to be sufficiently differentiated in values and social organization to present some fascinating challenges for a community integrative system subject to democratic normative constraints. While not of immediate relevance in Part II, the results reported in these two chapters are well worth keeping in mind as

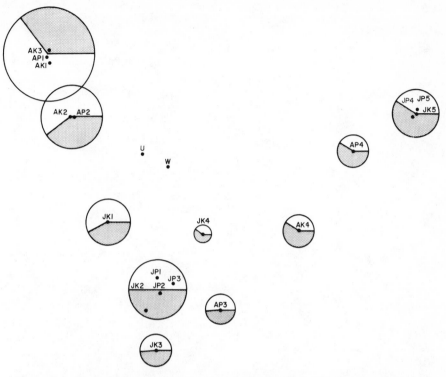

Figure 4.4 Typography of population groups' value space, with groups weighted by their population size and by their levels of civic competence. Circular areas are proportional to population fractions. Shaded areas are proportional to levels of civic competence. U: center weighted for population size. W: center weighted for civic competence.

we turn our attention to a more detailed examination of the community decision-making subsystem. Although we shall be speaking primarily of individual elite members and their relations with one another—that is, engaging in a more conventional network analysis—remember that elite members are socially rooted in one or another of the groups discussed in Part I and should, therefore, share certain values with them. In Part III, we shall have occasion to refer more explicitly to the results of Part I when we consider the interplay between the community and its elite.

PART 2

The Community Influence System

5

Locating the Top
Community Influentials*

This brief introductory chapter to Part II serves primarily to introduce the *personae dramatis*—the top community influentials of Altneustadt—with whom we will be much concerned in the remainder of the book. It confines itself to providing the theoretical rationale for the procedures we adopted in identifying the top influentials as well as describing two of their key attributes: the primary and secondary (if any) institutional sectors in which each elite member is active and his overall influence rank or generalized reputation as an influential in the total set of influentials. Subsequent chapters will focus on the manifold interrelations among the influentials in opposing coalitions, their divergent value orientations, types of resources upon which their influence rests, and their differential activation or involvement in different issue arenas and its effects.

THE IDENTIFICATION OF COMMUNITY
INFLUENTIALS AND THEIR RESPECTIVE
INSTITUTIONAL SECTORS

As we argued in the introductory chapter, the central element of structural analysis is not the individual person per se but the individual actor (or a set of actors) *in* a particular kind of *social position* (cf. Par-

* Parts of this chapter were drawn from Laumann and Pappi (1973).

95

sons, 1951). Thus, we come to a crucial question: How are we to identify the domain of relevant social positions for the community influence subsystem?

Objections to the reputational and issue approaches to identifying elite personnel are well-known. They mainly raise questions of validity and are less methodological than theoretical in nature. Adherents of the reputational technique argue that the issue approach has a conservative bias insofar as it is impossible to detect the major impact of nondecisions on the status quo. Adherents of the issue approach retort that the reputationalists only measure reputations rather than the actual ability of an individual to get his way, despite opposition from other actors. Both groups, however, are asking the same question: Who actually governs? This constitutes the main difference between these two techniques and the structuralist, or positional, approach. The positional approach does not ask "who are the powerful people?" but "which positions possess authority or generalized influence in the sense that their incumbents can make binding decisions in their respective institutional sectors or will be consequential in the resolution of community-level issues?" Without being clear about how these several approaches differ in their initial questions, nothing is to be gained by recommending, as has been done, some simple combination of these three techniques as the best procedure for identifying community elites.

Generally following Talcott Parsons' view of the community as a territorially grounded social system embracing all aspects of social life (cf. Davis, 1948: 312; Parsons, 1960: 250–279), we first identified prospective community influentials as incumbents of the highest positions of authority in organized collectivities whose primary functional responsibilities are in one of the four functionally specialized institutional subsectors at the community level of analysis (see Clark, [1968d] for a recent exposition of the AGIL paradigm applied to community institutions; also D'Antonio et al., [1961] for a less theoretically grounded, more "commonsensical" listing of types of community leadership personnel).

Given the abstract character of Parsons' original formulations, there are some operational difficulties in coding organizations as belonging primarily to one of the four sectors. We coded business firms and banks as economic institutions with *adaptive* primacy; top governmental administrative positions, judges, and legislative decision-making bodies as having *goal-attainment* primacy because they make binding decisions for the community as a whole; voluntary associations including unions and political parties as having *integrative* primacy as foci of interest group demands on the polity; and positions in educational, health, religious, and cultural organizations as having *pattern-maintenance* primacy. *Notars* in Germany are a specialty in the legal profession concerned with economically relevant activities, such as the preparation of contracts and property transfers, and, consequently, were treated as being in the adaptive sector (cf. Rueschemeyer, 1973). Although the Natural Science Research Center is the largest employer in Altneustadt, having many important economic consequences, we decided to code it as a pattern-maintenance collectivity, both because its goal objectives are themselves distinctively cultural in their focus and consequences and because, from the community's viewpoint, it poses the problem of the assimilation of its personnel with their distinctive cultural characteristics into a more inclusive pattern of community life. (See Appendix A, Part II, for more detailed information concerning the selection of organizations [corporate actors] in the various sectors.)

Parsons (1960: 59–69) argues that there are three levels in the hierarchical structure of organizations: the technical, the managerial, and the institutional. The last is concerned with the articulation of the organization with its larger institutional environment, both by securing its legitimacy in the community and making its *claims* on scarce community resources, often at the expense of other organizations' claims. On precisely these grounds, we can analytically treat the community influence structure as the focus of the integrative subsystem of the community. By adopting this theoretically grounded scheme for defining the universe of potentially relevant corporate actors for community integration, we avoid at least some of the pitfalls of less systematic schemes. Such schemes may ignore corporate actors who, while holding, in theory, great potential interest in collective community decisions, have not been active in advancing or defending their concerns during a given time period, perhaps because no issues relevant to them happened to arise (or were prevented from arising by the actions of others), and they are, therefore, not perceived as at all relevant to the community influence system. Our procedure at least enables us to evaluate empirically the relative participation and influence of diverse community elements and to note the points in the system where the existence of important, latent unresolved (or unheeded) demands may be found.

Not all community institutional subsystems, however, are equally likely to be organized into a structure of fully institutionalized and functionally specialized organizations with a full complement of explicitly identified leaders engaged in regularized transactions with one another. This is especially true in the integrative and pattern-maintenance sectors of the community which tend to have less crystallized, more fluid organization. We attempted to compensate for this bias of the positional approach by asking well-placed community informants to nominate other persons who enjoy reputations for influencing members on community affairs, but who do not presently occupy positions of authority in formally established organizations.

The analytic distinction we maintain between a social position and the particular actor who occupies that position is crucial. In general, incumbents of "influential" positions devote most of their time to the tasks associated with these positions. Empirical analysis, however, is complicated by the fact that a given actor may simultaneously occupy several "influential" positions in community decision making—that is, he may wear several hats. We propose to deal with multiple role occupancy operationally by distinguishing an individual's *primary* institutional location or position from his *secondary* position(s) on the basis of the amount of time he spends performing the duties of each.[1]

THE RANK ORDER OF INFLUENCE

Guided by these principles, we obtained a list of 51 community influentials in Altneustadt, 46 of whom were successfully interviewed (see Part II, Appendix A). We then asked: What is the relative influence status of these influentials? That is, can they be differentiated into a hierarchy of influence? This has been a classic concern, especially among those utilizing the reputational approach.

Two different questions were asked to measure general influence rank. First, the respondents were asked to name all the persons on our list whom they would say "are now in general very influential in Altneustadt." (See Q25 in Appendix C.) Second, they were asked to indicate the top five persons from those they had identified in the order of their influence on community affairs. (See Q26–Q28 in Appendix C.) The rank-order correlation between influence status on the basis of the simple

---

[1] People who spent most of their time in nonauthority positions were coded separately and, thereby, distinguished from individuals whose primary positions of authority were in established economic, political, voluntary, religious, educational, or cultural organizations.

number of mentions (Q25) and on the basis of a weighted sum of nominations for the top three influentials (Q26–28) is .84 ($N = 31$). Given the high correlation between the two procedures and the fact that the "simple mentions" method provided an order for the entire population of elite members while the "top three" method covered only the top 31 persons, we decided to use the simpler measure as our measure of influence rank.[2]

There is remarkable consensus among the 46 respondents concerning the top 7 influentials, the top 3 of whom received 46 and 37 votes, respectively. When we asked Herr Koenig, who was unanimously regarded as "very influential," to name the most influential person in the community, he replied, *"Das bin ich."* As we become better acquainted with him and the others in the following chapters, we shall see that this was not a mistaken act of hubris on his part.

In an effort to validate this influence rank order, at least indirectly, we considered the following evidence. At the beginning of the interview, before any mention of our list of influentials, respondents were asked to name persons and groups perceived to be on the supporting and opposing sides of five major community issues. Most people who were mentioned frequently were on our influentials list; 38 persons mentioned were not included in that list. Of these latter, however, all were seldom mentioned and only for one issue. We simply multiplied the number of times each person was mentioned as being on one or the other side of an issue by his influence rank (assigning a rank order of 55 to persons not included in the original list), summed the resulting numbers for each side, and divided this by the total number of mentions on the respective side. This number can be regarded as the average influence status of proponents or opponents—the lower the number, the higher the average influence status (see Table 5.1). We were able to predict the correct winning side for all five issues ($p = .03$) by picking the side with the higher average influence status. Incidentally, by looking at means and standard deviations of the influence ranks attached to each side of an issue, we can also assess the degree to which a given issue tended to be confined to the higher reaches of the set of influentials (that is, an internal elite disagreement) or was a broader-based community issue that involved the

---

[2] Each respondent was also asked to name other people he felt should be included on our list of community influentials. (See Q29 in Appendix C and Part II, Appendix A.) While a number of suggested additions were made, all but one were mentioned only once. The exception received five nominations and was, as a result, interviewed as one of the top influentials.

TABLE 5.1

The Average Influence Status of Proponents and Opponents of Five Community Issues, with Standard Deviations and the Winning Sides Indicated by Asterisks

Issue	Proponents		Opponents	
	Average influence status	Standard deviation	Average influence status	Standard deviation
Adaptive issue primacy:				
Industrial resettlement	13.7*	18.2	18.9	13.2
Goal-attainment issue primacy:				
Construction of new city hall	7.4*	14.8	22.5	14.9
Integrative issue primacy:				
Community annexation	10.6*	15.2	50.5	14.6
Pattern-maintenance issue primacy:				
Secular vs. confessional school	26.6*	17.8	28.3	23.3
Permission to hold Pop festival	29.2	21.0	15.8*	18.1

mobilization of personnel outside the top influential group. (Chapters 6 and 9 provide a more detailed description of the issues and the rationale for their selection.)

Now that we have described the procedures that we used in identifying the top corporate actors and influential individuals in our case community, we can become better acquainted with them in the next chapter.

6

The Coalitional Structure
of Altneustadt's Elite

The preceding chapters have described in some detail, first, the social structure and different value orientations of Altneustadt's adult population and, second, the rationale and procedures by which the community's most influential actors with respect to community affairs were identified. In this chapter, we shall take the first step toward describing the organization of this elite into a patterned set of social relationships. This chapter continues the emphasis on substantive description by describing the actual coalitions in which elite members find themselves when collaborating with and opposing one another in realizing their community objectives. With such concrete information in hand, the reader should then be in a much better position to evaluate subsequent chapters concerned with elaborating new and more general, formal strategies for describing the structure of the community elite network and how it functions in resolving community controversies.

Our tasks in this chapter will be fourfold. First, after describing the means that enabled us to describe the networks of social relations among our elite, we will describe the set of maximal, informally based cliques in the elite and the structure of their interrelationships by means of a condensation of the digraph of the 46 elite members. Second, we will consider the sociometry of the largest, dominant CDU coalition which may be subdivided into subcliques and a number of intersubclique mediators having special relations with one another and differing among themselves with respect to influence resources, value orientations, and political strategies. Third, we will take a look at the less extensive internal differentiation of the rival SPD opposition coalition. Finally, we will compare the various cliques on selected political and social attitudes, influence resources, political strategies, and preferences on certain community issues.

THE NETWORK OF INFORMAL RELATIONS

In the elite interviews, we asked the respondents to indicate the three persons with whom they most frequently interacted in *each* of three types of social relationships (*viz.*, business–professional, informal social and community affairs). Naturally the three persons named by a respondent in one relationship could be, and often were, different from those named in the other two relationships. On grounds of face validity alone, it would appear that the pattern of informal social choices would be especially likely to reveal informally based alliances and cliques within the elite. Both the sociometric literature on community power structures (cf. Hunter, 1953) and our own analysis of the interrelationships among various characteristics of the pairwise relations among elite members (see Chapter 8) also support this supposition. Consequently, we shall confine our attention to the directed choice matrix of informal relations among the elite and its derivative matrices in the following analysis.

As a first step in delineating the clique structure of the elite on the basis of their informal social choices, we turned to the mathematical theory of digraphs (cf Harary, Norman, and Cartwright, 1965, for a systematic introduction). This theory is concerned with postulates and theorems relating to "abstract configurations called digraphs, which consist of 'points' and 'directed lines' " (Harary *et al.*, 1965: v). Five digraph theoretic ideas are of special interest to us: an adjacency matrix (from which all our subsequent analysis proceeds), reachability, path distance, connectedness, and condensation.

Consider the following sociometric (adjacency) matrix in which the rows and columns represent three persons, v_1, v_2, and v_3, and the entries in the cells are either "1" or "0" to indicate whether or not v_1 (in rows) chooses (is in a relationship with) v_j (in columns). This matrix may be diagrammed, as in Figure 6.1 where points represent persons and directed lines (arcs) between two points represent a relationship. A point v_j can be reached from point v_i if there is a path from v_i to v_j, that is, if there is a set of directed lines from v_i to v_j. In our

MATRIX 6.1
An Adjacency Matrix

		Chosen		
		v_1	v_2	v_3
Chooser	v_1	0	1	0
	v_2	0	0	1
	v_3	0	0	0

illustrations, v_1 can reach v_2 in a path of length "1" and v_3 in a path of length "2", and v_2 can reach v_3 in a path of length "1", but v_2 and v_3 cannot reach v_1. The reachable set $R\ (v)$ of a point v is the collection of points that can be reached from v. The *path distance* between two points in a digraph is the *minimum* number of directed lines that must be traversed in order to reach the second point from the first. (The path distance between two points in a graph is the *minimum* number of lines, disregarding direction [i.e., the adjacency matrix is symmetric], that must be traversed in order to reach the second point from the first.)

Connectedness refers to the ways in which two points might be connected to one another by directed lines. Points v_i and v_j are 0-connected if there are no directed lines joining them in either direction; 1-connected if they are joined by lines disregarding their directions; 2-connected if they are joined by a path in one direction, but not in the other; and 3-connected if they are joined by paths in *both* directions. A *strong component* of a digraph (i.e., its maximal strong subgraph) is a subset of points in a digraph, all of which are mutually reachable—i.e., are 3-connected. The *condensation* of a digraph D occurs when one can partition the points into subsets $S_1, S_2, \ldots S_n$ such that a new digraph may be drawn in which there is a line from point S_i to point S_j if and only if in D there is at least one line from a point of S_i to one of S_j. The condensation of a digraph is its condensation with respect to the partition of its points according to its strong components (cf. Harary *et al.*, 1965: 405). Gleason (1969) has devised a computer program that computes reachability, path distance, and connectedness matrices from adjacency matrices containing up to 80 points.

In order to identify the set of cliques in the elite's informal social

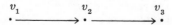

Figure 6.1   Graphic representation of Matrix 6.1.

network, we simply defined a clique as including all persons whose pattern of choices of informal partners for social interaction formed a *strong component* in the digraph—that is, all persons in such a grouping were mutually reachable from one another by directed paths of some length (in fact, usually no longer than "3" steps). Of course, this definition of what we mean by the word "clique" is no more than a statement of its formal equivalence to a mathematical entity in digraph theory that has certain properties. Indeed, this now enables us to assert that there are a number of theorems concerning such entities that are also formally true about "cliques" as well (cf. Harary, 1965: 50–85). One, however, should certainly raise the question of whether or not the postulation of definitional equivalence is empirically justifiable—that is, do the properties of strong components approximate those implied by the concept of "cliques" in common usage? We think they do, and one piece of evidence for this is the exceptional plausibility of the resulting groupings, according to strong components, when examined in the light of "softer" qualitative data about cliques in the elite concerning their compositional make-up, orientations, and activities.[1] The remainder of this chapter presents evidence demonstrating the empirical reasonableness and utility of this approach.

Three strong components (i.e., cliques) were identified in the digraph of informal social relations, together with eight "social isolates" who did not belong to any cliques. The largest clique ($N = 26$) included primarily members of the CDU or their fellow travelers and could be regarded on a variety of grounds as the dominant political coalition that "ran" the community. As we shall see later, this clique could be further subdivided to reveal its internal structure more clearly. The second maximal clique included three large businessmen whose operations were primarily in the county. The SPD maximal clique ($N = 7$) was the principal coalition opposed regularly by the CDU clique. The eight social isolates were scattered across a variety of specialized interest groups and

---

[1] It is certainly true that the coalitions we identified by our procedures would not by any means necessarily correspond to the subjective boundaries that individual elite members would draw around "our crowd." Undoubtedly, for a number of individuals, "our crowd" might include fewer or more people than those included in the coalition by our procedure, and there would probably be differences among individual respondents regarding the specific individuals to be included in "our crowd." While recognizing the validity of an objection to the possible lack of correspondence between "objective" and "subjective" definitions of coalitions, we believe that the following discussion will demonstrate the inherent plausibility of our procedure in delineating coalitions.

were unconnected by *reciprocated* informal ties to anyone in the three maximal cliques.[2]

CONDENSATION OF THE DIGRAPH OF INFORMAL RELATIONS

The condensation of the digraph of informal relations according to its strong components, portrayed in Figure 6.2, provides a very revealing picture of the essentially hierarchical structural organization of the elite. A directed line from one point (which may represent either a strong component [i.e., a clique] or a social isolate) to another in the condensed digraph indicates that there was at least one informal choice from someone in the "sending" point to someone in the "receiving" point, but such an informal preference was not reciprocated by anyone in the receiving point for someone in the sending point. Note that, if reciprocation had occurred, the two points would have to be collapsed into one because the defining characteristic of a strong component would then be met.

To facilitate discussion of the condensed digraph, it is useful to distinguish among three types of points. A *transmitter* point only sends

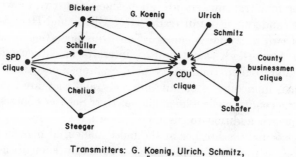

Transmitters: G. Koenig, Ulrich, Schmitz, Schäfer, Steeger

Carriers: Bickert, Chelius, county businessmen clique, Schüller, SPD clique

Receivers: CDU clique

Figure 6.2 The condensed digraph of the elite's informal social relations, according to strong components.

[2] Two respondents did not choose any other person in the elite as someone with whom they would have informal interaction. Consequently, they had to be excluded from the following analysis. They could be represented as disconnected points in the digraph portrayed in Figure 6.2.

choices to other points, while a *receiver* point only receives choices from other points. A *carrier* or mediator point both sends and receives choices from other points. Note again that the patterns of these choices are subject to stringent constraints because of the way in which condensation of a digraph according to its strong components is defined.

Turning to a substantive discussion of what this condensed digraph tells us, we should first note that all the transmitter points are social isolates, all of whom make unreciprocated choices of members of the dominant CDU coalition. Only one of these transmitters, Herr Steeger, chooses the SPD clique in addition to his CDU choice. He is a SPD city councilman, but, in contrast to the SPD clique, he is an *Altbürger* who also is of a less prestigious occupational background than the members of the SPD clique. Herr Steeger is a white-collar worker who is *not* employed at the National Science Research Center (NSRC). He shares all these objective characteristics with Herr Chelius, who is also a mediator between the two party cliques, but as a carrier, not a transmitter. Herr Chelius is chosen by the SPD clique and chooses the CDU clique. As a mediator between the SPD and the CDU clique, he may be much more successful than the transmitter, Steeger, who stands very low in the reputed influence rank order and is not seen by other members as participating actively in the resolution of community controversies.

The other four transmitters are all businessmen, two of whom are in construction and two in retail trade. Herr Ulrich and Herr Schäfer, the directors of two fairly large construction firms operating in and outside the city of Altneustadt, have limited interests in Altneustadt's affairs. They are interested in community politics proper only insofar as they relate to their immediate economic interests, and they are similar in this respect to the county businessmen clique. Herr Schäfer chooses a member of this clique, in addition to his CDU choice.

Herr G. Koenig, the brother of the most influential man in town (who is, of course, in the CDU coalition), is, curiously enough, not included in the dominant coalition although he himself directs a choice in that direction. In addition, he chooses the director of the NSRC who is, as we shall learn, quite atypical of the people working there as he does not have SPD sympathies.

Several social isolates and coalitions serve as carrier points. We have already mentioned the county businessman clique as having rather limited interests in community affairs and being exclusively oriented to the dominant CDU coalition, both in terms of their expectations of the civil administration's cooperation with their ongoing economic activities and in terms of sharing more general conservative values. Herr Dr. Bickert, an internationally known nuclear physicist with many important in-

ventions and patents to his credit, has only recently arrived in Altneustadt
to take over the general directorship of the NSRC and has, therefore, not
had much time to become very salient in community affairs—assuming
that he will take the trouble to involve himself in such matters beyond
the minimum necessary to coordinate the activities of NSRC with those
of the community's civil administration. The NSRC employs 3600 employees and controls a very large and desirable land area immediately
adjacent to the city limits.[3] NSRC policies must almost of necessity have
many ramifications of considerable consequences to the community. Perhaps the most important fact is that the NSRC, being a publicly supported facility, is not liable to any property taxes, the overwhelming
source of tax revenues for local communities. Thus, while it is a principal
generator of demands for city services, it makes no contribution to
relieving the community's tax burdens. Although chosen by members of
the SPD clique, Herr Dr. Bickert seems to be affiliating himself with the
CDU side of the elite structure, given his pattern of informal choices.
Herr Dr. Schüller, a long-term associate executive director of the NSRC,
physicist, and activist in community affairs, has also been very active
in Protestant church affairs. He is one of the two CDU city councilmen
from the NSRC. What all four mediators between the SPD and CDU
clique, the three carriers and the one transmitter, have in common is that
they deviate in key social characteristics from their political friends.

The SPD coalition, the principal oppositional coalition to the CDU
coalition, is composed of three NSRC scientists, two Protestant clergymen, the director of the engineering school, and a secondary school
teacher. This group has developed a fairly well-defined and coherent
policy of opposition to the policies of the reigning clique and have,
in fact, been successful on several important occasions in determining
the outcome of an issue, primarily through the expedient of mobilizing
public sentiment on particular issues rather than using informal, intra-
elite tactics, which seem to be preferred by the dominant CDU coalition.
The SPD coalition is publicly regarded as the spokesman of the interests
of the *Neubürger* associated with NSRC. The SPD coalition chose both
Herrn Dr. Bickert and Schüller, who are generally seen as the obvious
representatives of the organizational interests of the NSRC despite their
apparent lack of sympathy for the political views of their organizational
"subordinates." This coalition also chose Herr Chelius, an *Altbürger*,

---

[3] As a result of a recent decision made after the completion of our field work (and
discussed at the time with community leaders as one of five issues confronting the
community), this land area was one of the sections incorporated into a greatly
expanded territorial unit under city administration.

labor union representative, and SPD city councilman, whose sympathies are clearly with the traditional Catholic-dominated *Altbürger* except on certain economic issues. Both Herr Chelius and the SPD coalition direct informal choices to the CDU coalition, who do not, of course, reciprocate.

It was once said that all roads lead to Rome. Certainly, in this community, there is a universal convergence on the dominant CDU coalition as the ultimate recipient of informal choices. This upward flow of social choices toward the dominant leadership elements is certainly consistent with what we have come to expect on the basis of small group research and theory (cf. Homans, 1961). As we shall see in the next section, however, this coalition is itself composed of a more heterogeneously recruited set of people in terms of their primary institutional responsibilities and possesses a considerable degree of internal differentiation with respect to the pattern of informal interaction, relative standings in the reputed influence rank order, general value orientations, and preferences for community action. In contrast to the other cliques, the CDU clique is by no means as internally consistent in its objectives, perhaps precisely because of its heterogeneity. In short, it is not the incarnation of the specter of the monolithic ruling elite so often portrayed in the literature on community power structures but so rarely seen in practice. The coalition's strength lies in the relative ease and speed with which relevant information can flow from one part of the coalition to another as well as the fact that it is directly linked (in one direction at least) by some of its constituent members to *every* other influential grouping or individual in the elite system. The clue to its vulnerability may perhaps be found in the nature of its internal differentiation, to which we now turn.

THE INTERNAL DIFFERENTIATION OF THE DOMINANT CDU CLIQUE

First, a word or two should be said about procedure. Drawing a sociogram portraying the relationships among a set of individuals is really an art. Two investigators can easily come up with sociograms of the same set of relations among the same set of individuals that provide strikingly different *visual* impressions of the underlying (identical) structure. Such differences arise because the locations of persons in the sociogram, and the lengths and locations of lines among the actors (which merely denote the existence of relationships and *not* their relative proximities) are completely arbitrary. As a result, considerations of an essentially aesthetic and noncomparable nature, such as one's personal sense of visual appeal and neatness that may result in minimizing the number of lines that cross one another and identifying "dramatic focal points" around which the sociogram should revolve, determine the sociogram's overall design. Such a lack of the ability to replicate from one investigator to the next has been the principal reason why sociogramming, which enjoyed widespread popularity in the 1940s and early 1950s (cf. Moreno, 1953), has fallen into ill repute and been almost abandoned. Despite its limitations, however, we shall try our hand at the art of sociogramming because it provides an unusually rich means of providing a broadly grounded first approximation (i.e., a "good intuitive feel") for the basic empirical materials on our elite with which we will be working. Subsequent chapters will develop formal and replicatable strategies for describing the elite's structure. We believe that the plausibility of these latter strategies and the comprehension of the empirical results they yield will be greatly enhanced by looking first at the products of our artistic efforts.

In preparing a sociogram of a clique, we were guided by two principles of construction. First, wherever possible, two individuals should be adjacent to one another in the sociogram when at least one of them includes the other among his first three choices for informal interaction. Because we confined each respondent to only three choices among a long list of possible informal partners, he was obviously constrained in his ability to reciprocate informal choices, especially if he was very popular and the object of many "top three" choices by others. We have, therefore, relaxed our assumption of unidirectional choices (employed in condensing the digraph of informal relations in the previous section) and postulated that a given choice would ultimately be reciprocated if the chosen respondent could have exercised his option to indicate all the people that he would include in his informal circle of acquaintances. Second, we have identified the sociometric stars (i.e., the most frequently chosen persons by other clique members) as the focal points around which to arrange the other individuals directly tied to them and, then, those only indirectly tied to them. The two principles occasionally conflict. When they do, they are resolved in favor of locating the person relative to the sociometric star(s) to whom he is most closely tied.

Figure 6.3 is a sociogram of the dominant CDU clique. Each person has been uniquely identified with a code providing information regarding his influence status, institutional sector responsibilities, party membership, religious preference, and influence resources. (See the legend for Figures 6.3 and 6.4 for the complete explanation of the abbreviated code. See also Chapter 7, p. 138, for a more detailed explanation of the several codes.) Note that this coalition is quite broadly recruited from the ranks of the influentials, ranging from the most influential man in town, Herr Koenig, who is number "1," to Herrn Büsgen, Fahr, Riehl,

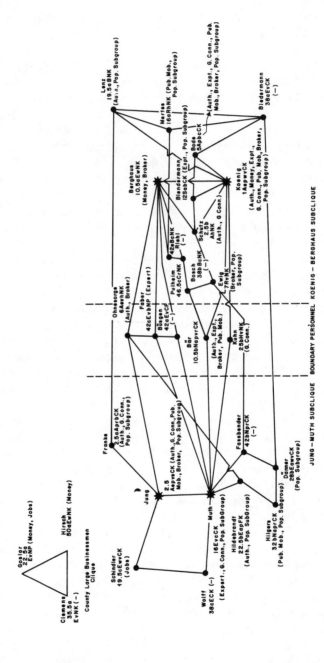

Figure 6.3 The internal differentiation of the dominant CDU clique, based on their informal social choices.

Key to Figures 6.3 and 6.4

Example

16 EvCK

| | | | | |
| | | | | Religion
| | | |
| | | Political party
| | Secondary institutional sector
| Primary institutional sector
Influence rank

Primary Sector, Secondary Sector (Primary sector is capitalized; secondary sector or sectors are lowercase)

E—Economy   (A—Sector)
A—Authority position in (G—Sector)
    political system
P—Political party   (I—Sector)
W—Economic association
V—Social clubs, sports
B—Education   (L—Sector)
R—Religion
C—Culture
H—Health and charity
S—Science
N—Respondent could not be
    coded into any primary sector

Influence Rank

Respondent's influence rank in the entire elite of 51 persons. Based on question 25, a measure of influence depending on other respondents' votes. Subscripts serve to distinguish respondents who were tied, that is, received the same number of votes.

Party—Political party of which respondent is a member.

S—S.P.D. (Social Democratic Party)
C—C.D.U. (Christian Democratic
    Union)
F—F.D.P. (Free Democratic Party)
N—Not a party member

Religion

K—Catholic
P—Protestant
N—None

Influence Resources—The attributed influence resources of each respondent, if any, are indicated in parentheses (see Chapter 11).

Money—Control over money and credit
Jobs—Control over land and jobs
Auth.—Official authority to make decisions
Conn.—Good connections with influential persons in and outside Altneustadt
Pub. Mob.—Public mobilizer, general respect as someone who can mobilize the public for good proposals in the interest of the city as a whole
Broker—Honorable broker who can mediate controversies impartially
Pop. Subgroups—Influence in particular population subgroups, such as voters of a particular party, members of a voluntary association, and so on
Expt.—Special expert knowledge in particular delimited areas of communal interest

and Frau Fassbender, who are tied for forty-second place. In addition, the members are highly diversified in terms of their primary institutional responsibilities, being drawn from all the institutional sectors in the community (i.e., small and large economic organizations, civil authority, religion, health, and education). In combination, they control all the types of influence resources relevant to community decision making (see Chapter 11).

The clique, on the other hand, is quite homogeneous with respect to party memberships and religious preferences. Of the 26 members of the clique, 16 belong to the Christian Democratic Union (CDU). Only one, Herr Hildebrandt, is a member of the Free Democratic Party, a small minority party normally in coalition with the CDU against the SPD. All the other members claim no political party membership, although we should not be surprised to learn below that their political views are basically in sympathy with those of the CDU. Actually, all of those who indicate no party membership do so because they occupy positions in the community that are supposed to be "above" party politics. Both Catholic priests, Ewig and Mertes; Herr Berghaus, the bank director; Herr Ohnesorge, the county civil administrator (manager); Herr Schütz, the city civil administrator (manager); Dr. Kuhn, the chief surgeon of the county hospital; and Herr Lenz, the county superintendent of primary schools, hold prominent public positions that appear to require party "neutrality." In terms of religious preferences, most members of the clique are Catholic, including the two Catholic pastors, one of whom, Ewig, is the Archdeacon and representative of the Cardinal in Altneustadt. Only two Protestants are included, Herr Büsgen and Fahr, who, as we mentioned earlier, are the least influential members of the coalition.

The clique can, however, be further divided into two subcliques that are connected to one another only indirectly by five "mediators" who are joined by paths of length "1" to a sociometric star in each subclique. The more influential of the two subcliques, at least with respect to city affairs, includes two sociometric stars, Herr Koenig, the most influential man in Altneustadt and its *Bürgermeister,* and Herr Berghaus, the director of Altneustadt's largest bank. Most of their coterie of associates are fairly influential city leaders whose primary institutional responsibilities are widely dispersed, including civil administration, religion, and education. Leaders from the economic sector are notably underrepresented. We have already encountered the two Catholic priests (Ewig and Mertes) and the superintendent of schools (Lenz). In addition to those people interested in educational and religious affairs, we must add Herr Riehl, the principal of the Gymnasium, and Herr Bosch, a teacher at the Gymnasium and director of the musical society. Herr Pulheim is musical director and organist for Pastor Ewig's church and quite active in the community's cultural affairs. Herr Bode is a judge in a neighboring city and majority leader of the CDU faction on Altneustadt's city council. Herr Blendermann, the only person from the NSRC in the coalition and currently vice *Bürgermeister,* is quite atypical of his colleagues at NSRC, being a Catholic member of the CDU and an economist involved in the higher administration of the NSRC. Finally, Herr Biedermann is the owner–manager of a firm of architects that has done work for the city and the county. One can easily see from this review of the composition of the Koenig–Berghaus subclique that the subclique is "specialized" with respect to its leadership, drawing heavily from traditionally oriented and conserving sectors of what we have called the pattern-maintenance institutions. These people have been most deeply involved in coping with the challenges posed by the *Neubürger*.

The second subclique, less influential in city affairs but much more consequential in county matters, also includes two sociometric stars, Herr Jung, the county *Landrat*, and Herr Muth, a *Notar* (lawyer) with primarily a county-oriented business clientele. Herr Jung and Muth are partners in a firm practicing commercial law (cf. Rueschemeyer, 1973). Their associates are heavily drawn from the larger farmers and businessmen whose plants are under county jurisdiction. (The three-person clique, located in the upper left-hand corner of Figure 6.3 close to the Jung–Muth subclique but not joined to it, includes Herr Goslar, the largest and wealthiest factory owner in the entire area and president of the Industrial Association, Herr Hirsch, director of a branch bank, and Herr Clemens, the manager of a large sugar beet processing factory. They are, in fact, *unilaterally* joined to Herr Schindler, the largest and most influential farmer and landowner in the county, and, thus, one can argue that they form an element in the Muth–Jung county-based subclique.)

Herr Jung, the principal intraclique rival to Herr Koenig, has been a "power" in the county since the end of the Second World War. He, in fact, enjoys the sobriquet, Graf von Altneustadt. During the 1950s, he was the president of the *Landtag* in Düsseldorf (the state capital) and was highly influential in "arranging" the location of NSRC in Altneustadt. Being over 70 and now somewhat less active in community affairs, Herr Jung's influence has suffered some decline in the past 5 years as a result of Herr Koenig's growing influence. There is considerable personal animosity between the two men—such that, at a recent publicly sponsored festivity to which all notables in the area were invited to celebrate Herr Jung's seventieth birthday, Herr Koenig failed to make a public appearance. Herr Franke, now the elected representative to the state legislature in Düsseldorf, has been regarded as heir apparent to Herr Jung. He is also *Bürgermeister* of a very small neighboring town, chairman of the county CDU, and elected representative to the county council. His interests are clearly oriented toward the county (note his links only to Herr Jung, his political sponsor, and Herr Lenz, county superintendent of schools) and to managing county–state relationships where he has extensive good connections. His interests are thus not limited to Altneustadt itself but to the county as a whole. He ranks high in overall influence within the community's elite system, primarily because of what "he can do" for Altneustadt at the county level and at the state capital.

Herr Muth is a man who, while not afraid to enter the public limelight when necessary to defend or advance his strongly held conservative views, generally prefers to operate through his excellent connections with those influentials whose activities are regularly oriented toward the public arena. Performing a structurally equivalent function for Herr Jung as Herr Berghaus does for Herr Koenig, Herr Muth functions as a publicly less visible and less controversial "silent partner" rooted in the economic subsector with excellent ramifying connections. (One might dare to offer the hypothesis that both subcliques possess a differentiation between their instrumental and expressive leaders a la Bales' (1958) distinction between the two types of leadership roles. The two rivals, Herr Jung and Koenig, are connected to one another only via intermediaries that are linked to Muth or Berghaus. Note also the quite different types of resources controlled by Muth and Berghaus in contrast to Jung and Koenig.) Thus, Herr Muth has good connections with small businessmen, tradesmen, and professionals, including Herr Hildebrandt, a veterinarian who serves on the county council and is chairman of the county FDP; Herr Wolff, a heating oil dealer active in community affairs; Frau Fassbender, chairwoman of the Community School's Catholic Women's Society and county chairwoman of the CDU Women's Auxiliary; Herr Fahr, another lawyer with good connections to Herr Berghaus, the banker; Herr Büsgen, the owner-manager of a firm of architects with a direct link also to Herr Berghaus; and Dr. Kuhn, the chief surgeon of the hospital, who is directly linked to Herr Koenig.

Also part of the Muth–Jung subclique but somewhat removed from the core are two small businessmen. Herr Hilgert, an owner of a small delicatessen, is a member of the city council, chairman of the community's Retail Advertising Council, and president of the most popular sports club in town (it has won the national amateur competition in soccer several times). Finally, Herr Dänner, a barber by profession, is chairman of the county tradesmen association and quite active in community affairs (see his secondary institutional activities).

The five mediators between the two subcliques are difficult to characterize in any summary fashion. First, note that four of the five are reputed to have good connections or expertise (in the case in question, legal training, a peculiarly integrative resource) or to be honorable brokers who are not biased in favor of one side or the other—all of these are resources that can function to integrate or coordinate a system of diverse and conflicting elements. Second, note that the mediators are drawn from quite diverse institutional sectors. Third, note that all direct linkages between mediators and the sociometric stars of the two subcliques follow the rule that a man having direct informal contacts to Herr Koenig cannot simultaneously be directly linked to his arch rival, Herr Jung (and vice versa). The linkages between the two "heavies" must apparently be mediated or buffered by the second "star" in each subclique. This pattern is certainly consistent with the principles of balance theory (cf. Newcomb, 1961).

More specifically, Herr Ohnesorge is the county's chief administrative officer who has considerable scope to his decision-making authority as well as a reputation as an honorable broker. He is linked directly to Herrn Jung and Hildebrandt, both of whom serve on the elected county council to which he is directly responsible. He is linked only to Herr Berghaus in the Koenig-Berghaus subclique, presumably because Berghaus is concerned with economic matters of countywide relevance and direct links to Herr Jung preclude direct links to Herr Koenig. Herr Fahr and Büsgen provide mediation between Muth and Berghaus. These linkages seem to be principally economic in character, as all of these men have responsibilities dealing with the mobilization of land and money for various building projects. A conservative *Altbürger* and retired middle-level railroad official, Herr Bär is a very influential member of the city council. He is directly connected to Herr Koenig, who is the key political leader of the CDU in city affairs, and to Herr Muth, who is himself also very conservative on most political issues and is a focal point in the county subclique. Finally, Dr. Kuhn, the chief of surgery at the hospital, joins Herrn Koenig and Muth in an informal linkage that is devoid of political and economic content, at least insofar as his particular institutional responsibilities are concerned.

From a more general perspective on the CDU coalitional structure as a whole, we might advance the hypothesis that the presence of these multiple mediators provides a number of alternative paths by which information about activities and objectives in one subclique can be communicated to the other. The redundancy in the connections joining the subcliques can be seen to strengthen the ability of the clique as a whole to respond coherently and promptly to diverse challenges originating at different points in the elite system. The impact of idiosyncracies in the characteristics of individual mediators that serve to filter or bias information flows is considerably reduced under conditions of multiple mediating pathways (cf. Guetzkow, 1965). The multiple mediators, drawn from diverse institutional areas, also increase the likelihood that specialized information from a given institutional sector will find suitable channels to flow from one subclique to the other, even in the face of the personal animosities of the two key influentials.

While our description of the CDU coalitional structure yields a picture of a structure that seems remarkably well-developed and adapted to meeting the needs of coordinating the divergent requirements of county-oriented, city-oriented, and county–city-oriented activities in the context of strong intracoalitional rivalries, we wish by no means to imply that this happy state of affairs must necessarily occur under all circumstances. In fact, the analysis suggests where one should look for structural vulnerabilities in such coalitions. We are really only just beginning analyses that would specify the conditions under which such highly adaptive structures will emerge. We do not know, for example, the conditions under which we can expect the emergence of a dual leadership subclique structure that serves, by hypothesis, to facilitate the coexistence of strong rival subcliques that rely on intra- rather than extra-elite influence resources. For the case in hand, we are looking at the end result of a process that has been going on for years. At critical junctures, if certain actors performing certain roles had not been available for various reasons, we could expect quite different outcomes. They range from the public blowup of the coalition into a set of contending factions going into the public arena to mobilize popular support at the expense of their erstwhile "friends" (rather than relying, as in the present situation, on intra-elite resources of good connections and honorable brokerage to mediate differences and avoid public fallings-out) to the complete elimination of rival subcliques in favor of a highly centralized decision-making core revolving around one or a couple actors who make all the important decisions without serious challenge from dissidents, either publicly or internally.

THE INTERNAL DIFFERENTIATION OF THE
RIVAL SPD CLIQUE

The sociogram for the SPD is presented in Figure 6.4. The story it portrays may be quickly told. It is readily apparent that the internal differentiation of this clique is considerably less complex than that of the CDU clique. Note first that the clique is very narrowly recruited from leadership elements in only one institutional sector, pattern main-

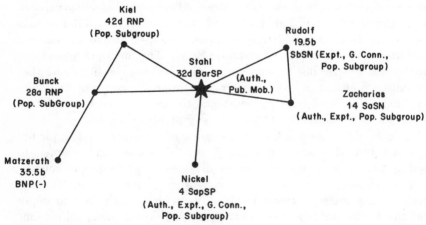

Figure 6.4 The internal differentiation of the oppositional SPD clique.

tenance, including religion, education, and science. All are *Neubürger* who have come to Altneustadt only after the founding of the NSCR. Five of the seven are Protestants, while the other two have no religious preference. Four are active SPD party members, while the other three claim no party membership (although their political sympathies are clearly with the SPD). As in the case of the CDU coalition, those who claim no party membership do so probably because they occupy positions in the community that are supposed to be "above" party politics. Both Protestant clergymen in Altneustadt, the Pastoren Bünck and Kiel, as well as Dr. Matzerath, the director of the engineering school, hold such positions. Note also that, save for Herr Stahl, all are seen as being influential among population subgroups—more specifically, the Protestant subcommunity and the natural scientists at NSRC.

There is only one focal point (sociometric star) in this clique. The evaluation of Herr Stahl's reputed influence status in the elite system as a whole is, surprisingly, rather low, even in comparison to the influence ranks of other members of the clique. (Contrast this to the relatively high influence statuses enjoyed by the four sociometric stars in the CDU clique.) In addition, Herr Stahl is of rather modest occupation, a teacher in the secular primary school (in comparison to the much higher occupational prestige, educational attainments, and income of all the other members of the clique) and is very active as a layman in church affairs (he is a presbyter of the Evangelical Church). Thus, he clearly serves as the necessary bridge between the leaders of the Protestant subcommunity in Altneustadt and the secular scientists, who have formed together an alliance against the domination of the traditionally oriented Catholic economic and political elite. As an SPD member of the city council, he functions as the principal mobilizer of public opinion in support of the wishes of his clientele group, articulating the SPD's demands for community action and criticisms of the dominant coalition, both within the council itself and in the hustings. Because he is not employed at the NSCR, he cannot be so easily dismissed as merely the spokesman for the natural scientists at NSCR.

Dr. Rudolf and Dr. Zacharias are both physicists at the NSCR and, as members of the city council, have developed especially sharp images, both within the elite and among the public at large, as ideologically oriented spokesmen for the demands of the highly sophisticated, secularized scientists. While both were assigned "expertise" as an influence resource, this expertise clearly meant nothing more than the elite's general recognition of their advanced scientific training—which, of course, has little relevance for most community questions. Both men were generally regarded as ideologues whose positions on issues were not sub-

ject to negotiation or compromise. Therefore, they enjoyed only a
limited popular base of support for their demands for social change in
Altneustadt.

On the other hand, Herr Dr. Nickel, a geologist at the NSRC, is much
more pragmatic and accommodating in his political role playing. He was
chairman of the SPD faction in the city council and was regularly consulted for his views by leading elements of the opposition, including Herr
Koenig, the *Bürgermeister*, and Herr Schütz, the city manager. His
ramifying pragmatic links with the opposition probably made him too
unreliable (i.e., ideologically impure) in the eyes of the other members
of the SPD clique. This may at least partially explain the fact that he
is not the sociometric star of the clique, despite his highly influential
status in the elite as a whole and his good connections with important
opposition leaders. For a challenger group (i.e., the "outsiders") that is
usually excluded from the councils of the most influential actors, the
best strategy might be an attempt to mobilize public support for their
views—that is, carry on their challenge in as public a forum as possible
—rather than turn to intra-elite influence attempts in which the challengers lack sufficient internal influence resources (see Chapter 11 for an
extended discussion of these matters) to provide even a reasonable probability of winning a contested decision. We shall document this interpretation in the next section in which we turn to a comparison of the
attitudes and leadership strategies of the several coalitions.

There is a final point. The SPD clique seems to be structurally much
more vulnerable than the CDU coalition. The sociometric star in this
clique is functioning only as a *mediator* between the religiously grounded
opposition elements and the secular opposition elements rather than as
the *leader* of the clique. The CDU sociometric stars, in contrast, clearly
perform important leadership functions for the subcliques, and mediators
are usually drawn from the ranks of less consequential elite members.
The mediation role in the SPD clique rests exclusively on Herr Stahl's
shoulders (again one should contrast this with the situation of multiple
mediators in the CDU clique). If something happened to Herr Stahl, the
SPD clique would face the prospect of its key constituent elements becoming disconnected and the alliance becoming endangered for lack of an
acceptable coordinating center. The presence of a number of actors, each
of whom have ideologically developed views of the "best way" to proceed against their common enemy, also implies an unstable leadership
situation in which there is a high potential for destructive competition
among the actors to determine who should exercise the leadership function for the clique as a whole.

DIFFERENCES IN VALUES AND POLITICAL STRATEGIES WITHIN AND BETWEEN THE VARIOUS COALITIONS

Value Differences and Coalitional Memberships

It has often been argued that consensual relationships are facilitated when individuals share common value orientations, beliefs, and attitudes and are hindered when they do not (cf. Laumann, 1973, for a review of the extensive literature on this point). *Value homophyly,* the term we shall use to refer to the variable degree of value, attitude, and belief similarity or congruence between two individuals, may promote or prevent a social relationship, depending on the type of relationship being considered. Obviously, high value homophyly is not required in a highly instrumental relationship, such as a business transaction between a buyer and seller. Homophyly increases in importance as the relationship becomes more functionally and affectively diffuse, that is, more and more intimate. Homophyly can be assessed for a large array of attitudes and beliefs. But only some of these are ever relevant for a given interactional context. That is, while intimacy may require homophyly in several value and attitude areas, the relationship between two individuals may not be seriously impaired if they happen to disagree on matters unrelated to their mutual transactions. In short, value homophyly is multifaceted and multidimensional in nature; and care must be taken to reflect this fact when measuring it.

With such considerations in mind, we tried to specify a range of social, political, and economic values and attitudes that, we hoped, were both salient and meaningful to individual elite members and, hence, relevant to the formation or avoidance of informal ties among them. Following Parsons' classic distinctions among the four functional problems confronting every social system (cf. Parsons, 1961), we identified four attitude items or scales that tapped an issue in each of the four functional domains. First, for the "adaptive" or economic issue, we ascertained the respondent's position on a much discussed issue in Germany today—co-determination (*Mitbestimmung*), that is, whether workers should be allowed to participate in managerial decision making (see S24, Appendix C). Second, with respect to the priorities among a set of competing goals or objectives toward which the community should be moving ("goal attainment" in the AGIL scheme), factor scores were assigned to each respondent such that a high score reflected a high commitment to the encouragement of Altneustadt's economic growth and expansion and a low score indicated a high priority assigned to the objective of administrative efficiency in the operations of the local government (see Q4, Appendix C). Third, several items were combined into an index of social egalitarianism (Duke, 1967) ("integrative" primacy in the AGIL scheme) that was intended to tap the respondent's attitude toward a key aspect of social and class stratification. Persons with high scores believed that existing social inequalities in the distribution of income and occupational prestige in Germany were justified, while persons with low scores did not (see S1, S8, S14, S16, and S23, Appendix C). Finally, several items were combined into an index of traditional familism ("pattern-maintenance" primacy) (see S4, S11, and S20, Appendix C). Persons with low scores supported traditional conceptions of family roles and obligations (e.g., believed that the husband should make the most important decisions in the family), while persons with high scores did not. These four attitudes were only very modestly intercorrelated, usually considerably below .25. For purposes of subsequent analysis, each attitude scale was trichotomized into high, moderate, and low scores.

We were interested in assessing the relative value homophyly of each pair of influentials, treating value homophyly as a multidimensional attribute. To this end, we submitted the data matrix consisting of the 45 elite members as rows and the 4 attitude items as the columns to a multidimensional scalogram analysis (MSA-II) (cf. Lingoes, 1967, 1973: 239–245; Laumann and House, 1970), which plots the respondents in an Euclidean space, their relative locations reflecting the similarity of their attitudes. That is, persons having similar attitudes in all four domains will be located close together, while those with dissimilar attitudes will be far apart. The computer routine found a satisfactory two-dimensional solution with a coefficient of alienation of only .02.

Figure 6.5 is the graphic portrayal of the two-dimensional MSA solution; the groupings of points according to their coalitional memberships have also been mapped onto it. It provides a highly condensed visual means of comparing the elite's coalitional structure with its underlying structure of value orientations. Scattered around the perimeter of the figure are 12 points, each of which represents a single value on one of the 4 scales. These points loosely cluster into three elongated ballons that represent roughly "liberal," "neutral" (i.e., centrist), and "conservative" viewpoints. The other 45 points are each associated with a particular elite member. The position of a given elite member relative to others in the plot and to the locations of the individual scale values roughly shows how close or distant each influential is to every other influential with respect to his value positions on these 4 scales considered simultaneously and also how close or distant he is to the 12 value positions. For example,

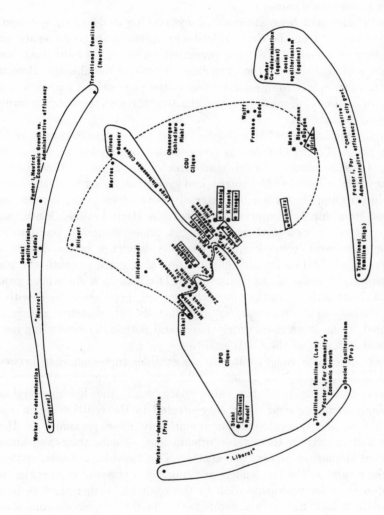

Figure 6.5 Multidimensional scalogram analysis of 45 elite members on four value orientations. Coefficient of alienation = .02.

Herr Chelius, Rudolf, and Stahl are *(1)* all quite similar to each other in their overall value profiles, *(2)* rather distant from most other members of the elite, and *(3)* rather close to the "liberal" set of value positions. (The SPD and large businessmen cliques have been delimited by solid lines, the CDU clique by a dotted line, and the social isolates by boxes around their names.)

The reader will be well-rewarded by making a detailed, systematic comparison between the elite's relative locations in the value space and the other information we have presented on them as individuals and members of coalitions in the preceding sections of the chapter. Here we shall have time only to direct attention to the more salient and important features of the relationship between the structures of the elite's informal relations and its value space.

First, compare the relative dispersions of the several coalitions in the value space. The SPD clique is concentrated on the liberal side of the value space in contrast to the much greater dispersion of the members of the CDU clique in the centrist and conservative areas of the space. The latter clique has a much greater diversity of value preferences that ranges from highly conservative men, like Herr Franke, Muth, and Biedermann, to men with more centrist, more moderate positions on major social and economic questions. This difference in the degrees of dispersion of the two rival cliques in the value space is consistent with our characterization of the "outsider" SPD clique as a challenger group that is rooted in a rather narrowly defined population base with a limited, but highly coherent, set of demands for collective action, in contrast to the much more widely based and potentially conflicting institutional interests of the CDU coalition.

There is only a rough, but still discernible, correspondence between the Muth–Jung subclique members who tend to be concentrated toward the conservative side of the value space, while the Koenig–Berghaus subclique members tend to be concentrated in the centrist region (i.e., middle) of the space. Note the remarkably close proximity of Herr Jung and Koenig in their value orientations, despite their well-known personal animosities toward one another. This provides grounds for viewing the rivalry of the two leaders as primarily a personal competition for the dominant leadership position in the coalition, rather than as being rooted in substantial, coherent differences in their economic and social world views.

The SPD clique, while concentrated in the change-oriented side of the value space, is, however, obviously differentiated internally between persons like Herr Stahl and Dr. Rudolf, who are ideological "purists," and those like Drs. Nickel and Matzerath and the Pastoren Bünck and Kiel, who are centrists with values not unlike those of the more liberal wing of the CDU coalition. These more centrally located men of the SPD clique serve as the mediating links between the two coalitions, hammering out compromises acceptable to both sides.

Next, we thought it useful to contrast certain characteristics of the elite members clustered in the central region of the space, the "moderates" ranging from Dr. Nickel to Herr Steeger and including 26 (or 59%) of the elite members, with those located in the periphery of the value space who hold more extreme positions on either the left or the right with regard to various social, political, and economic issues. Although the patterns were in the directions predicted, none met the conventional standards of statistical significance—in this case, a somewhat dubious criterion since we are dealing with a population universe.

First, we entertained the hypothesis, frankly derived from our impression of the way American politics operates, that the upper reaches of the influence hierarchy would tend to be dominated by moderates, while persons with more extreme views would be relegated to less influential statuses within the elite itself. In fact, we found that 7 of the top 10 influence ranks were occupied by moderates, while only 3 of the top 10 positions were occupied by persons from the periphery of the value space.

Second, we reasoned that at least two of the eight influence resources were especially likely to be differentially distributed between center and periphery. On the one hand, people with reputations as honorable brokers should have more moderate value positions than other elite members in order to be acceptable as "unbiased" mediators between opposing factions. In fact, five of the seven honorable brokers were located in the center of the value space. The two located in the periphery (Herr Bode and Ohnesorge) are also, in some sense, consistent with this expectation since they both serve as highly influential *intra-clique* mediators between the county and city factions of the CDU clique and are located between the moderate and more conservative sectors of the value space. On the other hand, one would expect persons with reputations as mobilizers of public opinion around particular issues to be located toward the periphery of the value space. In fact, five of the eight men reputed to be public mobilizers are located in the periphery. Moreover, two of the three located in the center are Herr Jung and Koenig, the rival leaders of the CDU clique, who far and away enjoy the largest and most unbiased bases of popular esteem and support of any in the elite (see Chapter 11, pp. 203–208). They are, in other words, the center's mobilizers of the moderates in the population at large.

Strategies for Performing Leadership Roles

In addition to differing among themselves as to the substantive goals toward which community policies should be oriented, we shall argue that members of any elite system differ among themselves with regard to their preferred strategies for identifying these community goals and for implementing them and with respect to their preferred leadership roles both within the elite coalitions themselves and vis-a-vis the public at large. Some leaders will have become interested in community affairs because they think of themselves as idealistic protagonists of certain self-evident social, political, religious, or economic values that require encouragement and protection against erosion by neglect or by the willful, misguided efforts of others. Other leaders will have adopted a more flexible, pragmatic strategy for assessing alternative community policies, believing that there may be a number of legitimate, but divergent community objectives that cannot all be maximized simultaneously. Bargaining and compromise should be seen as the appropriate techniques for handling differences of opinion among various interest groups by the "pragmatists." Such tactics are especially compatible with the use of informal means of persuading others within the elite to make suitable concessions in order to develop an acceptable compromise and the avoidance of public controversies that tend to freeze the bargaining positions of opposing sides (cf. Schelling, 1956; 1960). "Idealists," on the other hand, should find such "trading with the enemy" to be less acceptable and should prefer to mobilize public concern and support for their cherished point of view. They are less interested in developing a bargaining position from which to negotiate acceptable compromises for fear of conceding too much at the expense of maintaining their values. Finally, one can distinguish between leaders who are generally regarded as innovators or developers of new proposals for community action and leaders who prefer the role of the critic whereby they attempt to evaluate, refine, and, if feasible, improve innovative proposals for community action in the hope of making them more generally acceptable or of preventing their adoption if they are "undesirable" by some standard.

In sum, we propose to distinguish analytically among three functional features of an elite member's strategy for performing his community leadership role: first, his characteristic method of identifying general community goals and their implications for his preferred policy outcomes; second, his characteristic means of attempting to implement his conception of the community good; and, finally, his characteristic role as innovator or critic of new proposals for community action. These three features of leadership roles are intended as an elaboration and extension of Bales' (1958) functional analysis of leadership roles which suggested, first, that leadership roles perform various functions in task-oriented groups, and, second, that these functions, while complementary to one another and mutually necessary, are likely to be assigned to different actors because the requirements for adequate performance of a given function usually requires the development of capacities, skills, and behavior that are mutually incompatible or, at the very least, are unlikely to be equally developed in the same individual (see also Borgatta, Couch, and Bales, 1954). Note, firstly, that these features can be used to characterize the role strategies employed in any leadership position and have no intrinsic substantive policy content. Note, secondly, that this approach assumes that given actors tend to be consistent in the leadership strategies they employ from one situation to another on each of the three dimensions. While this assumption is probably true for most cases, it is also true that some elite members can and do alter their role strategies according to the situation in which they find themselves.

In order to assess an individual's characteristic strategies for fulfilling his leadership role, we asked our respondents three questions; each of these first described two alternative role strategies and then asked the respondent to indicate the two persons in the list of influentials who best exemplify the use of the first role strategy and the two who best exemplify the use of the second strategy. We then asked him to indicate which strategy he himself was more likely to use. Since our subsequent interpretation depends substantially on these role descriptions, the reader is urged to read with care Q41, Q42, and Q43 in Appendix C before proceeding.

These questions have a number of obvious limitations; consequently, the answers elicited must be used with caution. The questions ask for quite complex, summary judgments that are subject to errors and biases arising from the respondents' misunderstanding what is wanted, possessing insufficient information about the people on the list of influentials to make accurate judgments, and perhaps even being subject to some pressures to make the more socially desirable response, especially regarding their own preferences and those of their friends. Despite these limitations, there was a remarkably high correspondence between self-reported preferences and attributed preferences by others in the elite, suggesting that there may well be some "social reality" to these subjective judgments.[4]

By cross-tabulating the three dichotomized dimensions, one can iden-

---

[4] To be sure, we recognize that each of the three aspects of leadership role strategies are more appropriately seen as complex continua with many intermediate ("mixed") positions between the polar extremes. To assess more accurately an individual's location on the continua would have required a greatly expanded set of questions in order to develop reliable and valid scales. We justify this short cut only as a first approximation to see if the distinctions make much sense and to assist us in providing a meaningful characterization of the respondents. The respondents experienced no apparent difficulties in understanding what was wanted and making the judgments requested. That is, the questions seemed to provide meaningful tasks; and all the respondents had no trouble in doing them. The extensive qualitative information that we have on elite members is generally consistent with these summary judgments, reinforcing our confidence in the questions' utility.

tify eight possible combinations of leadership role strategies, only six of which actually occurred in our elite population. Table 6.1 provides a listing of the elite respondents according to their self-identified role strategies. It may well be that the combination, "idealistic critic," whether preferring public or private means of implementing his views, is an empirically empty cell or occurs exceedingly infrequently, at least among prominent community leaders. In explanation, one might argue that the logic of being an idealistic leader tends to imply active efforts to propose various new directions for community action that would serve to realize his values. Idealistic critics might arise only on the basis of "one-shot" activation over a proposal that represented especially strong threats to their deeply held values. Having resolved such an issue, the idealistic critic might again lapse into civic inactivity and, thus, not enter into elite circles. (Studies of community controversies over fluoridating the water in the United States suggest that some opponents of fluoridation might have fallen into such a category [cf. Rosenthal and Crain, 1966].)

Combining the information in Table 6.1 with the other information we have provided should give the interested reader a fairly detailed picture of Altneustadt's elite as a functioning entity. Several general observations are worth making here. First, as one might have anticipated for a well-established working elite, the bulk of the elite population falls into the categories of pragmatic proponents, although they are almost evenly divided between those who favor public means as opposed to more informal means of implementing their objectives. Noteworthy also is the fact that all the sociometric stars of the various cliques and subcliques see themselves as active proponents who primarily utilize public channels to achieve their objectives. Only Herr Jung says that he uses both informal and public means of implementing his objectives. In fact, 13 others in the elite agree with him; they split 9 to 4 in terms of seeing him as especially exemplary of the characteristic use of informal or public means of implementation.

Each clique and subclique, moreover, is internally differentiated with its own complement of publicists and leaders preferring more informal tactics of implementation. As Table 6.2 at least suggests (the numbers in the different cells are often too small to be always reliable statistically), the cliques and subcliques do differ among themselves in the degree to which they are composed of idealists and pragmatists, publicists and informal leaders, and proponents and critics of new proposals. Members of the SPD clique, as the challengers, are considerably more likely to see themselves as idealists (rather than pragmatists), preferring to use public means to implement their proposals (rather than informal

TABLE 6.1

General Strategy for Setting Community Goals: The Distribution of the Altneustadt Elite among Eight Self-Identified, Preferred Role Strategies for Performing the Community Leadership Role[a]

Proponent versus critic	Idealist strategy for goal implementation		Pragmatist strategy for goal implementation	
	Private	Public	Private	Public
Proponent	G. Koenig	Clemens	Bickert	(Berghaus)*
	Schmitz	Muth*	Biedermann	Bode
	Schütz	Rudolf	Blenderman	Bosch
		Schindler	Bär	Bünck
		Stahl*	Chelius	Franke
		Zacharias	(Jung)*	Hildebrandt
			Lenz	Huppertz
			Matzerath	(Jung)*
			Schäfer	Ohnesorge
			Wolff	(Koenig)*
				Mertes
				Nickel
				Pulheim
	$N = 3$	$N = 6$	$N = 10$	$N = 13$
Critic			Büsgen	(Berghaus)*
			Hilgert	Ewig
			Kiel	Fassbender
			Schüller	Hilgert
				(Koenig)*
				Ulrich
				Riehl
				Steeger
	$N = 0$	$N = 0$	$N = 4$	$N = 8$

[a] Parentheses ( ) indicate that the person said that he employed both strategies; asterisk * indicates a sociometric star in one of the cliques or subcliques.

means), and to be proposers of new initiatives (rather than critics of proposals as they are introduced). The CDU coalition, on the other hand, is internally differentiated among the several subcliques and boundary personnel. The dominant Koenig–Berghaus subclique primarily consists of pragmatic, public mobilizers of new initiatives. The rival Muth–Jung subclique contains more idealists, critics of the proposals of others, and

TABLE 6.2

Percentage Self-Reported Idealist–Pragmatist, Informal–Public Means, and Proponent–Critic of New Proposals, by Cliques and Subcliques

Cliques subcliques	Percentage of idealists	Percentage of public means	Percentage of proponents of new proposals
Dominant CDU clique			
(*N* = 25)	11.5	61.5	65.4
Koenig–Berghaus			
subclique			
(*N* = 12)	8.3	66.7	75.0
Boundary personnel			
(*N* = 5)	—	20.0	60.0
Muth–Jung subclique			
(*N* = 8)	25.0	62.5	50.0
SPD clique			
(*N* = 7)	42.9	71.4	85.7
Total percentage			
(*N* = 32)	18.8	62.5	68.8

people who prefer informal tactics of implementation. The boundary
personnel, on the other hand, include no idealists, only one public
mobilizer, and are about average in seeing themselves as proponents of
new proposals.

Positions on Community Issues and
Coalition Membership

McClosky (1964), Converse (1964), and others have provided convincing evidence that elite members typically possess relatively high
levels of internal coherence and consistency in their ideological orientations in contrast to those of the public at large, which tend to be much
more loosely structured, almost random combinations of beliefs, attitudes, and preferences. Moreover, it is not surprising that they have
shown that an elite member's value orientations are fairly predictive of
his voting preferences and of partisan behavior in contested issues. Both
the earlier coalitional analysis and the analysis of the value space can
be shown to be closely linked to the partisan behavior of the elite in
five hotly contested community issues. In Chapter 9, we provide an
extended discussion of the rationale for selecting community issues for
study according to their relevance to the four functional subsystems of

the community and a description of the five issues selected for intensive study in Altneustadt. For each issue, we were able to determine which side each elite member himself favored, regardless of whether or not he participated actively in its resolution, and which elite members were perceived by the others to have been especially active in fighting for or against a proposal. Obviously, an elite member's subjective preference on an issue was not in itself a sufficient guarantee that he would actually become active in fighting for or against it. In order to convert his predisposition into action, a number of other factors had to be present, including the time available for such activities, relatively high priority in his hierarchy of preferences, and possession of the relevant influence resources to bring to bear on the issue (see Chapter 11, pp. 212–214).

On four of the five issues, there were dramatic differences among the coalitions and among people located in the various sectors of the value space with respect to which side individual elite members favored in a given controversy. As one would certainly have expected, an elite member's location in the value space was especially useful in predicting his positions on the two pattern-maintenance issues. The SPD coalition and the liberal side of the value space were overwhelmingly in favor of the change-oriented sides of the two issues, while the CDU coalition and the centralist and conservative sectors of the value space were generally opposed to the proposed changes. These two issues had been selected precisely because they were so closely related to the principal axis of cleavage in the pattern-maintenance structure of the community and because they were expressive of potent, underlying value preferences (see Chapters 3 and 4). It is, therefore, hardly surprising that there is such a close relationship between the different generalized value orientations and the positions taken on concrete issues that might be derived from these differences in *Weltanschauungen*. Note, however, the strict conceptual and methodological independence of these several measures that provides at least some support for the plausibility of our general characterization of the community elite's dynamics of activation and opposition.

The value space, on the other hand, was essentially irrelevant in predicting which sides were taken on the issues of community incorporation and construction of the new city hall. The resolutions of both issues were almost entirely confined to the precincts of the elite itself, in sharp contrast to the pattern-maintenance issues that had aroused (or were regarded as likely to arouse) widespread public controversy and mobilization. Both community incorporation and the construction of the new city hall had highly variable practical political consequences for the two subcliques of the CDU coalition as well as the large businessmen and SPD cliques. The extension of the city boundaries into the county promised considerable political advantage for the Koenig–Berghaus city sub-clique and the SPD clique and threatened the political base of the county-oriented Jung–Muth subclique and the political access of the large businessmen clique, which enjoyed especially favorable treatment at the hands of the county faction. As a result, an ad hoc political alliance between the city CDU subclique and the SPD clique developed opposing the rival county CDU subclique. The construction of the new city hall was a pet project of Herr Koenig, who saw it as a monument to his civic leadership, while the SPD clique joined with the county crowd in criticizing its extravagance, location, and inadequate provision of "needed" facilities desired especially by the SPD clique and its supporters.

Note that both issues were very much instrumental issues revolving around technical and "practical" political considerations that were simply not especially relevant to basic value orientations. They basically posed questions concerning the "best" way to implement general policy decisions that had already been made. They did not raise questions about which of several conflicting "ultimate" community goals or objectives, each of which were directly expressive of fundamental value commitments, should be chosen.

The issue of a new industry relocating in Altneustadt generated no consistent patterning on the basis of value orientations or coalition memberships. In fact, this hypothetical issue posed a serious challenge to the existing coalitional structure because it set individuals in the same subcliques against one another. This was especially true for the CDU clique which included the full range of economic notables with their potentially divergent economic interests. People with primary institutional responsibilities in the economic sector were especially likely to be seen as becoming activated on the issue, but they were sharply divided internally over whether they favored or opposed the new industry coming to town. Large employers regarded with disfavor the invasion of "their community" by a substantial competitor for a labor pool already in short supply. Retail shopkeepers and tradesmen, on the other hand, welcomed the newcomer as a boost to their businesses because it would generate economic expansion and population growth. People in the other institutional sectors simply lacked an equivalent means of calculating the advantages and disadvantages to aid them in making consistent extrapolations of how the newcomer with its attendant population in-migration would affect their long-term political interests or basic value commitments. Interestingly enough, although most elite members expressed personal enthusiasm for Altneustadt's industrial development, they felt that many of their peers were likely to be strongly opposed to such changes on economic or other grounds.

CONCLUSION

While hopefully not overburdening the reader with more than he really needed or wanted to know about Altneustadt's elite, we have attempted to provide a detailed overview of its coalitional structure, the internal differentiation of its cliques, the principal axes of its value consensus and differentiation, and its cleavages into opposing camps on different issues. With the information provided in this chapter, the reader should be in a much better position to evaluate critically the plausibility and adequacy of our subsequent formal analyses which are more concerned with developing a general theoretical and methodological strategy for delineating elite structure and dynamics on the basis of radical condensations of selected data.

7

Opening the Black Box: Relations among the Community Elite: A Method for Describing Their Structure*

In this chapter, we shall take the first step in developing a more rigorous methodology for structural analysis of the elite decision-making system. In contrast to the macrostructural approach to network analysis proposed in Chapter 3, our strategy here will be much more conventional and microstructural in focus. Specifically, it will examine the interrelationships among a delimited set of individual actors. Armed with the extensive qualitative information of the preceding chapters on the community and its elite members, their values, coalitional relations, and activities, the reader should be in a strong position critically to evaluate the adequacy of this methodology in describing the underlying social structures of the decision-making elite. To facilitate such critical interchapter comparisons, we have employed the same identifying codes for elite members throughout. The reader is urged to make these comparisons for himself as a check on our inferences and generalizations.

The following three chapters are intended as an interrelated set analytically focused around the concept of social structure. This chapter, first, reviews the theoretical and methodological rationale for the description of community influence structures and then presents the empirical re-

* Portions of this chapter are drawn from a previously published article (Laumann and Pappi, 1973), reprinted with the permission of the *American Sociological Review* and the American Sociological Association.

sults of employing these procedures in our case study. The next chapter then takes up a proposed causal model of influence structures. The following chapter outlines a structural–functional theory of community issues, using an empirical description of Altneustadt's consensus—cleavage structure to illustrate the principles of this theory.

THE THEORETICAL RATIONALE FOR THE DESCRIPTION OF COMMUNITY INFLUENCE STRUCTURES

To review briefly our introductory chapter's theoretical discussion, we defined *social structure* as a persisting pattern of social relationships among social positions (cf. Laumann, 1966, 1973). A *social relationship* is any link between incumbents of two social positions that involves mutual, but not necessarily symmetric, orientations and activities, whether of a positive, neutral, or negative affect or whether of superordination–subordination or equality in the relative status of the participants (cf. Homans, 1961; Parsons, 1951; Blau, 1964). If *social differentiation* is defined as the differing allocation of tasks and responsibilities among positions in a social system, then a *differentiated social structure* is one whose actors tend to confine their consensual relationships to others performing similar tasks. In other words, similar positions will tend to cluster, that is, to be in closer proximity in the structure, as a function of the higher density of their social ties relative to those with more dissimilar positions. One interesting implication of this definition is that the degree to which a social structure is differentiated into clusters of positions is itself a variable.

A more important implication of these definitions is that models of social structure will differ to the extent that different social relationships are used as the linking mechanisms for the set of social positions, such as informal social contacts as compared to professional or business contacts. We wish, therefore, to devise a methodology that reveals how the pattern of given types of social relationships is structurally differentiated along specifiable dimensions or facets (cf. Guttman, 1959). This usage of the term "structural differentiation" will be seen to parallel Parsons' (1966) usage.

Our treatment of the question of how to describe social structures rests on a fairly explicit physical analogy. There are always a number of pitfalls in taking any analogy too literally. Certainly one must be warned against making assumptions such as the following: In Structure Z, Position A is *twice* the distance from Position B as from Position C. We can, however, assert that, assuming a reasonably good smallest space solution, Position B is, relatively speaking, farther from Position A than Position C. In short, we can make statements at the level of the rank order of positions.

For purposes of interpreting the underlying dimensionality of elite social structures based on consensual relationships, we turn once again to the specification of Postulate II, Chapter 1, on distance-generating mechanisms that was used to analyze the population subsystem's structure of intimate ties:

> Similarities in social positions, interests, attitudes, beliefs, and behavior facilitate the formation of consensual relationships among incumbents of social positions.

The corollary is that the more dissimilar two positions are in status, interests, attitudes, beliefs, and behavior of their incumbents, the less likely is the formation of consensual relationships and, consequently, the "farther away" they are from one another in the structure. Ample theoretical and empirical justification exists for accepting such a postulate as a reasonable starting point for structural analysis (cf. Homans, 1950, 1961; Newcomb, 1961; Blau, 1964, 1974; Fararo and Sunshine, 1964; Laumann, 1966, 1973; Turk, 1973).

THE METHODOLOGY OF STRUCTURAL ANALYSIS: GRAPH THEORY AND SMALLEST SPACE ANALYSIS

We shall focus on three social relationships among our influentials that provide critical vantage points from which to view a community's influence structure. (See Q33, Q37, and Q38, Appendix C, for the sources of information on these relationships.) First, from an instrumental point of view, we shall describe the pattern of *business–professional relationships*, since, in both the functionalist and Marxist literature on community decision making, these are seen as important sources of common interests and claims on the polity and should, therefore, help determine the lines of coalition and cleavage in the community. Respondents were asked to report the three other persons on the list of influentials with whom they were most often in contact in pursuing their primary institutional responsibilities. These are the task-linked, or instrumental, relationships that tie various organizations and collectivities together. Second, we shall describe the pattern of "social" or expressive relationships as it reflects the common interests arising from the influentials' instrumental activities in their primary institutional areas and the shared values, attitudes, and concerns arising from their participation in other spheres of community life. These latter derive from such secondary characteristics of the influentials as their religious and educational backgrounds and residence status (*Alt-* versus *Neubürger*). Finally, we shall describe the pattern of *"community affairs" relationships* which are, at the minimum, informational links among persons with regard to community affairs, and one may hypothesize that they result from the business–professional and social relations structures and the distinctive political arrangements of the community (cf. Rossi, 1960). (The next chapter will explore these hypotheses in greater detail.)

Obviously, all these concerns derive quite directly from the sociometric approach to the study of community power structures beginning with Hunter's work. In a paper written in 1959, Peter Rossi (1960: 132) quite correctly observed:

> Similar amounts of thinking and effort have not been expended on invention of an appropriate methodology for studying other kinds of organized relationships among the members of a community. Although on the abstract level sociometric devices might seem useful tools in the study of large communities, on the empirical level they prove impractical.

Truly remarkable advances, however, in the methodology of sociometric or network analysis for large systems have been made since 1959, rendering Rossi's judgment considerably less cogent for the situation today. (See Coleman and McRae, 1960; Rapoport and Horvath, 1961; Harary, Norman, and Cartwright, 1965; Hubbell, 1965; Alba and Kadushin, 1970; Holland and Leinhardt, 1970; Kadushin, 1970; Rosen and Abrams, 1970; Bonacich, 1972a,b; Lorraine and White, 1971; Levine, 1972; White, Breiger, and Boorman, 1976.)

A major objective of recent sociometric efforts has been to develop theoretically grounded, routine procedures to identify cliques, defined according to varying criteria of interrelatedness or "choice" patterns (see, for example, our discussion of the condensation of a digraph in Chapter 6, pp. 103–108), in a large set of persons. A corollary objective has been to develop graphic techniques for describing how these cliques and persons who belong to no cliques are, in turn, interrelated.

The "sociogram" whereby individuals are represented by points and choice relations among individuals by directed lines was an early effort at graphic representation of the structure of interpersonal relationships (cf. Hunter, 1953; Moreno, 1953; Loomis and Beegle, 1950). While presenting some artful sociograms of Altneustadt's elite, the preceding chapter also noted the limitations and pitfalls of such an approach. We shall now consider a more rigorous means by which to represent relational structures graphically. Essentially, we have combined two recent developments, graph theory and smallest space analysis, to describe our three relational structures.[1] (Systematic introductions to these developments and a discussion of their merits are found in Harary *et al.* [1965] and McFarland and Brown [1973].) For our limited purposes, the brief introduction and illustration of the mathematical theory of digraphs and graphs in Chapter 6, pp. 102–105, will suffice to define the key concepts of an adjacency matrix, reachability, path distance, connectedness, and condensation. Since we were interested in the presence of a particular relationship between two persons, regardless of whether or not it was reported by both persons as a mutual choice, we disregarded the direction of choices by the simple expedient of symmetrizing the adjacency matrices (i.e., we converted the original choice matrices from digraphs to graphs).

An inspection of the reachability matrix (consisting of "1" if [person] v_j is reachable from [person] v_i in a certain number of steps and "0" if v_j cannot be reached from v_i) immediately tells us which persons were disconnected from which others in the total set of influentials—that is, their pattern of choosing and being chosen were such that they could not reach certain others in the structure. In our data, respondents could be reached from all other respondents in the social and community affairs graphs in some finite number of steps, while five respondents in the business–professional structure could not be reached by some others. The maximum number of steps along a shortest path from one influential to any other was five, in both the business–professional and the social relations graphs, and six in the community affairs graph. Herr Koenig, who, as the reader will recall from the last chapter, ranked as the most influential man in town, could reach in two or fewer steps 91% of the others in the community affairs structure and 73% of the others in the social relations structure and in the business–professional structure, respectively. Thus, from one point of view, we could conclude that our influence structure is highly integrated since nearly every leading influential can reach and be reached in each of the three networks by every other influential in the community. Many disconnected individuals or sets of individuals would indicate a less integrated influence structure, with presumably greater difficulties in coordinating community affairs or resolving issues that divide community opinion.

---

[1] See Alba and Kadushin (1970) for a rather similar approach based on graph theoretic notions but using a different graphic technique.

GRAPHIC REPRESENTATIONS OF INFLUENCE STRUCTURES

By submitting each path distance matrix (calculated from the symmetrized adjacency matrix) to a symmetric smallest space analysis (cf. Roskam and Lingoes, 1970; Guttman, 1968), we obtain an acceptable Euclidean two-dimensional representation of each matrix. The program takes into account the rank order of the path distances (and not their absolute size); it attempts to preserve this rank order while arranging the points in a space of few dimensions. In each representation, the derived Euclidean distances among the points (persons) are a monotonic function of the original path distances among the points. We propose to interpret these pictures according to the theoretical principles suggested in the discussion of characteristics of individual influentials and differentiated social structures. Figures 7.1, 7.2 and 7.3 are the graphic representations of the smallest space solutions. Each person has been uniquely identified with a code providing information regarding his influence status, institutional sector responsibilities, religious preference, party membership, and influence resources. (See the legend for Figures 7.1, 7.2, and 7.3 for the complete explanation of the abbreviated code.)

In general, we shall employ two basic principles for interpreting the

Key to Figures 7.1, 7.2 and 7.3

Example
10.5a E w C K
| | | | |
| | | | Religion
| | | Political party
| | Secondary institutional sector
| Primary institutional sector
Influence rank

Primary sector, Secondary sector (Primary Sector is capitalized; secondary sector or sectors are lowercase.

E—Economy   (A—Sector)
A—Authority position in   (G—Sector)
    political system
P—Political party
W—Economic association   (I—Sector)
V—Social clubs, Sports
B—Education
R—Religion
C—Culture   (L—Sector)
H—Health and charity
S—Science
N—Respondent could not be coded into any primary sector

Influence Rank
Respondent's influence rank in the entire elite of 51 persons. Based on question 25, a measure of influence depending on other respondents' votes. Subscripts serve to distinguish respondents who were tied, that is, received the same number of votes.

Party—Political party of which respondent is a member
S—S.P.D. (Social Democratic Party)
C—C.D.U. (Christian Democratic Union)
F—F.D.P. (Free Democratic Party)
N—Not a party member

Religion
K—Catholic
P—Protestant
N—None

Resource base
See Chapter 11, pp. 187–189 and Figure 11.2.

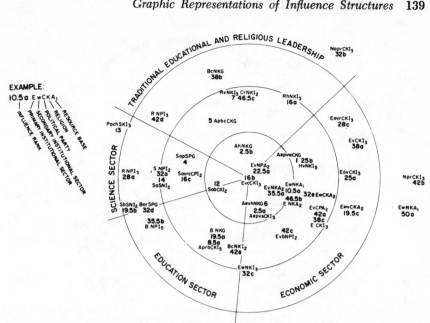

Figure 7.1 Business–professional network, smallest space analysis, Euclidean metric, two-dimensional solution, Guttman–Lingoes coefficient of alienation = .148.

spaces: the principle of integrative centrality and the principle of sector differentiation. The *principle of integrative centrality* holds that persons playing key integrative or coordinating roles in a given structure will tend to be located in the "central region" of the spatial representation of that structure—this will, on the average, minimize their distance from (access to) any other person in the space—while persons located increasingly in the periphery should be of declining functional importance in performing integrative activities for that structure and possibly of increasing importance in representing narrowly defined or interest-specific demands on that structure. This principle of interpreting the spatial solutions implies the identification of a coordinating central region (delineated by a circle with a short radius whose center is the centroid)[2] whose membership varies from one structure to another, depending on the nature of the relationship on which it is constructed, and a series of increasingly large concentric rings reflecting, heuristically speaking, "zones" of declining integrative importance.

The *principle of sector differentiation* divides the space into relatively homogeneous regions radiating from the center and including personnel who typically occupy key positions in the same institutional sector and who, therefore, are likely to share common concerns. These sectors represent potential, if not actual, "natural" coalition zones for community

[2] See Footnote 4, Chapter 3, for a definition of the centroid of a spatial solution.

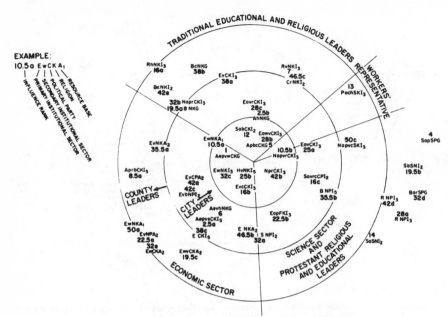

Figure 7.2 Social relations network, smallest space analysis, Euclidean metric, two-dimensional solution, Guttman–Lingoes coefficient of alienation = .158.

issues. Persons in a given functional (institutional) subsystem may, at times, appear on opposite sides of the central region. When they do, they are likely to be in opposition on some common functional issues. The less localized or regionalized a scatter of points (persons) sharing a common institutional locus, the more likely it is that they will be divided on issues of common institutional concern. The more localized a cluster of persons in a common institutional sector is, the more homogeneous they will be in attitudes and values and the more they will function as a co-ordinated proactive or reactive claimant group (coalition) on community issues.

By combining these two principles, we can offer two additional specu-lations about the structure of the integrative center. First, we hypothe-size that a position's location toward the center of the space but in a particular sector may be seen to reflect its potential integrative role as a representative for that sector's interest since, on the one hand, its posi-tion close to the center makes it relatively more influential, and, on the other hand, its location in an institutional sector ties it to other positions in that sector. Second, integrative centers may be seen as being highly biased in composition, overrepresenting certain sectors at the same time that they underrepresent or completely exclude others. To the extent

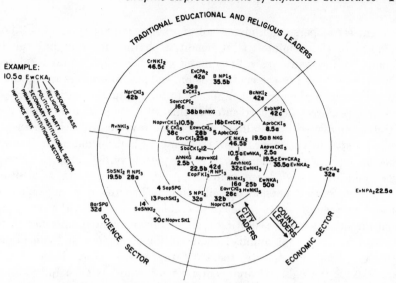

Figure 7.3 Community affairs network, smallest space analysis, Euclidean metric, two-dimensional solution, Guttman–Lingoes coefficient of alienation = .131.

that certain sectors are excluded from central zone locations (i.e., all their personnel are located in the periphery), we may infer that their impact on decision-making outcomes will be minimized. In other words, the decision-making structure, while performing Almond's function of aggregating interests, has an aggregative bias in favor of some interests and against others (cf. Gamson, 1968: 53–54).

Looking at the three spaces (Figures 7.1, 7.2 and 7.3), we readily see that they do differ among themselves in important ways. The central core of the *business–professional space* includes only the top-ranked community influentials who occupy positions of authority at the city and county administrative levels and personnel who control the largest economic and financial interests in the general area (and who, incidentally, do not in general enjoy as high a reputed influence status as the governmental leaders). These two groups presumably have much common intercourse concerning the coordination of government decisions that have bearing on economic matters (such as zoning, housing policy, and so on), and vice versa. Control over adaptive resources (money, land, and jobs) and authority (right to make binding decisions) are the principal influence resources represented in the center. Small businessmen, religious, educational, and research center personnel are relegated to the peripheral zones but in clearly demarcated sectors at some considerable distance from one another.

The central core of the *social relations space* is composed of a rather different set of personnel, almost all of whom are long resident, Catholic members of the dominant CDU coalition in the city that has run the community for many years. It is noteworthy that high reputed influence is not concentrated in the central region. Influence resources in the center are primarily authority and different forms of intra-elite influence—no adaptive resources are represented in this core group. The differentiation of the economic sector is almost the precise reverse of the business–professional space as it moves from the center, which includes small downtown businessmen and merchants, to the periphery, which includes managers and owners of large manufacturing, financial, and agricultural enterprises located outside the city limits. The research personnel are located by themselves at some considerable distance from the center and from the other sectors, reflecting their highly segregated existence in the "social life" of the community. The traditional religious and educational elite are located opposite them in the space. Herr Blendermann, 12SabCK, is the only research center person who has been fully assimilated, in the sense of being located in the central zone of the social space, but he differs from his colleagues at the research center on nearly every key count—he is a Catholic rather than a Protestant, a political economist rather than a natural scientist, and a convert from the SPD to the CDU since his arrival in Altneustadt.

Finally, the central core of the *community affairs space* includes a higher density of personnel than the other spaces whose members are recruited from much more heterogeneous institutional sectors and political and religious backgrounds and among whom all the types of influence resources are represented. As one should expect, center personnel are more homogeneous on their reputed influence status in that they tend to be seen as belonging in the upper reaches of the influence hierarchy. The sector divisions, especially toward the periphery, are very similar in character to those of the other two spaces.

If we correlate reputed status as a community influential with distance from the centroid of each of three spaces, we find significant correlations for the business–professional structure (.40) and the community affairs structure (.30) but an insignificant correlation of .17 for the social relations structure. If we are prepared to regard reputed influence status as a crude indicator of relative "integrative" status in the community social system, then we can take these correlations as at least consistent with, but by no means dramatic confirmation of, our principle of integrative centrality. We might speculate further that integrative status may mean rather different things in these three relational contexts. Reputed status as a community influential is clearly more relevant to the business–profession and community affairs structures, but it is not especially relevant for the social integration of the community elite. If we had assessed "social prominence and esteem," in the sense of Robert Dahl's (1961) "social notables," for all the influentials, we might well have found that this ranking was a more appropriate indicator of integrative status in the social relations structure and was significantly associated with centrality in that structure.

We can make two general statements summarizing our findings regarding the sector structural differentiation of Altneustadt. First, pattern-maintenance personnel are divided into two clearly identifiable regions or clusters at roughly opposite ends of an axis running through the center, with research center personnel located at a relatively greater distance from the center (reflecting their weaker influence on community decision making) and traditional religious and educational leaders at the other end of the axis, some of whom enjoy closer proximity to or inclusion in the integrative cores of the three spaces. It is this axis of differentiation among pattern-maintenance personnel that reflects the principal axis of recurrent, intense cleavage on community issues. Second, there is somewhat less differentiation of the adaptive sector since economic personnel tend to cluster in the central region and an immediately adjacent peripheral zone rather than to fall into sharply separated clusters on opposite sides of the central region. The portrayal of the social relations space in Figure 7.2 reflects most clearly the somewhat weaker potential for an oppositional axis of adaptive personnel in which Herr Chelius, 13 PachSKI$_3$, the only workers' representative in the SPD and the only union member found in the elite, is located diametrically opposite the largest factory owner, Herr Goslar, 22.5a EvNPA$_2$, and a number of other large businessmen. As expected for this predominantly middle-class community, economic interest differentiation is not so extensively developed and seems to involve primarily differentiation of small business, mercantile interests located in the city from the larger manufacturing and agricultural interests located outside the city limits, rather than labor–management differentiation.

CONCLUSION

In this chapter, we have adopted a graph theoretic strategy, in combination with a data-reduction technique (i.e., smallest space analysis), to describe the structures of interrelations among elite members in different interactional contexts. Both procedures serve two purposes: First, they radically restrict the amount of information taken into account in the structural analysis (e.g., by assuming merely the presence or absence of a link between two individuals without regard to the obvious differences in the amount of information or affect being exchanged that characterize different links). Second, their internal logics impose some relatively strong assumptions about the nature of the data being analyzed (e.g., that elite members will, in fact, find the shortest paths among themselves and will use them or that path distances between different elite pairs can be compared with one another at least at the level of rank order). Because we are dealing with a population universe, the elements of which are all, by theoretical assumption, interdependent, we cannot turn to sampling theory or conventional rules of statistical inference to guide us in accepting or rejecting different interpretations of the results. All that can be done in "verifying" our conclusions is to compare systematically the smallest space solutions reported in the figures in this chapter with the more discursive, qualitative information provided in the preceding chapter. We find such comparisons to be very reassuring, but we urge the reader to check our conclusions for himself.

The next chapter necessitates our making even stronger simplifying assumptions. Assuming that the results to this point are convincing, however, we are prepared to make them in the hope of gaining greater insight into the fundamental nature of the decision-making system by eliminating irrelevant details that serve only to obscure it.

8
A Causal Modeling
Approach to the Study of
a Community Elite's
Influence Structure*

With Lois Verbrugge

INTRODUCTION

To summarize the argument of the preceding chapters, we have developed a general structuralist framework for analyzing community influence systems based on Parsonsian assumptions about the nature of social systems. Our central objective was to develop a methodology reasonably faithful to the underlying assumptions at the same time that it yielded an empirically accurate structural description of the community influence system. Once the set of influential positions in community affairs and their incumbents had been identified, the structure of the influence system was defined as the persisting pattern of relationships that link positions (or incumbents) to one another, directly and indirectly. A direct link between two positions was said to exist when one or the other incumbent reports a high frequency of communication about community affairs with the other. By using a graph theoretic approach (cf. Harary *et al.*, 1965), both direct and indirect links were taken into account in calculating the path distances between every pair of incumbents.

* This chapter is a shortened version of a previously published article (Laumann, Verbrugge, and Pappi, 1974), reprinted with the permission of the *American Sociological Review* and the American Sociological Association.

Treating the matrix of path distances as ordinal-level proximity estimates of the relative distances among positions, we used smallest space analysis to portray the pattern of interrelationships graphically. Assuming that the resulting Euclidean representation of the community influence structure (see Figure 7.3, Chapter 7) reasonably approximates its "true" structure, we will attempt in this chapter to extend the preceding analysis by developing a general causal model of the determinants of such a structure and then to evaluate the model's adequacy for our case study.

To accomplish these objectives, we have had to reorient our approach to the problem and to depart from that found in the literature. Conventional study of community elites has focused on the characteristics of individual elite members, however identified, either contrasting their distributions on some characteristics with those of the community at large or contrasting the composition of opposition groups in the elite. For example, Hunter (1953) demonstrated that the white community elite of Regional City was differentially recruited from the economic elite, while the black elite was heavily drawn from the professions, and both were obviously unrepresentative of the populations of their respective subcommunities and the city as a whole. Employing a different approach to identify community influentials, Dahl (1961) showed that different types of people become involved in community controversy, depending on the type of issue (see also D'Antonio et al., 1961).

In using individual elite members as the units of analysis, however, one quickly encounters analytic problems because of the small numbers typically involved in a given elite—that is, the problem of vanishing cell frequencies. More fundamentally, one loses sight of the central sociological questions regarding the structure of relations among individual actors. While the theoretical literature has usually made it quite clear that the relationships among actors, rather than the actors themselves, are the objects of special concern for sociological analysis (e.g., Blau, 1964, 1974, 1975; Nadel, 1957; Cartwright, 1965), remarkably little empirical research has been based on that premise, especially in community power studies.[1]

---

[1] There have, of course, been many sociometric studies of community elites, but the usual intention of such strategies has been limited to identifying the clique memberships of individuals. Once identified, the coalitional structure is typically used as a descriptive framework for discussing the activities of the elite in specific controversies. Although they start from a relational framework, such discussions typically return to the individual elite members as the focal analytic unit (see Kadushin [1968] for an important exception to this generalization). In an interesting, methodologically innovative study, Linton Freeman (1968) and his associates used a

We propose, therefore, to take as the unit of analysis the *interpoint distance* between a pair of points (i.e., elite incumbents), as estimated in our smallest space solution. (Note here that, in general, we will be speaking of n $(n-1)/2$ interpoint distances, where n equals the number of elite members.) The problem then is to predict the relative distances among all pairs of incumbents as a function of other attributes of the pairs of incumbents. The crucial question in such a strategy is how to measure attributes or variable characteristics of relationships between elite pairs.

A GENERAL CAUSAL MODEL FOR THE COMMUNITY INFLUENCE STRUCTURE

Figure 8.1 represents our path model of the determinants of the community affairs structure (CA), which we are assuming to be our best estimate of the "true" community influence structure.[2] The business–professional structure (BP) represents objective interest differentiation

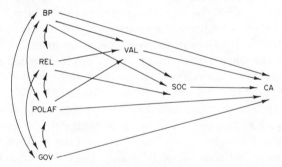

Figure 8.1 Path model of the community influence structure. BP = business-professional structure; REL = religious similarity–dissimilarity; GOV = governmental structure; POLAF = political affiliation similarity–dissimilarity; VAL = value similarity–dissimilarity; SOC = informal social relations structure; CA = community affairs structure.

factor analytic approach to the problem of clustering individual elite actors, organizations, or issues on the basis of their differing involvement in common community concerns. While bearing on our interests, their approach concentrated primarily on a technique for clustering individuals or organizations in terms of some underlying commonalities. Their subsequent discussion attempting to account for the occurrence of specific clusters was handled almost entirely on an ad hoc, "common sense" basis. We hope to propose here a more general framework for describing the structuring principles that undergird elite influence systems.

[2] This chapter will discuss three such models. The first portrays our expectations based on our "theory" of the process by which community influence structures are de-

in a community. This operationalization emphasizes occupational and sector-specific interests compared, for instance, with class interests. As the reader will recall, for each individual elite member, we identified the three others in the elite whom he contacted most often in performing his primary institutional responsibilities. For example, businessmen tended to report other businessmen and governmental officials. Even here, however, we found differences in the choices of the business community, based on firm size, buying–selling relationships, industrial type, and capital requirements. Religious leaders, on the other hand, typically reported other religious and lay leaders of the same faith, as was the case for other institutional sectors. Thus, a pair of actors with a relatively small interpoint distance in the BP structure, as compared to a pair with a larger interpoint distance, are assumed to have more shared (common) institutional activities and concerns.

Most community analysts, whether Marxist or functionalist, have argued that objective interests in a community should influence the structure of the community influence system since different interests often present conflicting claims on scarce community resources. The implication is that the proximity of objective interests should be reflected in the proximity of people who represent these or related interests. Conversely, when the objective interests of interest groups are opposed, their representatives should stand farther apart in the community influence structure. Accordingly, we have drawn an arrow directly from BP to CA, reflecting our hypothesis of a direct effect of BP on CA.

Similarities in actors' institutional tasks and responsibilities have often been shown to lead to similarities in their value orientations and world views (or value homophyly, cf. Perrucci and Pilisuk, 1970; Newcomb, 1961). Dissimilar institutional activities, on the other hand, should lead to dissimilar (but not necessarily conflicting) value orientations. Big businessmen, for example, are expected to develop common definitions of situations and views of the world that set them apart from small businessmen, religious, educational, or political leaders. These latter groups are expected to differ from one another as well. Thus, we postulate a positive direct effect of a pair's proximity in the business–professional structure (BP) on that pair's proximity on a set of value orientations

termined (Figure 8.1). The second (not drawn) is a heuristic model that contains all possible paths in a just-identified model to be discussed. Finally, the third model is derived from our empirical analysis that indicates certain paths are too small substantively to warrant inclusion (Figure 8.2).

(VAL) of special relevance to community affairs. Moreover, similar value positions should directly affect a pair's proximity in the community affairs structure. Following this reasoning, we show a direct effect of VAL on CA in Figure 8.1.

One's choice of a partner for informal social activities and more intimate relationships is expected to reflect both common institutional (or instrumental) activities that bring the pair together and similar value orientations. The proximity of a pair in terms of their informal relations (SOC) should, in turn, affect their relative proximity as potential coalition partners in the community affairs network. Hence, we postulate direct effects of BP and VAL on SOC, and of SOC on CA in Figure 8.1.

The development of informal relations between two actors, however, is not simply a function of shared institutional activities of an instrumental character. It should also reflect similarities in ascriptively assigned characteristics, such as common religious preferences, length of residence in the community, and other shared particularistic characteristics, some of which may be potent sources of value differences in the community (see Chapters 3 and 4; also Laumann, 1966, 1973). Hence, we postulate a positive direct effect of religious similarity (REL) on the informal social structure (SOC) and value homophyly (VAL).

Every community has a distinctive pattern of groupings of governmental actors as a result of legal arrangements that specify how governmental units such as the city council, mayor's office, and county executive office, are to be constituted, what their formal relationships are to be, and which units have authority to make particular binding decisions. Council members of the opposition party, for example, must serve on the same city council with majority party members and have formal relationships with the mayor and city administrator. We would, therefore, expect the relative proximities of pairs of actors in the CA structure to be a function of whether or not they share formal positions in the governmental system (GOV) concerned with the resolution of community issues and their implementation. By the same logic, pairs of actors sharing identical political party affiliations (POLAF) might be expected to be in closer proximity in the CA structure than pairs of actors of different political party persuasions.

As is conventional in path diagrams of causal models, all independent variables for which we offer no hypothesis regarding their causal ordering are connected by double-headed arrows indicating that the extent to which the variables are empirically intercorrelated will be taken as given.

The remaining sections of the chapter will be concerned, first, with describing how we propose to measure the variables in the causal model outlined in this section, and second, with presenting the results of applying this model to our case study of Altneustadt.

MEASURING THE VARIABLES IN THE
CAUSAL MODEL

All the variables in the causal model are meant to describe the relative distances between all possible *pairs* of influentials, in contrast to the more conventional analysis which attempts to characterize attributes of individuals, such as their ages, socioeconomic statuses, or religious preferences. Since there were 45 influentials in Altneustadt's elite structures, we will need to estimate $\binom{n}{2} = 990$ interpoint distances for each structure.[3]

The dependent variable, community affairs structure (CA), is the 990 Euclidean interpoint distances derived from the smallest space solution based on the matrix of path distances described in the preceding chapter.[4] The estimates of the interpoint distances in the business–professional structure (BP) and social structure (SOC) are the Euclidean distances for these two structures, which are also described there.

Although the political party affiliation (POLAF), religious similarity (REL), and formal governmental (GOV) structures represent quite

[3] In the business–professional structure, we had complete information on only 41 influentials. Consequently, there were only 820 interpoint distances in this structure.

[4] We have not performed statistical tests of significance because they are inappropriate when dealing with a population universe. Readers who might wish to do so should bear in mind that the $n(n-1)/2$ interpoint distances do not constitute an equivalent number of independent observations. Professor David D. McFarland of the University of Chicago, whom we consulted regarding appropriate degrees of freedom, responded as follows:

> Insofar as I am aware, there exists no sampling theory applicable to the present context, and hence no statistical basis for performing significance tests at all, let alone formulae for appropriate degrees of freedom. In any case, there is considerable redundancy among the $n(n-1)/2 = 990$ interpoint distances among $n = 45$ points lying in a two-dimensional Euclidean space. From the $2n = 90$ coordinates, one could deduce not only all of the 990 interpoint distances, but also certain additional information such as the 45 distances of the various points from the origin of the coordinate system. Thus, even if one were able to obtain the necessary sampling theory, the appropriate degrees of freedom would be something less than 90, and nowhere near 990.

See also Proctor (1969) on some related issues.

different attributes of the relationships between pairs of influentials, they may be treated together here, since we adopted the same strategy for describing each of them. First, we created a 45-by-45 matrix; each row and corresponding column of it referred to a particular influential. Then we entered a "0" for each pair of influentials who were of the same political party affiliation (Christian Democratic Union, Social Democratic Party, Free Democratic Party, or none) and a "1" for each pair whose political party preferences differed. A similar matrix was constructed for the religious similarity structure, in which "0" indicated a pair sharing a religious preference (Catholic, Protestant, or none) and "1" a pair differing in religious preferences. Finally, for the formal governmental structure, we assigned a "0" for a pair of influentials who were members of the same governmental body, such as the city council or county council, and a "1" if they did not have a legally required relationship. For example, all members of the city council, regardless of their party memberships and personal preferences, must have some dealings with one another as well as with the city manager and mayor. The mayor and city manager, in turn, must have interaction with the county manager and state representative, while the county manager must interact with the elected county council. (Note that only those members of the city and county councils who were regarded as especially consequential and part of the top set of influentials were included among the 45 influentials.)

Our operationalization of these structures is admittedly crude since the dichotomous variables suppress considerable variation in the degree to which any two influentials are *(a)* involved together in political party or religious affairs, or share common orientations, and *(b)* constrained to interact in the context of their formal governmental responsibilities. Nevertheless, we believe that these structures do describe major channeling mechanisms by which influentials come to be linked. The matrices indicate, however imperfectly, three important hypothetical constructs— the ascriptive and politically grounded solidarities in the community elite and the formally established institutional structure of community decision making.

With regard to value homophyly, we have already discussed in Chapter 6, pp. 119–123, the rationale for treating it as a multidimensional attribute that may be used to estimate the relative proximities of influentials with respect to the similarities and differences among them regarding their general value orientations and attitudes toward significant societal issues. We used the Euclidean interpoint distances from the MSA space reported in Chapter 6 (Figure 6.5) as our estimate of value homophyly (VAL) among influentials.

ESTIMATING THE MODEL

The central hypotheses concern the dependence of the community affairs network on other networks and similarities or differences among elite pairs. It is intuitively useful to think of the measures of business–professional contacts, informal social contacts, and contacts in governing bodies as probabilities (or relative rates) of information and influence flow between pairs of influentials. These contact measures ultimately derive from reports of interaction, but the proximity scores based on these reports reflect likelihoods, since all pairs are assigned a distance, regardless of whether or not they have direct contacts in real life.

All the predictor structures are assumed to exist prior in time to the CA network. They facilitate and "direct" its formation. Social ties (SOC) are also seen as being aided by common objective interests, similar values and opportunities for frequent meeting. The social network is, therefore, assumed to depend on networks measuring those factors. Finally, political and social attitudes (VAL) are shaped and honed by economic position and political affiliation and, to a lesser extent, by religious affiliation. Consequently, value homophyly is postulated to depend on these variables.

Although networks may have reciprocal impact on each other (e.g., mutual concern and conversation about a city issue may strengthen a friendship), we shall only explore here a recursive system. This "one-way" vision of relationships may be incomplete, but the hypothesized directions included do enjoy theoretical support. Because even the recursive model may be incomplete, we have adopted a heuristic approach, which permits some changes in the model based on its empirical exploration.

With successive dependent variables, a path analytic solution is appropriate (Duncan, 1966). It permits us to do more than simply account for variation and discuss partial coefficients since we can explore the "routing" of causes through direct and indirect effects. We must, however, assume additive, linear relations among the variables. There is no evidence that these assumptions are unreasonable.

In the path analytic model, we must, in addition, assume that *(1)* each disturbance term is uncorrelated with included predetermined variables in its structural equation. This is sufficient for determining the model's identification. Further assumptions are that *(2)* each disturbance is uncorrelated with excluded predetermined variables and *(3)* with other disturbances. These assumptions allow us to utilize ordinary least squares (OLS) in an overidentified model (Goldberger, 1970). Because our data are for a universe, we are not concerned with the additional features of

TABLE 8.1

Correlation Matrix for Proximity Structures[a]

	Var	SOC	BP	VAL	GOV	REL	POLAF	Mean	Range
CA	X_7	.458	.195	.241	.154	.240	.220	.604	.03 –2.01
SOC	X_6		.384	.296	.118	.317	.439	.846	.01 –2.13
BP	X_1			.164	.012	.151	.335	.769	.01 –2.03
VAL	X_5				−.011	.043	.130	.536	.001–1.45
GOV	X_4					.027	−.018	.113	0–1
REL	X_3						.234	.579	0–1
POLAF	X_2							.499	0–1

[a] All correlations involving BP are based on 820 pairs, due to missing data for four persons. Other correlations are based on 990 cases.

these assumptions (unbiased estimates from [1] and minimum-variance coefficients from [3]), which are appropriate for sampled data. If zero-order correlations among variables are not reproduced by the model, then the second and third assumptions are not correct and the size of those relationships can be estimated. The correlation of a disturbance with excluded predetermined variables is serious, since it suggests that the researcher should add a path in his model, which he expected to be zero.[5] Correlated residuals are less worrisome: They reflect an omitted variable (or variables) with effects beyond those of the included predetermined variables for the two dependent variables in question. The researcher may have some idea what these absent predictors are, but may have no good measure of them in his data. We will evaluate the assumptions for our final model later.

We began with a just-identified model (not shown): CA was regressed on the six predictor structures, SOC on five, and VAL on four. Paths less than .05 were dropped—a criterion of substantive significance, not statistical significance. This resulted in deleting the paths p_{71}, p_{72}, p_{53}, and p_{54} (see Table 8.1 for names of X_is). The remaining model (Figure 8.2) is overidentified in two of the three structural equations (those with CA and VAL as dependent variables). (The rule used for overidentification is: The number of predetermined variables exceeds the number of explanatory variables included in the structural equation.[6]) For CA,

[5] Alternatively, he might be able to find a variable correlated with the excluded predictor in question and to include it, if it provides a more reasonable explanation than the excluded predictor.

[6] A variety of renditions of the identification rule exist, depending on the author's definition of an "identified" model and whether the conditions are only necessary ones or both necessary and sufficient. The rule used here for overidentified models

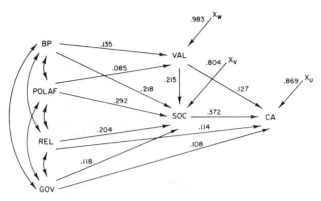

Figure 8.2 Path diagram showing dependence of community affairs network on predictor network. See text for description of variables.

there are six predetermined variables $(X_1 - X_6)$, but only four predictors appear in the equation (ignoring the residual X_u):

$$X_7 = p_{73}X_3 + p_{74}X_4 + p_{75}X_5 + p_{76}X_6 + p_{7u}X_u. \tag{1}$$

For VAL, there are four predetermined variables $(X_1 - X_4)$ but only two predictors in the equation:

$$X_5 = p_{51}X_1 + p_{52}X_2 + p_{5w}X_w. \tag{2}$$

The equation for the social network (SOC) is identified, with all predetermined variables included (VAL is predetermined with respect to SOC):

$$X_6 = P_{61}X_1 + p_{62}X_2 + p_{63}X_3 + p_{64}X_4 + p_{65}X_5 + p_{6v}X_v. \tag{3}$$

This model was estimated by OSL, under the aforementioned assumptions.

Table 8.1 presents the correlation matrix for all variables. Path analysis uses this as its initial data and splits each utilized correlation into direct effects, indirect effects, and unanalysed components (involving correlations among the left-hand set of predetermined variables). The larger a positive correlation is, the more similar the two networks are. Informal social contacts are strongly associated with community affairs and business–professional contacts. The social network also appears to be

is only a necessary condition, and, in econometric terms, it is an order condition. It appears in Duncan, Haller, Portes (1968). (There it is used for nonrecursive models, but the rule is equally applicable to our recursive ones.) Other counting rules are discussed in Johnston (1972), Mason and Halter (1971), and Wonnacott and Wonnacott (1970).

moderately related to religious, political, and value similarities. Business–professional ties and political similarity are also strongly related, suggesting both initial recruitment of persons of similar political persuasions for related economic and professional positions and/or reinforcement (or inculcation) of similar political attitudes among persons sharing similar institutional responsibilities. All but two correlations are positive. In general, then, proximity in one arena of behavior, attitudes, and social contacts implies proximity in others. The two exceptions, however, are also suggestive. Similar political affiliations and value homophyly are essentially unrelated to shared governmental positions. This result suggests the degree to which pluralism is adopted in filling governmental positions.

The paths in Figure 8.2 can be calculated by expressing the three equations in terms of known correlations (r_{ij}) and paths (p_{ij}) (equivalent to standardized partial regression coefficients). The several sets of simultaneous equations are solved for p_{ij}, and the residual paths are then computed. (See Duncan [1966] and Land [1969] for examples of this sequence.) Table 8.2 shows the (unstandardized) path regression coefficients and the (standardized) path coefficients (Land, 1969: 8). (Standard errors are not reported since the data represent a universe.) Since several variables in the model derive from smallest-space plots, the unstandardized coefficients do not explain how change in proximity in one structure affects proximity in another. The standardized coefficients resolve the problem of varying units of the variable, but they do not

TABLE 8.2
Path Regression Coefficients and Path Coefficients for the Model

Variable	Number	Path regression coefficient[a]	Path coefficient[b]	Dependent variable
SOC	X_6	.289	.372	CA
VAL	X_5	.120	.127	CA
		.262	.215	SOC
BP	X_1	.123	.135	VAL
		.241	.218	SOC
POLAF	X_2	.058	.085	VAL
		.244	.292	SOC
REL	X_3	.075	.114	CA
		.172	.204	SOC
GOV	X_4	.111	.108	CA
		.155	.118	SOC

[a] Unstandardized
[b] Standardized

solve the problem of an explanation. (They show how much of a standard deviation in the dependent structure changes for one standard deviation change in a predictor structure.) Our interest is, therefore, in the relative size of effects, their indirect and direct components, and the overall fit (R^2) of the model.

Table 8.3 presents direct effects, indirect effects, and correlation due to common (or associated) causes for all dependent variables with their predictors. All zero-order correlations are closely reproduced—this is not surprising here, since absent paths are small. (Perfect reproduction occurs in a just-identified model under assumptions [1]–[3].) The second and third assumptions are constrained to be adequate because of the heuristic procedure whereby small paths are deleted. Formal evaluation of them (not shown) produces small correlations of residuals with excluded predictors and other residuals. The assumptions are supported, and we are satisfied with the model's specification.

RESULTS AND DISCUSSION

The model explains 24.5% of the variation in the influence structure of the elite in Altneustadt. This is remarkably high, given the simplicity of several predictors (e.g., the dichotomous measurement of certain similarities among pairs). (Models of individual behavior seldom produce high R^2. Pairwise behavior is still microlevel behavior, and we do not expect boosts in R^2 due to such minimal aggregation.)

In assessing direct and indirect effects on CA, we note that social ties have the largest effect on the community affairs network (.442). Most of that effect is direct (.372). Friendship offers intimacy and trust, which apparently enhance serious discussion of community affairs. Proximity in the influence network is also directly enhanced by value (.127) and religious (.114) similarity and by common membership in governing bodies (.108). These three predictors have small indirect effects, mediated by the social network (SOC).

Business–professional contacts are, by themselves, not propitious settings for community affairs discussions. If friendship develops, however, or if the pair share common values and discover this, business ties become an appropriate setting for political discussions. Occupational ties do encourage social ties, because of the frequent interaction and expression of mutual interests they afford. Close, continued work ties foster similar values over time. (Clearly, the relationship is reciprocal since the initiation and persistence of close work ties are somewhat contingent on

TABLE 8.3

Direct Effects, Indirect Effects, and Unanalyzed Components of Predictors on Dependent Variables

Dependent variable	Predictor	Direct effect	Indirect effect	Subtotal	Unanalyzed component	Total	Zero-order correlation	Difference (obs-computed)
CA	BP	—	.109	.109	.069	.178	.195	+.017
	POLAF	—	.126	.126	.078	.204	.220	+.016
	VAL	.127	.100	.227	.015	.242	.241	−.001
$R^2 = .245$	SOC	.372	.070	.442	.017	.459	.458	−.001
	REL	.114	.076	.190	.050	.240	.240	.000
	GOV	.108	.044	.152	.004	.156	.154	−.002
VAL	BP	.135	—	.135	.028	.163	.164	+.001
	POLAF	.085	—	.085	.045	.130	.130	.000
$R^2 = .033$	REL	—	—	—	.040	.040	.043	+.003
	GOV	—	—	—	.000	.000	−.011	−.011
SOC	VAL	.215	.054	.269	.028	.297	.296	−.001
	BP	.218	.029	.247	.136	.383	.384	+.001
	POLAF	.292	.018	.310	.128	.438	.439	+.001
$R^2 = .354$	REL	.204	—	.204	.113	.317	.317	.000
	GOV	.118	—	.118	.003	.121	.118	−.003

similar values.) The business–professional contacts in the data, there-fore, reflect a selective process that has already occurred; and we explore only how they affect political contact by fostering more similar values.

The community affairs network represents conversations among elite members that have political consequences. To the extent that informa-tion and persuasion do flow along those ties, the network depicts the structure of political decision making in Altneustadt. The results for this model demonstrate the absence of coalitions among the elite based on political, occupational, or religious status. The most important factor is informal, social ties, which are somewhat based on status and value similarities, but not strongly so. Friendship is the aid to influence among those with power.

Exploring the sources of the social (SOC) network, we find that busi-ness contacts, value similarity, religious and political similarity all foster friendship ties to a similar degree. The role of business contacts was discussed earlier. Similar values are an important precursor of friendship (Izard, 1960; Lazarsfeld and Merton, 1954; Newcomb, 1961). Few friend-ships persist or become intimate when values differ sharply. (A large literature also treats the reverse effect: that acquaintance and friendship foster more similar values over time. See Davis, 1963; Heider, 1958; Homans, 1950; Newcomb, 1961; and the review in Lindzey and Byrne, 1968.) The impact of common membership in a governing body on friendly relations is small. People are recruited for such bodies by a political process. Once there, each proceeds to fulfill his mandate. Net of occupation and attitude similarities, that common membership has only a small effect on friendship.

An interesting finding is the existence of a higher R^2 for the social net-work (.354) than for the influence network (which includes SOC as its strongest predictor). All the predetermined proximity structures (BP, POLAF, REL, GOV, VAL) have direct effects on the social network, whereas only three of them directly affect the influence network. More-over, the direct effects of REL, GOV, and VAL are greater determinants of the social network than of the influence network.

Exploring the sources of value similarity (VAL), we do not expect the model to be highly predictive; indeed, the R^2 is only .033. Values are persistent features of an individual, slow to change, difficult to state, yet pervasive in their behavioral effects. We have discussed how occupa-tional ties might foster greater similarity of values, and we note the very modest path from BP to VAL. Political and religious groups in the West recruit people of highly heterogeneous backgrounds. Moreover, they do not usually require or inculcate broad consensus on political and social attitudes for affiliation. Consequently, we can anticipate only small effects of these affiliations on an individual's values. More relevant to our immediate concerns, similar political and religious affiliations can be expected to have little effect on the value similarity of the pairs. In fact, the path solution shows no effect for common religious affiliation and a barely important effect for common political affiliation. Common membership in a government body is less persistent than the other affiliations and does not induce similar values among members. (If anything, it should reinforce different ones.)

The crucial feature of the solution is the impact of informal social ties on the influence structure. Politically relevant information and persuasion tend to flow along friendship ties. Other types of contact and similarity have small direct and indirect effects, the latter mainly filtered through informal social ties. These other "proximities" (BP, POLAF, REL, GOV, VAL) *are* important for the persistence of informal friendly contacts among elites, but they have little direct impact upon the influence structure. The important feature in the structure of political communications among the elite is informal social ties which, while affected by other ties and similarities, are not entirely determined by them.

Perhaps, in summary, the most striking and important disparity between our theoretical and empirical model is the empirical absence of a direct path from the business–professional structure to the community affairs structure. At least in this community, all the effect of the community's objective interest differentiation is exerted indirectly through its effect on channeling informal social ties and creating value homophyly. Facetiously, we might say that this is an empirical instance of Marx and Engel's famous dictum that the government is merely the executive committee of the bourgeoisie. More specifically, one might speculate that the relatively small size of the community gives each elite member, at least in principle, the opportunity to meet every one else in the elite. Elite systems, however, by their nature, are small in size relative to their total populations and, indeed, are probably a declining proportion as population size increases (cf. Coleman, 1973). A review of the literature on elites of communities of larger size (e.g., Hunter's study of Atlanta [1953] and Banfield's study of Chicago [1961]) does not suggest that formal, institutional ties among elite members predominant over informal ties. Perhaps only in highly differentiated communities with fluid coalitions continually changing around disparate issues could we expect objective interest directly to affect the community affairs structure on the grounds that informal ties simply do not have time to crystallize in such environments. Such decision-making systems would tend to be fairly disorganized, unstable, and unpredictable in their decision outcomes.

SOME FURTHER CONSIDERATIONS AND
CAVEATS

We have proposed an explicit model of the antecedent factors that determine the *pattern of interrelationships among a set of community influentials* acting as community decision-makers (what we have called the "community affairs influence structure"). Our unit of analysis has been elite pairs rather than individual influentials.

In constructing the causal model, we had to make many simplifying theoretical and methodological assumptions that will no doubt provoke serious disagreements and, hopefully, encourage efforts to correct and refine them. Certainly, the meaningfulness and adequacy of the model's seven variables must be evaluated. Unlike the extensive work on path models of the status attainment process (cf. Hauser, 1970; Duncan, Featherman, Duncan, 1972), no previous work that we know of has used such measures and could, therefore, yield assessments of their validity and reliability. Beyond a reasonable degree of face validity and plausibility for the measures, we can only point to the analyses presented in the preceding chapters and to those yet to come to demonstrate the measures' general validity insofar as they could be meaningfully interpreted and linked to evidence on the rival coalitions and the consensus–cleavage lines in Altneustadt's community elite. Even if these measures are accepted as valid, we still have no estimate of their reliabilities, especially for the VAL, BP, SOC, and CA variables. As Siegel and Hodge (1968) have quite rightly pointed out, the reliability of measurement, so often ignored in sociological investigations, can be important in evaluating and interpreting path models.

Moreover, the seven variables differ in their logical status in a number of respects. Perhaps the most important difference is whether they measure actual and/or potential interaction among influentials or similarities among them (cf. McFarland and Brown, 1973: 277, for a discussion of this distinction). Four of the measures, including BP, SOC, CA, and GOV, are based on reported or inferred rates of actual interaction between pairs of influentials. The other three, including POL, REL, and VAL, refer only to similarities in group memberships or value orientations that may, of course, induce higher rates of interaction but, nevertheless, represent at best only "necessary but not sufficient" conditions for the emergence of actual interaction links. The "similarities" variables measure the opportunity structure for interaction, while the first set of variables measures "realized" interaction.

Surely the greatest problem, however, is the causal model itself, with its simple additive, linear assumptions. Although all the variables have been measured at one point in time, we have postulated a temporal ordering among them that some might find questionable. We have ignored the obvious possibility of mutual or feedback effects between variables. This simplification is especially questionable with respect to the relationship between value homophyly and the informal social network where one might reasonably expect to find mutual influence of friends on value orientations. Our model simply postulates a selective effect of value homophyly on the choice of partners for informal interaction. As a first approximation, however, we believe that our model does represent the usual assumptions, often implicit in the literature, made about the relationships among the variables (e.g., Clark, 1968b; Perrucci and Pilisuk, 1970).

One could, of course, treat the problem of predicting the influentials' proximities in the community affairs structure as a task for a multivariate prediction equation that makes no assumptions whatsoever about the causal order of the variables. In such an approach, one would merely be concerned with predicting actual and potential coalition partners— the greater the proximity, the higher the likelihood of a link being formed in community affairs. From our viewpoint, however, this is a less interesting and demanding theoretical task than what can be tackled with the path analytic approach.

Obviously, much remains to be done in developing and evaluating the proposed approach. We hope, however, that the results reported here show the promise of shifting theoretical and research attention away from the individual to the relationship as the unit of analysis.

9

Consensus and Cleavage:
The Resolution of Issues*

Readers concerned with analyzing community conflict over the resolution of various community issues may well ask how our structural analysis deals with such matters. Our emphasis on describing the structure of the black box responsible for community integration from a Parsonian standpoint seems to confirm the often repeated charge that the framework is simply too static and cannot handle conflict and change adequately (cf. Dahrendorf, 1961: 77–82; Gouldner, 1970: 353–355; Sztompka, 1974). Although we cannot answer all these objections satisfactorily, we would like to consider these questions.

Recall our discussion of Figure 1.1 in Chapter 1, which schematized our theoretical framework. We wanted first to open the black box of "throughput" to analyze its internal contents. We wanted then to use this knowledge to clarify *(a)* the structure of consensus and cleavage in the integrative system and *(b)* the resulting outcomes in binding collective decisions on particular issues and the extent and sources of community tensions.

* Portions of this chapter are drawn from a previously published article (Laumann and Pappi, 1973), reprinted with the permission of the *American Sociological Review* and the American Sociological Association.

TOWARD A TYPOLOGY OF COMMUNITY ISSUES

In order to specify a bit more precisely the nature of these outcomes and tensions, it is useful to distinguish between two broad types of community issues and their related outcomes. On the one hand, *instrumental issues* are concerned with controversies over the differing allocation of scarce resources, such as land, jobs, and money, and find their particular focus in the adaptive and integrative sectors of community concern. Lipset (1963) and others have spoken somewhat more narrowly of "class politics" when discussing such issues. For such issues, there usually is a fairly obvious calculus of costs and benefits to various interested parties. As a result, a fairly straightforward, even quantitative, analysis of objective interest differentiation is facilitated. Conflict over such issues tends to be moderate, often characterized by bargaining and compromise among the contending parties. The specific outcome is the direct result of their relative power or influence. Some political scientists have even thought it possible to devise means for the "rational" or "optimal" resolution of such controversies.

Consummatory or *expressive issues*, on the other hand, are concerned with controversies regarding the maintenance or change in the organization of basic values, commitments, and orientations that guide or control community affairs. Such controversies, sometimes termed "status politics" (cf. Lipset, 1963), are usually highly charged with emotional affect and have an "all or none" nature that usually precludes or makes very difficult negotiated settlements among the contending parties. Thus, the nature of the outcome and the level of community tensions often directly depends on how a given issue comes to be defined as one or the other type of issue. As we shall see, this distinction is closely related to the functional perspective on community issues elaborated later.

One of the most unsatisfactory aspects of the literature on community decision making has been the basically atheoretical, ad hoc selection of community issues for analysis such that comparative study of community decision making is difficult, if not impossible. One can identify two favored strategies for identifying and selecting community issues for study. In the first strategy, the investigator identifies a set of recent issues in a community from newspaper accounts and community informants and selects particular ones for intensive study that meet some criterion of "importance to the community," such as the level of public controversy and mobilization (cf. Dahl, 1962; Polsby, 1963; Freeman *et al.*, 1968). In the second strategy, the investigator selects an issue in which he already has some interest, perhaps because of his interest in a preferred outcome, such as fluoridation of the water supply (cf. Gamson, 1966a; Rosenthal and Crain, 1966) or urban renewal (Hawley, 1963; Clark, 1968e), and which has come up for resolution in a number of communities. He wants to ascertain what factors determine a particular outcome. While both strategies enjoy the obvious advantage of relatively clear, unambiguous operational procedures, they both suffer from being strongly tied to all the historical particularities of the specific issues studied and pose serious problems, especially in the first strategy, for comparative analysis.

As Polsby (1963: 96; also see Wolfinger, 1971: 1078) pointed out some years ago, "There seem to be no satisfactory criteria which would identify a universe of all decisions (issues) in the community." The problem of defining the universe of content from which to sample issues is especially important when one wants to identify "nonissues"[1] or to check whether or not the actual issues are a biased sample. We think that it is impossible to define a universe of content without an adequate frame of reference for studying community power. At present, only two frames of reference seem to be available: the interest group approach and the functional approach. The interest group approach looks for possible partisan groups in a community and identifies possible issues according to some notion of the objective interests of these groups. Since we used the functional approach for analyzing the decision-making structure, it follows that we should use the same approach to define the universe of content of possible issues. We, however, agree with such commentators as Ossowski (1963), Lenski (1966), Stinchcombe (1968), and Sztompka (1974), that Marxian and functionally oriented perspectives are by no means as radically incompatible as has sometimes been assumed. There are, of course, obvious differences of emphasis and concern between them. Marxian oriented analysts tend to see instrumental issues as the fundamental substrata of actual or potential community controversy, while functionalists tend to stress expressive issues, seeing group dis-

---

[1] Often assuming a ruling elite model of community decision making, critics of the issue approach (e.g., Bachrach and Baratz, 1962, 1963) have pointed to the "nonissue" problem in communities dominated by a ruling faction that has so much control over the community agenda that "important" and consequential matters never come up for general community discussion and decision. This is a problem that, presumably, an objective theory of structural differentiation and implied sources of oppositional interests resting on an externally postulated model of community structure would help to resolve in much the same way that Freudian personality theory is intended to permit the diagnosis of an individual's personality problems independently of his own ability ("self-insight") to "see his problems." Unfortunately, the elements of such a theory are rudimentary at best and subject to much controversy in their own right.

agreements over fundamental values as arising from considerations, such as status group differences, in addition to their different relations to the economic structure.

While it may sound hopelessly ambitious at this stage of development, a theoretically grounded scheme for defining and classifying community issues is needed that permits: *(1)* a definition of the universe of content of possible community issues; *(2)* a means of defining the biases in the set of issues that actually arise in a community during a given period (that is, communities confront issues sequentially and, therefore, in any period of time, may not face issues from the full range of the issue space); *(3)* a translation of the historical individuality of a given issue into a more theoretically meaningful category that permits comparative analysis; and *(4)* the generation of hypotheses linking the type of issue to structural characteristics of the community decision-making system. We hope that we took a step toward constructing such a scheme in deciding to classify community issues according to their functional primacy in the AGIL paradigm of functions confronting any social system (cf. Parsons, 1951, 1961; Clark, 1968d; Mayhew, 1971).

Obviously, issues will often have implications for several functional sectors of the community social system. Much in the same way that we proposed to distinguish between primary and secondary functional foci for our influentials, issues may be seen to have primary and secondary impacts in different institutional sectors. Which of the possible functional definitions of an issue becomes focal or primary will depend on a series of considerations about its emergence in a particular community at a particular point in time with particular sponsors and opponents.[2]

With our preceding structural analysis of community influence, we should be able to predict how given issues will be resolved by determining the functionally specialized sectors likely to be activated by a given

---

[2] Coding of an issue into its appropriate functional sector is not a simple matter of identifying the institutional sector of the collectivities most likely to be affected. For example, a school bond issue is obviously concerned with the educational system, which is usually treated as functionally specialized with regard to pattern maintenance. The issue, however, may develop in two quite different directions. It may be regarded as a purely instrumental issue: whether or not the community can afford to pay for another school, given its current obligations. Its functional locus is, therefore, integrative insofar as it concerns establishing its claim of priority in the allocative scheme (budget) of scarce community resources among competing alternatives. The issue, however, may become expressive by focusing not on costs and alternatives foregone but on what type of school program is to be implemented in the new building. In this case, prospective changes in the organization of pattern-maintenance activities are at issue, and, correspondingly, quite different sorts of community actors and influence resources must be activated to resolve the issue.

functional issue. We can also assess the likelihood of the sector being divided on an issue by examining the relative spread or clustering of personnel in a particular institutional sector in the spatial solutions and their locations with respect to the central integrative core. If there is significant sectoral or integrative differentiation, we can predict the winning coalition as being the one that is favorably located relative to the integrative core, controls more "appropriate" influence resources (e.g., adaptive resources, such as money, jobs, and land, may be of little consequence in a pattern-maintenance issue in which persons controlling commitment and integrative resources may have the competitive advantage), and includes a higher average level of reputed community influence.

THE SELECTION OF COMMUNITY ISSUES
IN ALTNEUSTADT

With these general considerations in mind, five issues were selected for intensive study according to two criteria. First, each issue must have had a major impact on community affairs within the past 3 or 4 years or one might realistically argue that it would have such an impact if it were to become a matter for consideration in the near future. Second, the issues as a whole had to be distributed across the four functional problem areas identified in the AGIL paradigm. The issues meeting these two criteria were the following:

a. relocation of a large industrial firm to Altneustadt (economic or adaptive primacy) (see Q12, Appendix C);
b. construction of a city hall (political or collective goal-attainment primacy) (see Q10, Appendix C);
c. incorporation of outlying communities into an expanded city administrative unit (integrative primacy) (see Q11, Appendix C);
d. establishment of a secular primary school as opposed to the existing confessional school (latent pattern-maintenance primacy: education and religion) (see Q9, Appendix C);
e. permission to hold a pop festival in Altneustadt (latent pattern-maintenance primacy: public morality, status of youth as a "minority" group with low access to the center of power, intergenerational conflict) (see Q13, Appendix C).[3]

---

[3] Altneustadt actually confronted issues, b, c, and d in the past several years. Because, however, it had not confronted issues with special relevance to the economic subsystem in the recent past and because we saw the city as having especially acute pattern-maintenance problems due to the rapid in-migration of distinctive new-

The underlying notion here of sampling issues from various institutional sectors was meant to provide an opportunity to determine if the elite tended to be correspondingly differentiated into coalitions functionally specialized for "control" in specific sectors or if there was a functionally and structurally undifferentiated unitary elite core (dominant coalition) that made the crucial decisions for all institutional areas (perhaps with specialized "lower-level" personnel to implement these decisions). (See Table 5.1, Chapter 5, for average influence status of opponents and proponents on the five issues.)

GRAPHIC REPRESENTATION OF THE
CLEAVAGE STRUCTURE

Figures 9.1, 9.2 and 9.3 present the same three spatial representations of the business–professional, social relations, and community affairs structures that we considered in Chapter 7, only we now have drawn in

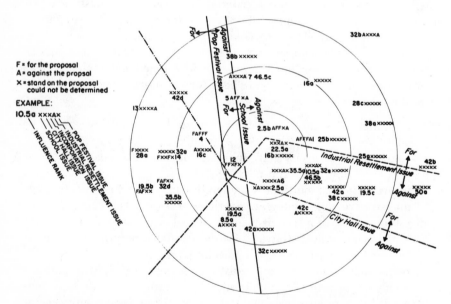

Figure 9.1   Consensus-cleavage "fault lines" for the business–professional network, smallest space analysis, Euclidean metric, two-dimensional solution, Guttman–Lingoes coefficient of alienation = .148.

comers, we decided to develop two hypothetical issues (a and e) for these two sectors. (See Perrucci and Pilisuk [1970] for another recent study employing hypothetical issues.) Both issues were quite realistic in that they could easily become matters of public or elite debate in the immediately foreseeable future, and, in fact, they generated considerable disagreement among our respondents.

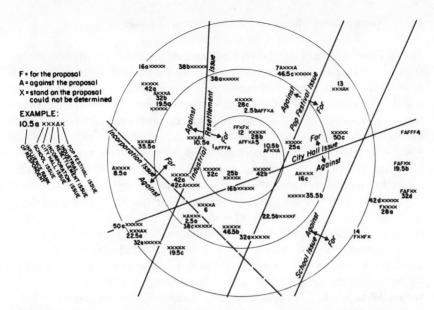

Figure 9.2 Consensus-cleavage "fault lines" for the social relations network, smallest space analysis, Euclidean metric, two-dimensional solution, Guttman–Lingoes coefficient of alienation = .158.

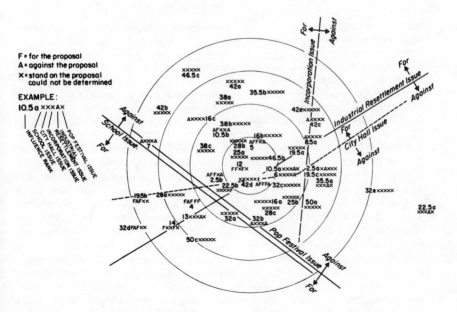

Figure 9.3 Consensus-cleavage "fault lines" for community affairs network, smallest space analysis, Euclidean metric, two-dimensional solution, Guttman–Lingoes coefficient of alienation = .131.

"fault lines" for each of the five issues that more or less divide the respective spaces into proponents and opponents on each issue. Before discussing these consensus–cleavage structures in greater detail, we should discuss the operational independence of our various procedures. First, at the beginning of the interview, each respondent was asked a series of questions about each issue probing such matters as the individuals and groups he perceived to be most strongly in favor of or opposed to the issue, his own position on the issue and his degree of actual or likely participation in the decision process on the issue, as well as his estimate of the level of conflict over the issue and whether the conflict was public or confined to the "inner circle" of community influentials. The names of the participants, pro and con, were spontaneously generated by the respondents—the list of influentials we had identified was not presented until much later in the interview. Second, in order for us to designate an influential as an active proponent or opponent of an issue, at least two respondents had to have spontaneously mentioned him in one or the other capacity. (In most cases, attributed and self-reported position and involvement in the issue were the same, but, in a number of important cases, they were not. Persons on the losing side tended to report themselves on the winning side.)[4]

---

[4] Since this stringent coding rule tended to identify only the most publicly prominent leaders on the opposing sides, many of the elite had to be coded as "indeterminate" for any given issue on the basis of the perceptions of others. Did this mean that the fault lines, based on codings of only some elite members, were completely arbitrary? To check this possibility at least indirectly, the following procedure was adopted for the community affairs space (Figure 9.3). All elite members were coded "for" or "against" an issue depending on which side of a fault line they were located. These new codings were then cross-tabulated against the elite members' self-reported positions on the corresponding issues. Agreement was highest for the incorporation issue in which 79% were placed on the side of the issue in the figure that corresponded to their self-reported stands. Agreement was not quite as high for the pop festival and the industrial resettlement issues (69% and 64%, respectively), partly because, we suspect, they were hypothetical issues, and elite members could only guess which side of an issue other elite members would take. It declined further for the city hall issue, where only 56% were correctly placed, but note again that this issue was regarded as the least controversial of all issues posed, and few elite members reported special interest or involvement in it. Only the fit for the school issue was poor (24% agreement), but this lack of agreement is more apparent than real. More than 90% of the elite members claimed to be for the secular school (the side that won), many more than could actually have favored it given the controversial, divisive, and extended character of the public debate. Many persons reporting themselves on the winning side were, in fact, perceived by other elite members as having been active on the losing side. In general, we detected a general tendency for people to report themselves on the winning sides of all issues even though their knowledgeable peers saw them as having been on the

An inspection of the several pictures, especially those for the social and community affairs, makes it readily apparent that the fault lines of the oppositional structures and the personnel active on each of the issues do change from one functional issue to another and that some persons, most notably those in the central integrative zones, are likely to be active in more than one issue. In fact, only one person, the most influential man in town (Herr Koenig), was perceived to be involved in all five issues.

For purposes of discussion, we shall look more carefully at the community affairs space (Figure 9.3). The fault lines are almost identical on the two pattern-maintenance issues, the school and the pop festival, with the newcomers at the research center and their allies opposed to nearly everyone else. Although these issues differ considerably in their substantive content, they generated the most public controversy and mobilization of the issues considered. The integrative issue (community incorporation), on the other hand, united all city factions against the county political leadership, while the polity issue of building a new city hall was an intra-elite controversy (there was low public controversy surrounding this issue), aligning the "city hall crowd" located in the central zone against the periphery who, of course, lost. Finally, the industrial resettlement issue split the economic sector, with the large employers possibly fearful of such a large competitor for a limited labor supply and of their possible unfavorable dislocation in the influence structure opposed to the small retail tradesmen and business people who would probably welcome the expanded business opportunities arising from the population growth likely to be generated by the new employer. (Similar conclusions regarding the fault lines could be drawn from inspecting Figures 9.1 and 9.2.)

Thus, for even this moderately small community, we see that structural differentiation is extensive enough to generate relatively stable coalitions that are activated differentially depending on the functional issue. Much that we have already said (in Chapter 6) about the internal structure of the coalitions, their influence resources, value orientations, and preferred leadership strategies would support our interpretations. Hopefully, the evidence presented here has sufficiently indicated the ways in which our procedures greatly facilitate the systematic description of structural cleavage and consensus (e.g., by identifying who would be "impossible" coalition partners). In addition, this evidence seems to

---

losing side. Apparently here, as elsewhere, no one likes to be regarded a loser. We are, therefore, inclined to place much more trust in attributed positions than in self-reported positions.

be reasonably consistent with the explicit structural–functional model we have been developing. Consensus–cleavage structures do, of course, change over time. We believe that these techniques could be used to generate meaningful snapshots at different points in time which, in turn, could be juxtaposed to describe stability and change in community influence structures over time.

10

Bringing Groups Back in: The Structure of Interrelations among Corporate Actors in the Community

THE COLLECTIVITY STRUCTURE OF COMMUNITY INFLUENCE

One of the obvious limitations of the analysis thus far is its focus on individual elite members and their social positions to the virtual exclusion of the involvement of collectivities in the community decision-making process, except by inference. One cannot help but wonder what impact departure or death of specific elite members would have on the overall structure of the community influence system. Individuals would seem, at first glance, to be very slender reeds upon which to build the edifice of the community decision-making system. Of course, once individuals are treated as agents for community-active groups and collectivities, greater confidence in the relative stability of the influence system is possible by appealing to the fact that most collectivities usually have more or less routine procedures to replace leadership positions that become vacated.[1] We hasten to add, however, that individuals do, of course,

---

[1] In a provocative article on the relative power of natural persons and corporate actors, James S. Coleman (1973: 1) makes the following observation: "To increase benefits, natural persons in society give over usage rights, that is, direct control over actions, to corporate bodies through investments or membership. In so doing, they have gained these benefits at the price of loss of power." Deriving his ap-

173

make a difference in that they vary in their relative efficacy in performing leadership and representative roles for their respective collectivities.
We are persuaded, however, that, although great men (cf. Hook, 1943) do
occasionally arise and have profound impacts on social systems, we can
assume that the more normal state of affairs is for rather ordinary men
to be performing such roles with satisfactory competence (cf. March
and Simon, 1958) and that they usually may be replaced without necessi-
tating a fundamental reorganization of the influence structure. We should
now like to turn to a more direct analysis of the group influence structure
in Altneustadt.

In addition to asking about influential individuals in Altneustadt, we
asked our respondent-informants to indicate the organized collectivities
and less structured population categories that actively participated in the
resolution of the five community issues. These collectivities were spontaneously named, that is, without the assistance of any list of groups.
Subsequent to the set of questions on the issues, we presented the respondents with a comprehensive listing of 98 organizations and groupings
from which they were to choose those that were "generally very influential" in Altneustadt.[2] We were quite successful in achieving complete
coverage of identifiable organizations and groups in the community, for
only 12 organizations were spontaneously mentioned in the questions
about the issues that were not included in our group list, and none of
these received more than a few mentions.

Higher status or elite members of a community have been consistently
found to have much higher rates of participation in a broad range of
voluntary associations than average or lower status members of the community (cf. Cutler, 1973). The Altneustadt elite is no exception to this
generalization. Even using the crude indicator of number of member-

proach from the formal analysis of collective decisions through mathematical
methods as well as organizational studies, such as Michels (1959) and Lipset *et al.*
(1956), he is concerned with discussing methods of calculating the extent of loss
of power of individuals in society to corporate actors as well as particular means
that persons use to regain power. While not directly relevant to our concerns in
this chapter, Coleman's work does raise important considerations in evaluating the
assumptions of individuals serving as agents of corporate actors.

[2] To facilitate the use of the list, we divided the collectivities into three broad divisions including (*1*) named economic organizations (e.g., specific firms, such as
Goslar and Prey Box Manufacturer and Düsseldorf Mustard Co.) and occupational
groups, such as artisans and large farmers, (*2*) political, administrative, religious,
and educational organizations, such as the Engineering School and the Catholic
Pastors' Community Council, and (*3*) other organized social groups, such as Catholics, retired people, the Tennis Club Blue–White, and the carnival societies.

ships in formally constituted voluntary associations, the Altneustadt elite has an average of 6.8 memberships in contrast to the general community's average of .9. Indeed, the most influential member of the elite reported membership in no less than 16 organizations, and these did not include memberships in more informally defined groupings. We are interested in characterizing the patterning of overlapping memberships of elite members in collectivities ranging from the most formally constituted and organized to the clearly identifiable, but informally organized, groupings. Only those groups that were explicitly identified by at least one elite member as being influential in community affairs will be included in the following organizational analysis.

Our strategy for describing the underlying structure among collectivities is again to apply a graph theoretic analysis in which the collectivities are defined as points and the link (line) between collectivities (points) represents the presence of an elite person who is *active in both collectivities*. An active member of a collectivity was either an executive officer or a member of the organization's executive committee, or was someone who defined himself as active in that organization's affairs.[3] Seventy collectivities met our initial requirement that they be regarded by at least one elite member as influential in community affairs. On the basis of the reachability matrix, however, five organizations had to be dropped as being isolates (that is, they could not be reached from any other organization). Once these five organizations were dropped, the remaining 65 organizations were *all* mutually reachable in four steps or less (i.e., path distances of 4 or less).

[3] Note that we are excluding from consideration those numerous elite memberships that are merely passive in character (e.g., rank and file status in the organization). Of course, there are a number of other ways in which the interpenetration of or linkages among organizations and collectivities could be described—ranging from determining relative rates of overlapping memberships of rank-and-file members from a large cross-section survey of the community or the determination of the overlapping organizational memberships of the entire executive boards of every organization under consideration to monetary transactions among organizations or rates of formal correspondence among them. Each strategy would generate proximity measures that would yield somewhat different configurations of organizations since these measures reflect somewhat different social processes. Moreover, each would encounter different strengths and weaknesses in operationalization. Our strategy was selected primarily on the pragmatic grounds that the data were already available, but it was also strongly recommended on the grounds that an individual having active membership in two organizations is in a particularly effective position to serve, minimally, as a communication channel between the two organizations and might even serve in a coordinative capacity as well (cf. Perrucci and Pilisuk, 1970).

GRAPHIC REPRESENTATION OF ALTNEUSTADT'S COLLECTIVE ACTOR STRUCTURE

This symmetric matrix of path distances among organizations was then submitted to a smallest space analysis (Roskam and Lingoes, 1970). An acceptable smallest space solution was achieved in two dimensions (Kruskal's stress = .141; Guttman–Lingoes' coefficient of alienation = .171) and is portrayed in Figure 10.1. We can make sense of the underlying structure of the figure by applying our two principles of interpretation discussed in Chapter 7: *(1)* the principle of sectoral differentiation and *(2)* the principle of integrative centrality.

Collectivities of the same functional type tend to share common regions of the space. Economic organizations fall almost exclusively in the right-hand side of the space and may be further subdivided into two wedge-shaped sectors including *(1)* small retail and artisan businesses and their associations and *(2)* the larger manufacturing concerns (e.g., Goslar Company and the flour mill), their industrial association, and the

Key to Figure 10.1

Influence

Influence rank of the collectivity in the set of 65 collectivities. Based on votes by the elite members regarding which collectivities were influential. See footnote 4 for further elaboration. Subscripts serve to distinguish collectivities that were tied, that is, received the same number of votes.

Sector

Collectivities were coded into one of several sectors, based on the primary function of the collectivity.

Sectors consist of the following:

Voluntary Associations
    CV—Charitable Voluntary Association
    SV—Social Voluntary Association
    RV—Religious Voluntary Association
    PV—Political Voluntary Association
    EV—Economic Voluntary Association
EO—Economic Organization
R—Religious Organization or Subunit
P—Population Subgrouping
O—Occupational Subgrouping
Ed—Educational Organization
A—Civil Administrative Unit
Pp—Political Party Unit
Pe—Elected Political Unit
S—Natural Science Research Lab.

Name

Names correspond roughly to the title of the collectivity, if it is an organization, or to a description of the collectivity, if it is not an organization. In some cases, titles have been translated rather freely, either to preserve the anonymity of the organization, or to give a better sense in English of what the organization does.

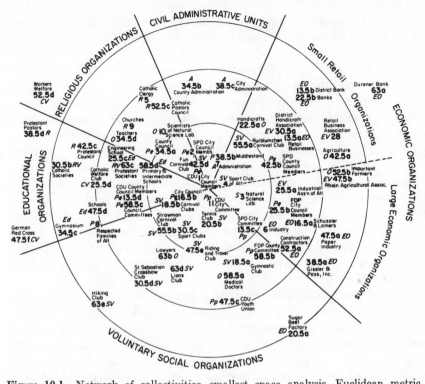

Figure 10.1 Network of collectivities, smallest space analysis, Euclidean metric, two-dimensional solution, Guttman–Lingoes coefficient of alienation = .171.

largest employer in Altneustadt, the natural science research installation. Proceeding clockwise around the space, we encounter a region including predominantly sport clubs and other social voluntary associations, their relative proximities to economic organizations versus other kinds of collectivities being "determined" by their differential recruitment from various parts of the social space. *Rurblümchen,* for example, is a carnival society located in the region of small businessmen and artisans from whom it primarily recruits its membership, while the Lion's Club and the St. Sebastian and St. Anthony Crossbow Society are high status, socially exclusive clubs relatively close to "socially respected Altneustadt families." On the left-hand side of the space are the various pattern-maintenance organizations including educational and religious organizations and personnel, which are, in turn, somewhat segregated from one another into differentiable regions. We close the circle with various civil administrative units concerned with implementing community goals. Finally, the central core of the space primarily includes collectivities especially concerned with integrative functions, such as the various factions of the city and county councils and the executive committees of the three political parties.

The principle of integrative centrality asserts that organizations most concerned with integrative functions should be located toward the center of the space, while the farther away collectivities are from the center, the more narrowly specialized their function and the less concerned they are with community-level integrative issues except to the extent that they pertain to their functional activities. We were able to evaluate the relative influence status of our 65 organizations by employing a procedure essentially comparable to that employed for ranking our individual elite members. Respondents were asked to rank order the top five groups of those they identified as generally very influential in Altneustadt. The summed influence scores[4] had a product–moment correlation of .416 ($p < .01$) with distance from the centroid of the two-dimensional solution, providing some corroboration of our principle of integrative centrality.

At least one way of validating these influence ratings of collectivities is to predict the outcomes of the five issues from knowledge of the collectivities' relative influence statuses. Following the same procedures used to relate elite members' influence ranks to issue outcomes (Chapter 6, pp. 99–100), we multiplied the number of times a given collectivity was mentioned as being on one or the other side of an issue by its influence rank, summed the resulting numbers for each side, and divided by the total number of mentions on the respective sides. This number can be regarded as the average influence status of proponent or opponent collectivities—the lower the number, the higher the average influence status. Four of the five issue outcomes were correctly predicted with this procedure ($p = .188$) (see Table 10.1).

Even the error in prediction arose from the rather special circumstances surrounding this issue. All the informants who named an opposition group on the city hall issue mentioned only one or two collectivities, either the SPD members of the city council or the SPD city committee (the executive committee of the party). No other community organization or population group was seen as opposed to building the city hall. On the other hand, these informants named many more community

---

[4] The summed influence score for each organization or collectivity was determined by multiplying the number of first-rank votes by "4," second-rank votes by "3," third-rank votes by "2," and simple mentions by "1," and summing the resulting products. There was widespread agreement on the crucial importance of the group of CDU city council members as being the most influential collectivity in community affairs.

TABLE 10.1

The Average Influence Status of Proponent and Opponent Collectivities on Five Community Issues, with Their Winning Sides Indicated by Asterisks

Issue	Proponent collectivities' average influence status	Opponent collectivities' average influence status
Adaptive issue primacy:		
Industrial resettlement	16.1*	18.4
Goal-attainment issue primacy:		
Construction of a new city hall (error in prediction)	11.9*	5.8
Integrative issue primacy:		
Community annexation	17.4*	42.5
Pattern-maintenance issue primacy:		
Secular versus confessional school	12.8*	14.7
Permission to hold pop music festival	21.7	14.0*

organizations as active sponsors of the new hall in addition to the dominant CDU faction on the city council (the most influential group of all 65 collectivities), which had the final responsibility for deciding the issue. Thus, the average influence rank for the winning side was depressed by the inclusion of these various groups on the support side. If we had used an influence scale that took into account the relative distances between ranks, this anomalous result would probably not have occurred.

THE CLEAVAGE STRUCTURE OF CORPORATE ACTORS

We are now in a position to examine the cleavage structure among the corporate actors and collectivities for the five community issues. Figure 10.2 portrays the same solution as in Figure 10.1, but we have now indicated the "fault" lines for the various community issues. The identification of proponent and opponent collectivities was made on the basis of their reputed positions spontaneously reported by our elite respondents in the issue series of questions toward the beginning of their interviews (See Q9–13, Appendix C). Again we see that the fault lines are located in different parts of the space as a function of the type of issues being examined. The fault lines for the two pattern-maintenance issues, the secular school and the pop music festival, are roughly coincident, dividing the pattern-maintenance oriented collectivities into two opposing factions. The issue of industrial resettlement divides the more inclusive economic region into two parts, with large economic enterprises and employers being opposed to the location of a large manufacturer of electrical

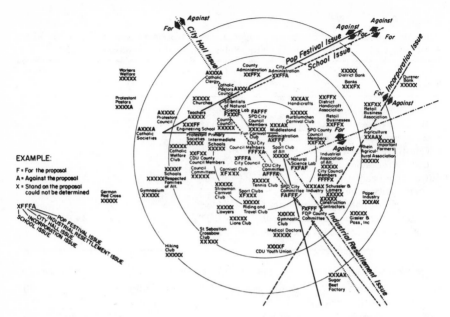

Figure 10.2 Consensus-cleavage "fault lines" for the network of collectivities, smallest space analysis, Euclidean metric, two-dimensional solution, Guttman–Lingoes coefficient of alienation = .171.

equipment in Altneustadt and small businessmen and commercial interests being generally in favor of the move. The incorporation of outlying towns and land area into greater Altneustadt is opposed by agricultural interests located in the outlying region while all city-oriented collectivities, regardless of their oppositional statuses on other issues, are unanimously in favor of extending city control to these areas. Finally the building of a new city hall, the goal-attainment issue, divides the integrative center in half, split precisely along the lines of the political party cleavage between the CDU and the SPD.

It is worth noting at this juncture that, as in Figures 9.1–9.3, which portray the cleavage structures among individual elite members, collectivities that are opposed to one another on a given issue tend to be located relatively close to the fault line for that issue. Groups (and individuals in the spaces previously discussed) located at some distance from the fault lines were typically not reported by our elite respondents as having been especially active on the issues in question. We might hypothesize, however, that individuals and groups falling into the "for" or "against" category but not actively involved in the resolution of the issue would at least share views on the issues similar to those of the activated individuals and groups. At least for the individual members of the elite, we can test this speculation since we asked them to report their own position on each of the five issues, regardless of their active participation in the resolution of the issue. An inspection of their distribution in the space (excluding the active participants) generally supports this speculation.

CONCLUSION

Although the overall structure and organizing principles of the spatial solutions for the individual elite members and for the corporate actors are very much alike, there are some noteworthy differences. Elite members who are employees of the Natural Science Research Center are located in a clearly delineated sector of the business–professional, social relations, and community affairs networks. In the group space, however, the different corporate actors representing the research center are no longer close together. The center itself is located in the economic sector— it is, after all, the largest employer and economic consumer in town. The scientists as a group, on the other hand, are found in the sectors specialized around pattern-maintenance issues, including religious organizations and educational institutions. Thus, one can claim that the principle of sector differentiation is more important in structuring the group space than in the relative positioning of individual elite members in the elite person spaces. As a result, the coalitions and opposition groups reveal themselves much more clearly in these latter spaces, while the principle of sector location overrides the coalitions in the group space. Corporate actors appear to be much more functionally localized than individuals, who often perform roles in several functional sectors. A central question for future research is how sensitive our models of influence structures are to different methods of estimating interpoint proximities, whether based on individual- or group-level data sources.

PART 3

The Interface between Community and Elite

Part 2

The Interface
between
Communities and Site

11

The Resource Bases of Community Influence: A Strategy for Studying Their Distribution, Efficacy, and Convertibility*

INTRODUCTION

Perhaps the most elusive conceptual problem in discussions of community influence systems has been the definition of what is meant by the term "influence," and, more particularly, the operationalization of individual actors' and groups' relative impacts on a community's decision-making process. Many investigators have found it expedient to differentiate a community's elite on the basis of their reputations for influence on community decision making, often coming up with a presumptively unidimensional rank ordering of the elite according to their relative influence (e.g., Hunter, 1953; Gamson, 1966b). Other investigators, however, have correctly pointed out that influence is not an inherent characteristic of individuals or groups, but refers to an *asymmetric relationship* between actors (individual or corporate) with respect to a higher likelihood of compliance with the wishes of the more influential actor as the result of an influence transaction (e.g., Dahl, 1961). Thus, it is at least theoretically problematic whether or not this inequality in the relative influence of two actors may vary from one interactional context

* A version of this chapter was read at the VIIIth World Congress of Sociology, sponsored by International Sociological Association, in Toronto, Canada, August 19–24, 1974.

to another although we might presume it to be stable and invariant across many empirical contexts. Relative influence is based, among other things, on an actor's (individual or corporate) control over scarce resources that may be brought to bear in a given decision situation as specific inducements (or punishments) for an individual to behave in compliance with the influencer's wishes.[1]

In this chapter, we shall develop a theoretical analysis of influence resources and some propositions about their distribution in and relevance to community influence systems. Our more practical objective is to develop empirical procedures that can be employed in studying community influence systems. Although our intent is generality of treatment, we shall also describe the systematic application of our procedures in our case study in order to facilitate exposition and demonstrate, we hope, the utility of the approach. As always, the empirical results reported later should be seen more in the nature of an empirical illustration of our theoretical discussion than a test of our propositions.

More specifically, we have set ourselves five tasks in this chapter. First, we will briefly review several attempts to develop systematic distinctions among resource bases and to link them to the influence process. We will then propose a typology of influence resources and discuss our measurement procedures. In this connection, we will also develop a general theoretical model of the conversion of economic and value-based demands on the community influence system into specific authoritative decisions that have feedback effects on the community's structure of interests. Third, we will describe the distribution of influence resources in the community elite and examine some empirical propositions about their differential distribution within and across institutional sectors of the elite and the several oppositional coalitions in our case study. Fourth, we will examine the interface between the community's population at large and the elite, with respect to the differential distribution of different types of resources. And, finally, we will demonstrate the relation of different types of resources to a series of "outputs" or consequences of holding specific resources, including the prediction of the overall rank position in the hierarchy of reputed influence, reachability in the networks of linkages among influentials in the business–professional, social, and community affairs structures, and differential activation of leaders possessing different types of resources in resolving five community controversies.

---

[1] Our definition of resource is consistent with that of Rogers (1974: 1425): "A resource is any attribute, circumstance, or possession that increases the ability of its holder to influence a person or group."

A TYPOLOGY OF COMMUNITY INFLUENCE RESOURCES

There is a voluminous literature attempting to develop systematic distinctions among resource bases and to link them to the influence process. Examples include French and Raven's (1959) five bases of power (reward, coercive, referent, legitimate, and expert) with special reference to interpersonal influence processes, Parsons' four media of exchange (viz., money, power, influence, and commitment) at the societal level of analysis and his "influence paradigm" (cf. Parsons, 1969), and Clark's (1968c: 57–67) list of 13 resources for power, prestige, and norm formation.[2] All of them have varying degrees of theoretical elegance and empirical plausibility. Unfortunately, there have been virtually no empirical studies that have systematically attempted to assess resource bases and to build propositions about their distributions and consequences with special reference to community social systems. (There are resource studies in experimental social psychology [cf. Cartwright, 1965], but their referent is the small group and, more recently, a theoretical effort to specify the resources and consequent power of individual and corporate actors [cf. Coleman, 1973].)

In order to generate a comprehensive analytic scheme that would help us to specify the relevant range of community influence resources to be considered, we identified two fundamental aspects of influence resources that have often been seen as relevant. As Weber first suggested, the *locus of influence base* distinguishes between resources that inhere in the social position itself (e.g., the authority of office) and those that inhere in the personal characteristics of the actor exercising influence (e.g., personal charisma). This distinction seems to be of particular importance in determining the relative stability of an influence resource in terms of its conditions of access, use, and ability to be transferred (alienation) from one actor to another. Fully institutionalized roles usually have explicitly formulated rules regulating entry and succession of incumbents, and, thus, they tend to insure some continuity and predictability in the control of a given resource over time. In addition, the use of the resource is often hedged with rules regulating the circumstances under which and the purposes for which it may be used. Resources inhering in individuals,

---

[2] Clark's 13 resources include money and credit, control over jobs, control of mass media, high social status, knowledge and specialized technical skills, popularity and esteemed personal qualities, legality, subsystem solidarity, the right to vote, social access to community leaders, commitments of followers, manpower and control of organizations, and control over the interpretation of values (see also Gamson, 1968: 59–109; Nuttall, Scheuch, and Gordon, 1968: 352–356).

on the other hand, are subject to considerably greater unpredictability regarding the circumstances by which they came to be under a particular individual's control and how they will be used and transferred, if at all possible, to a successor. We should note here, however, that this distinction does *not* imply that there be a necessary disparity in the relative efficacy of positional versus personal resources in influence transactions.

The second aspect of resource bases that is of special interest concerns their *effective scope, generality,* or *convertibility.* Here we distinguish between resources that can be utilized in a wide variety of concrete influence situations as positive or negative inducements, such as money, and those that are more restricted (or particularistic) in their efficacy to a limited range of appropriate situations in which they can be utilized. (Note the parallelism of this distinction to Parsons' universalism–particularism, Clark's generality of resources, and Dahl's influence domain.) Again we should note that this distinction does not imply a necessary disparity in the relative efficacy of generalized versus specific resources in specific influence transactions.

Treating these two axes characterizing influence resources as analytically independent, dichotomous variables, we cross-tabulated them to yield a fourfold typology of resource bases (see Table 11.1). The eight

TABLE 11.1

Analytical Scheme for Classifying Influence Resources

Effective scope or convertibility	Locus of influence base	
	Positional (institutionalized role)	Personal characteristics of incumbent
Generalized	a. Official decision-making authority as elected public official or occupant of a high position in public service b. Power of disposal over fluid economic resources, possible giver of credit	c. General respect as someone who can mobilize the public for good proposals in the interest of the city as a whole d. Honorable broker who can mediate issues in a nonpartisan way
Specific	e. Power of disposal over less fluid economic resources, such as land or jobs f. Special expert knowledge of certain limited fields of community interest	g. Good connections with influential persons inside and outside of community h. Influence in certain subgroups of the population, such as voters of a particular party, members of a voluntary association, and so on

resource bases were chosen so that two of them would fall into each of the four cells. While not necessarily exhaustive of all the relevant community-level influence resources, the tabulation does seem to include the salient resources most often discussed in the literature. It is especially difficult to construct an exhaustive typology of the personal resources. Since power or influence may depend on so many personal characteristics, even Max Weber (1922: 28) characterized power in contrast to authority as a concept that is *"soziologisch amorph."* Robert Michels (1925: 65–73) also discussed a plethora of *"akzessorische Eigenschaften der Führerschaft."* To avoid these cafeteria lists, we confined our personal characteristics to those that have a relational aspect, that is, help the individual to be a more effective member of an elite system.

HYPOTHETICAL MODEL OF THE PROCESS OF RESOURCE CONVERSION

With these distinctions in mind, we can now introduce our hypothetical model of the process of converting resources into binding collective decisions. Its construction rests on a synthesis of the theoretical discussion to this point as well as an incorporation of some of our empirical results (to be reported later) that helped to clarify and specify our original abstract formulation. Figure 11.1 provides a synoptic overview of the model.

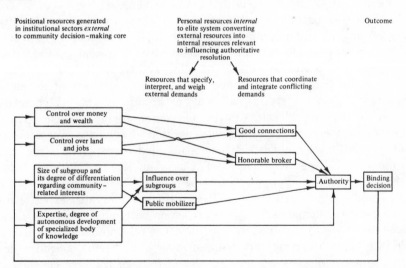

Figure 11.1 A hypothetical model of the process of resource conversion into binding collective decisions.

The model attempts to represent two aspects of the process of converting resources into binding community decisions. The first aspect concerns the functional logic of resource conversion; the second considers several alternative mechanisms of resource conversion that may be employed, depending on the nature of the issue to be resolved. It is important to remember that the community decision-making system is the focus of the integrative subsystem of the community social system (cf. Parsons, 1960) and is, therefore, especially concerned with establishing binding priorities among competing alternatives for the expenditure of scarce community resources and their subsequent implementation (i.e., the focus of the goal-attainment subsystem).

Actors in the other two institutional subsystems of the community generate a variety of demands for specific community decisions that either will be directly beneficial to themselves in moving toward specific objectives or will conform to their preferred values. Associated with these demands for action are external influence resources that are generated in each institutional subsystem. In the economic subsystem, control over money and land and jobs are the key resources and are, of course, highly skewed in their distributions across economic actors. Similarly, a community's population may be subdivided into groupings with different ultimate social values concerning the desirable state of society or with differing immediate interests (recall our discussion in Chapter 4). The relative importance of these subgroups will be a function of their relative size in the population and the degree to which they are conscious of their distinctive values and interests that are at variance with those of others. (Of course, this presupposes that the rules of the game in the community decision-making system permit electoral strength of a group to be translated [converted] into relevant elite resources.) A special case of influence resources generated outside the elite system itself includes those actors in the pattern-maintenance sector who are masters of an autonomously developed, specialized body of knowledge that is generally recognized as being efficacious in the solution of specific problems. These experts will, therefore, be in a special position of influence over decision making when rendering "expert judgments" that nonexperts are not in a position to challenge effectively (cf. Carr–Saunders and Wilson, 1944; Parsons, 1968).

The problem, of course, is how these variously generated external resources and the demands for collective action with which they are associated can be converted into *relevant* influence resources that will play a role in resolving a community issue in favor of a specific collective decision to act or not to act. The *functional logic of resource conversion* basically asserts that these externally generated resources must somehow become converted into resources relevant to the elite influence subsystem. It was only as we considered carefully our empirical results that we discovered, quite by accident, the need to distinguish between two types of influence resources internal to the elite system itself.

The first type of personal resource internal to the elite is concerned with specifying, interpreting, weighing, and representing externally generated demands for community action. Elite actors having either influence over subgroups or reputations as public mobilizers possess resources relevant to this function. The second type of personal resources internal to the elite is concerned with coordinating and integrating conflicting demands. Elite actors possessing good connections or reputed to be honorable brokers are especially relevant to this function. Once a profile of interest group demands on an issue has been specified or articulated and weighed ("coordinated") as to the various interest groups' relative amounts of influence resources that can be mobilized, then authoritative action can be undertaken, leading to a binding collective decision. As noted in Figure 11.1, this decision output feeds back into the community system at large by modifying in some way, positively for some and negatively for others, the interest group demands.

The second aspect of our model in Figure 11.1 is an effort to portray two alternative mechanisms of resource conversion, depending on the issues to be resolved. Earlier (see Chapter 9) we made a distinction between instrumental and consummatory or expressive issues. *Instrumental issues* are concerned with controversies over the differing allocation of scarce community resources, such as land, jobs, and money, and find their particular locus in the adaptive and integrative sectors of community concern. Consummatory or *expressive issues* are concerned with controversies regarding the maintenance or change in the organization of basic values, commitments, and orientations that guide or control community affairs. We hypothesize that the mechanisms by which external resources are converted via internal elite personal resources into specific outcomes differ, depending on which type of issue is being processed. Instrumental issues, because they have a "more or less" allocative character that can be the subject of bargaining and compromise among the contending parties, will tend to activate the elite resources of good connections and the honorable broker. Consummatory issues, on the other hand, because they have an "all or none" character that makes bargaining and compromise difficult, if not impossible, among the contending parties, tend to activate the internal elite resources of influence over subgroups and the public mobilizer directly influencing those in authority positions.

The two aspects of our hypothetical model, its functional logic and alternative mechanisms of resource conversion, are not at the same level of generality. The mechanisms of resource activation actually depend not only on the types of issues to be resolved, but also on other characteristics of the community influence structure itself. These additional sources of constraints might imply other conversion sequences among the different types of resources. Such modifications of the process logic, however, would not alter the functional logic of our hypothetical model, with its separation of the resources into extra-elite positional resources, the personally based, intermediary resources of the elite system itself, and the positionally based, implementative resource of authority.

We must note an especially important modification of our model of the processes of resource conversion. For periods of time and for certain issues, any elite system, even a democratic one, may function as a self-contained autonomous system in its own right, with decision outputs to the community at large but with practically no inputs from the other institutional sectors (cf. Gouldner, 1959). In such situations, the integrative elite core and its authoritative elements are not merely a passive mechanism transforming externally generated demands (arising from the so-called "productive forces") into binding collective decisions. The elite system not only recognizes and aggregates external demands, but it may play a creative role in community decision making by anticipating and articulating latent demands of the community at large and designing innovative strategies for "solving" community problems. In addition, there are functional requirements and constraints for the generation and maintenance of the elite actors' personal influence resources that lead to biases in decision making, that are not predictable by considering only the extra-elite demands for action.

As already mentioned, our model of resource conversion is partially derived from our original theory and partially from the results of our analysis. The distinction that we are now emphasizing between the types of resources found within the elite system and those generated in institutional subsystems external to the elite coincides reasonably well with our earlier distinction between positional and personal resources (discussed in Table 11.1) but permits a better interpretation of the involvement of the resources in the different steps of the influence–conversion process. The structuring of the integrative, personal resources according to the two tasks of specifying and interpreting external demands and of coordinating influence processes was suggested by the results of the analysis of the community at large—elite interface and the reachability data discussed later.

Finally, we should note one unanticipated result of our empirical analysis that has not yet been discussed. A well-known hypothesis states that the more general resources are, the more easily they can be converted into power or influence (cf. Clark, 1968c: 57–67). Money is often taken as one of the best examples of a highly general resource easily converted into relevant influence in many different contexts, including community decision-making situations. Our data strongly suggest, on the contrary, that money was not only unconvertible into a usable influence resource in Altneustadt, but may actually have been converted into "negative" influence. In short, in addition to the generality of the resource, one must take into account the norms regulating the legitimate ways in which given resources can be converted into other influence resources (cf. Rogers, 1974: 1430–1431). Such norms are important system parameters to specify in advance, especially for meaningful cross-cultural comparisons.

OPERATIONALIZING THE MODEL

With this guiding framework in mind, we can now consider how its key components—that is, the resource bases and their differential allocation among elite participants—were operationally identified in the case study. It is quite reasonable to assume that the elite population is highly sophisticated regarding matters of influence and its use. Consequently, we decided to treat them as well-placed informants about themselves and their peers and to adopt the most direct expedient of simply asking them to make a judgement, for each influential they knew well enough, as to which one of the eight resources he primarily controlled. (See Q40, Appendix C, for the text of the question asked.) Each respondent also indicated what he believed to be his own resource base. The list of resources provided in the question is an attempt to synthesize the previously mentioned lists, formulating them in terms that our "lay" respondents would find meaningful. Apparently we were reasonably successful in this effort since none of the respondents had any difficulties in understanding what was wanted or in doing the task. There was a definite tendency for the respondents to attribute resources more frequently to persons in the higher reaches of the influence hierarchy (more about this later) where members are more visible and to neglect somewhat the less influential members of the elite. Table 11.2 presents a tabulation of the total number of resources held by the 50 influentials for which we have information. In order for an individual to be regarded as possessing a particular resource base, at least three respondents had to mention him as having that resource.

TABLE 11.2
The Percentage Distribution of Resource Bases Held by the Top Fifty Influentials in Altneustadt[a]

Resource bases held	Percentage distribution
None	24%
One	26%
Two	26%
Three	12%
Four	4%
Five	4%
Six	2%
Seven	2%
Total	100%
(N)	(50)

[a] An influence resource was attributed when a person got three or more votes for this resource.

There was consensus (in the sense of at least 50% of the judges attributing the same base) for more than 64% of the influentials with regard to their putative influence base. Where individuals were attributed more than one influence base, this usually was justifiable given their overall profiles of characteristics—that is, on the basis of other information we had about elite members, we could ascertain that they actually possessed several bases of influence. (So that the reader can evaluate for himself the following statistical analysis, he should recall that the sociograms in Chapter 6 indicate the resources held by every elite member, according to these coding rules.)

It is worth stressing at this point that we have determined only that an individual is believed to control some *unspecified* amount of a given resource. We have not ascertained how much of that resource he controls relative to others also believed to possess the resource. The question of relative amounts of resources under the control of a set of influentials is an obviously important one with far-reaching implications. Unfortunately, to date, we have been unsuccessful in coming up with a satisfactory answer to it. All we can do at this point is to confine our analysis to the crude distinction between those with and those without a resource.

Since the question proved to yield meaningful responses from the respondents, we could now ask whether or not there was a systematic pattern in the distribution of resources among the influentials. Of course, we did not have any theoretical expectation of a correspondence between the two dimensions generating the analytic scheme portrayed in Table 11.1 and the dimensionality of the empirically derived description of the differential allocation of these resources among the influentials (to be discussed later). We did expect, however, that the positional resources would be differentially allocated among influentials according to their institutional specialization, following Parsons, and that the personal resources would be allocated according to the nature of the roles elite members played in different coalitions.

We adopted a frankly exploratory strategy to study the differential allocation of resources by treating our list of community influentials as a set of common stimuli to which our respondents could respond with eight alternative responses. Indexes of dissimilarity were calculated for all possible pairs of influence resources by determining percentages within resource categories across the 50 stimuli. These indexes were uniformly high, ranging between 53.8 and 97.5, suggesting considerable differential allocation of influence resources across the elite "stimuli." Formulated in other terms, such high indexes suggest considerable specialization of control over resources among the elite. A smallest space analysis of this matrix of indexes of dissimilarity yielded a good fit of the original matrix in two dimensions (coefficient of alienation = .108), which is portrayed in Figure 11.2. The farther away two resources are in the space, the more dissimilar they are in their patterns of distribution across the elite population.

The first axis neatly divides the resources into three categories: economic or adaptive resources, informal influence or integrative resources, and an authority or goal-attainment resource. Only special expert knowledge is not an intra-elite influence resource and shows up in the "wrong" location. If the rank order of the resources in the first axis from right to left is correlated with the rank order of the correlation coefficients of each resource with a general reputation for influence (see Table 11.7), one obtains a *rho* of +.596 (a coefficient of .643 is significant at the .05 level with $n = 8$ using a one-tailed test). This provides at least suggestive evidence that the first axis arranges resources according to their relevance to "generating" general community influence among the elite. The second axis seems to arrange these resources along a generality–specificity dimension, that is, from (universalistic) resources that can be utilized in a wide range of situations, such as money or general respect as an "honorable broker" capable of composing differences, to more restrictively utilizable (particularistic) resources, such as land or jobs and "good connections." "Authority" appears to be intermediate in

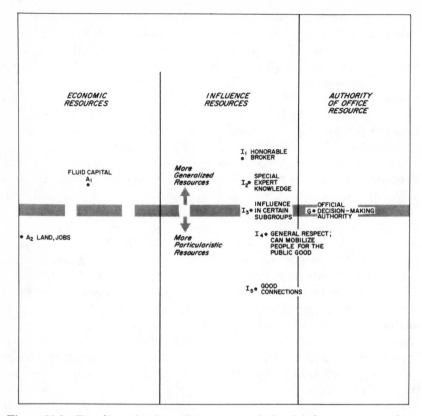

Figure 11.2 Two-dimensional smallest space analysis of influence resource bases. Guttman–Lingoes coefficient of alienation = .108.

its generality (perhaps reflecting the legally prescribed boundaries of authority domains).[3]

The three resources closest to the central axis in the influence resource cluster do not follow our interpretation of the second axis. Since special expert knowledge is again located in the "wrong" place, we should mention that we had intended to measure expert knowledge relevant to the implementation of community decisions. Our respondents, however, perceived it more generally such that most of the scientists were attributed

---

[3] A cautionary note should be interjected here: Given the wide scatter of points and the fact that there are only eight points, interpretation of the underlying structure cannot be as certain as when there are many points in a given region to help define its "meaning." With that caveat in mind, there is, nevertheless, a remarkable correspondence between our theoretical expectations and the empirical results.

expertise on the basis of their scientific training which was, of course, not especially relevant to community affairs. If this "error" had not occurred, this resource would have been more closely correlated with authority because the other individuals attributed expert knowledge were public officials.

Another way of looking at the way resources co-vary among the elite is to examine the intercorrelation matrix (see Table 11.3) in which control over each resource is treated as a dichotomous variable. Again a person is said to control a resource only if three or more respondents attribute the resource to him. A careful examination of the matrix shows essentially the same configuration with regard to the grouping of resources that was portrayed in Figure 11.2. Control over economic resources tends to be highly specialized with individuals possessing these resources generally not having any systematic relation to any other resource (except for the association between control over money and reputation as an honorable broker!). Authority, on the other hand, tends to cluster with a variety of personal resources including influence over voting blocs in the population, having good connections, and being a public mobilizer, honorable broker, and expert in some field of community concern. In a real sense, these latter resources may be seen as being ultimately convertible into authority (the right to make binding collective decisions) through the electoral political process. It is difficult to imagine how one could acquire public authority lacking all of these resources; in fact, we find that all of the 17 influentials with authority have at least one of the other resources listed. Indeed, these 17 people have an average of 2.4 resources *in addition* to their authority.

THE DISTRIBUTION OF RESOURCES

The Distribution of Resources by Institutional Sectors

Thus far, we have been concerned with the differential distribution of resources among the elite as a whole. We now turn to a more precise delineation of resource allocation according to primary institutional sectors to which elite members may be assigned. The reader will recall that, in identifying prospective elite members, we used the positional technique whereby individuals were selected because they were incumbents of the highest positions of authority in organized collectivities whose primary responsibilities were in one of the four functionally

TABLE 11.3
Intercorrelation Matrix of Eight Influence Resources

Influence resources	Influence resources							
	Authority	Public mobilizer	Good connections	Influence over subgroups	Expert knowledge	Honorable broker	Money	Land, jobs
Authority	—							
Public mobilizer	.378[a]	—						
Good connections	.323[a]	.222	—					
Influence over subgroups	.408[a]	.293[a]	.224	—				
Special expert knowledge	.388[a]	.266	.346[a]	.425[a]	—			
Honorable broker	.319[a]	.453[a]	.261	.141	.178	—		
Control over money and credit	-.056	.072	.054	-.172	.007	.306[a]	—	
Control over land and jobs	-.212	-.129	-.138	-.320[a]	-.166	-.119	.185	—

[a] $p < .05$.

specialized institutional subsectors at the community level of analysis. This list was supplemented with individuals nominated by well-informed community informants as being especially influential in community decision making but, for one reason or another, were not currently incumbents of formal positions of authority in influential collectivities. Of course, some individuals simultaneously occupied several influential positions. We attempted to resolve the problem of multiple role occupancy by distinguishing an individual's *primary* institutional location from his *secondary* position(s) on the basis of the amount of time he spent performing the duties of each (see Chapter 5, pp. 96–98, and Appendix A, Part II, for a more extensive discussion of these procedures).

An obvious hypothesis derived from Parsons (1969) is that the various resources should be differentially distributed among the institutional sectors according to their functional relevance to each sector. This hypothesis may be further specified to refer particularly to positional resources that are associated with institutionalized roles (see Table 11.1). Personal resources will be less predictably distributed across the institutional sectors because of the more random mechanisms (at least with respect to institutional functioning) that generate them. Thus, we would expect the adaptive resources of money and land and jobs to be more often located in the economic sector, authority in the polity, and special expertise in the pattern-maintenance sector. So-called "influence resources" (see Figure 11.2) will tend to be more randomly distributed among the elite although some concentrations in the polity may be anticipated.

In Table 11.4, we have cross-tabulated the primary sector locations of our 46 influentials with their attributed resources. The disparity between the number of cases (which refers to the number of individuals in that sector) and the number of mentions (which refers to the number of resources allocated to people in that sector) is, of course, explained by some individuals having multiple resources, typically having acquired them because of their activities in "secondary" institutional roles. For example, one large businessman who controls land and jobs also happens to be on the city council which provides him with public authority. Given the small size of this population universe, one should examine the pattern in the table cautiously as a shift of several individuals from one cell to another can sharply affect the pattern. No tests of significance are appropriate. With these caveats in mind, it seems reasonably clear that the observed pattern broadly conforms with our theoretical expectations. Positional resources tend to be overrepresented in their respective institutional spheres, while personal resources are distributed more evenly across the different sectors.

TABLE 11.4
Primary Sector Location and Influence Resources[a]

Influence resources	Primary sector locations of elite members					
	Economy 1[b] %	Economy 2[c] %	Polity %	Science %	Pattern maintenance %	Total %
Authority	7.1	—	25.6	18.8	12.5	17.0
Public mobilizer	—	11.1	12.8	—	12.5	8.5
Good connections	7.1	—	12.8	12.5	6.2	9.6
Influence over subgroups	21.4	44.4	23.1	31.2	31.2	27.6
Special expert knowledge	14.3	—	10.2	31.2	—	11.7
Honorable broker	—	11.1	12.8	—	6.2	7.4
Control over money and credit	7.1	22.2	2.6	—	—	4.2
Control over land and jobs	21.4	—	—	—	—	3.2
No resources	21.4	11.1	—	6.2	31.2	10.6
Number of mentions including cases with no resources = 100%	14	9	39	16	16	94
Mean number of resources	1.1	1.1	3.5	2.5	0.9	1.8
Number of cases	10	7	11	6	12	46

[a] An influence resource was attributed when a person received three or more votes for this resource.
[b] Professionals and managers—owners of large business firms and farms.
[c] Smaller businessmen and bankers.

Influence Resources and Oppositional Cliques

To place community influentials into various institutional sectors to which they owe primary allegiance in no way confronts the problem of how the elite is organized into a set of working coalitions that combine or pool their resources for the purpose of achieving their common objectives, often at the expense of others' objectives. Community decision making must ultimately decide among competing alternatives, and the exercise of influence is, therefore, very much concerned with mobilizing relevant resources to influence decision outcomes. Rarely is an individual possessed of sufficient resources, under his immediate control, to determine by himself a particular outcome, particularly if it is not already the object of widespread community consensus. Working in concert with like-minded others is much more likely to yield success in particular decision situations. Indeed, collaboration with the same people over time is likely to make mobilization of resources even more effective, since it permits the development of common strategies and resource specialization in an internally differentiated clique that is bound together by diffuse, informal social ties as well as more instrumental ones.

Table 11.5 presents the distribution of influence resources among the cliques, as identified in Chapter 6, pp. 105–106. What is truly noteworthy here is that the dominant city CDU subclique and the SPD clique, the two groups most regularly in contention, have very similar distributions of resources—except that the SPD coalition lacks honorable brokers and economic resources. (The lack of economic resources is not serious, as we shall learn later, because economic resources are not associated with effective influence in the community decision-making system.) Both coalitions are even similar in the average number of resources controlled by their respective members. The crucial point is, of course, that, while the countervailing power of the opposition is composed of similar types of resources, it is highly deficient in the *amounts* of the resources that it can successfully mobilize against its CDU opponents. We must hasten to point out that the SPD coalition is by no means an inconsequential opponent—it has won important battles. The CDU coalition is dominant in the community decision-making system, but is by no means pre-emptive in its influence.

The large businessmen clique is clearly specialized with respect to economic resources and confines itself to the limited role of attempting to influence community decisions of special relevance to their economic enterprises. They possess no authority or other resources and, in fact, would certainly have difficulty in realizing their wishes on other issues unless they happened to be shared by the dominant CDU coalition

TABLE 11.5
The Influence Resources of the Coalition Cliques

Influence resources	Coalition cliques						
	Dominant city CDU subclique %	Mediators of CDU subcliques %	County CDU subclique %	Large businessmen clique %	SPD clique %	Social isolates %	Total %
Authority	14.8	18.2	17.6	—	20.0	20.0	18.8
Public mobilizer	7.4	9.1	5.9	—	6.7	13.3	7.9
Good connections	11.1	9.1	17.6	—	13.3	—	10.1
Influence over subgroups	22.2	18.2	29.4	—	33.3	40.0	27.0
Special expert knowledge	11.1	18.2	5.9	—	20.0	13.3	12.4
Honorable broker	14.8	18.2	5.9	—	—	—	7.9
Control over money and credit	7.4	—	—	50.0	—	—	4.5
Control over land and jobs	—	—	5.9	25.0	—	6.7	3.4
No resources	11.1	9.1	11.8	25.0	6.7	6.7	10.1
Number of mentions including cases with no resources = 100%	27	11	17	4	15	15	89
Mean number of resources	2.2	1.7	1.9	1.0	2.0	1.8	1.9
Number of cases	11	8	5	3	7	8	43

with whom they are associated. Wealthy in economic resources as they are, they apparently have not been able to convert these resources into others more relevant to the exercise of public authority. While these businessmen made informal choices among members of the CDU coalition, these were not reciprocated. The social isolates, as one might expect, tend to be overrepresented in the resource of influence over subgroups. They can be regarded as representatives of more specialized, intermittent demands on the community decision-making system who are not organized into perdurable coalitional blocs.

From these results, we might infer the hypothesis (also suggested by Galbraith's [1952] argument on countervailing power) that persistent oppositional coalitions in a given power arena tend to mobilize similar types of resources. They differ primarily in the amount of such resources they can successfully control.

THE ELITE–COMMUNITY INTERFACE AND TYPE OF RESOURCES

By focusing almost exclusively on the community elite, many studies of community power structure neglect a critical part of the equation of influence: to wit, the reciprocal role of the public at large in generating and maintaining certain types of influence resources for elite members to employ in within-elite and elite–public-at-large influence attempts. Taking a somewhat different tack, Gamson (1968) has also directed attention to the importance of political trust of population subgroups in the political system and its leaders in explaining the political behavior of these groups and, ultimately, community decision making. We have an unusual opportunity to examine some aspects of this question with data gathered from our sample of eligible voters ($N = 820$) in Altneustadt regarding their responses to the 27 most influential members of our elite population (see Chapters 3 and 4 and Appendix A for a study description). Three questions were designed to tap different aspects of the public's trust or confidence in specific elite individuals. The first, *instrumental trust*, asked to whom in the list of 27 persons the respondent would turn for help in preventing a measure from being passed in the city that he considered very unjust or harmful (cf. Almond and Verba, 1963). The second, *personal trust*, asked to whom the respondent would turn in this list for advice or help if he had a personal problem, such as finding a residence, purchasing or selling a piece of land, and so on. The third, *general trust*, asked on whom the respondent relied in this list for very good judgment in community affairs—that is, which persons would most likely influence the respondent's attitude on a community issue. Each question permitted a maximum of 5 persons to be named. The sample averaged 1.3, .6, and 1.0 names per respondent for each question, respectively.

For purposes of this analysis, we simply determined the proportion of the population who identified a given individual in response to each of the three questions on the assumption that the higher the proportions of mentions a given individual received, the greater the public's trust in him. As one might have expected, these 27 proportions were, on the average, quite low (3.5%, 1.6%, and 2.6%, respectively) and were very highly intercorrelated ($r_{12} = .835$, $r_{13} = .977$, and $r_{23} = .832$). Consequently, we decided to combine them into a single measure of general popular trust and esteem in which we simply pooled all the individuals who identified a given influential on *at least one* of the three questions as someone he would turn to for advice or help. The resulting pooled data yielded 5.9% as the average proportion of the population who mentioned given influentials as people they could turn to for advice or help.

TABLE 11.6

Zero-Order and Multiple Correlations of Eight Influence Resources with Measures of Popular Trust and Esteem and Clientele Bias

	Community–Elite interface	
Influence resources	Popular trust and esteem[a] (1)	Index of clientele bias[b] (2)
Authority	.343[c]	.115
Public mobilizer	.362[cd]	−.228
Good connections	.645[cd]	−.177
Influence over subgroups	.248	.326[c]
Special expert knowledge	.264	.215
Honorable broker	.074	−.141
Control over money and credit	−.234	−.389[c]
Control over land and jobs	−.427[c]	−.156
Number of resources[e]	.509[c]	−.072
Multiple R	.796[c]	.608
N	26	26

[a] Excludes the most influential man in the elite because he is an extreme outlier on this variable.
[b] Excludes a county farmer because he is an extreme outlier on this variable.
[c] Significant at the .05 level.
[d] Coefficients remained significant at the .05 level in the multiple regression equation.
[e] This variable was omitted in the multiple regression equation.

Column 1 of Table 11.6 tells an interesting story. Popular trust is especially associated with good connections, authority, and being a public mobilizer. Note, however, that both adaptive resources are *negatively* associated with general popular trust and esteem. In addition, the more resources an influential controls, the more trusting is the public opinion of him. An especially intriguing nonassociation is that between reputation as an honorable broker and popular trust and esteem ($r = .074$). One might surmise from this that the role of honorable broker is very much confined within the elite itself (see also Columns 2–4 of Table 11.7) and is not a matter of popular perception. The eight resources in combination predict very successfully (multiple $R = .796$) the level of popular trust and esteem each influential enjoys.

We can take our exploration of the interface between the public at large and the elite a step farther. The proportion of the population who express trust and confidence in given individuals can be interpreted as estimating only the relative sizes of influentials' potential clienteles—a matter certainly of considerable significance in an electorally oriented influence system. (We hasten to remind the reader that we have not confined our description of the community influence system to such a limited conception.) Another important question immediately arises: How representative or concentrated are these clienteles with respect to the public at large? That is, the extent to which a given clientele is overselected from specific population subgroups and underrepresented in others should give some indication of that influential's role as a representative of special interests or as a more broadly based representative of general community interests—in other words, some indication of the biases in his popular support and clientele. Moreover, can we infer some implications of these clientele biases for the types of resources he controls?

First, let us consider positional resources. In general, we might expect those possessing adaptive resources, especially money, to have clienteles that are more representative than those possessing other sorts of resources simply because of the generality of money as a medium of exchange and its utility for most parts of the population in pursuing myriad objectives. Land and jobs, being a resource of more restricted utility—that is, more specialized or particularized—should be held by influentials having more specialized clienteles. Special expert knowledge, also a more particularized resource according to our scheme in Table 11.1, should be held by influentials having specialized clienteles.

One would naturally assume that possessors of authority, a more generalized resource, should have more representative clienteles. Unfortunately, however, the test of this hypothesis is complicated by the fact that incumbents of high administrative posts, such as the city manager, are expected to be responsive to all elements in the population while holders of electoral mandates are expected to be more responsive to the voting blocs that place them in positions of authority. In fact, we found that the average index for the higher bureaucrats was only 17.4 in comparison to an average index of 29.3 for holders of electoral mandates. Thus, the zero-order correlation of authority and representativeness of clientele is indeterminate. With respect to personal resources, as Table 11.1 suggests, influence over subgroups and good connections should have more specialized clienteles, and the public mobilizer and honorable broker should have more representative clienteles.

To anticipate ourselves a bit, we should point out that these speculations are theoretical ones without regard to the empirical fact that particular types of resources are controlled by specific individuals who often possess several different types of resources (see Table 11.2). These multiple resources have conflicting implications for the degree of specialization of an influential's clientele. In general, we expect an association between the number of resources an influential controls and the representativeness of his clientele, since the more resources he possesses, the greater utility, for one or another purpose, he has for all elements of the population.

We used the percentage distribution of the total population across our eight population subgroups (excluding students) (see Chapter 3, pp. 67–68) to compute indexes of dissimilarity (cf. Duncan and Duncan, 1955), comparing a clientele's distribution across the eight population subgroups for a given influential with the sample's as a whole. The index has a very straightforward interpretation: Its computed value is the proportion of a clientele that would have to redistribute themselves among the eight categories to have the same percentage distribution as the total sample's distribution. Obviously, the closer to "0" the index for a given clientele is, the more representative it is of the public at large. The average index of dissimilarity for the 27 influentials was 27.6, with a range between 7.8 and 59.6.[4]

---

[4] The man with an index of 59.6, a large farmer in the county, was an extreme outlier. In addition, only five persons mentioned him as someone they would turn to —thus, the population base by which to calculate the index was too small to get a reliable estimate of his index of dissimilarity. On the other hand, the most influential man in town was not an outlier in this sense, although he was on all the other variables discussed in Tables 11.6 and 11.7. Consequently, in our analysis of the index of clientele bias, we included the most influential man in town and excluded the large farmer in the county. In the other column(s) of Tables 11.6 and 11.7, the most influential man in town, being the extreme outlier, was excluded from the correlational analysis.

There is a correlation of $-.592$ ($p < .001$) between size of an influential's clientele and its index of dissimilarity—that is, the larger the clientele, the more representative it is of the public at large. This result is *not* tautologically implied as a direct result of our procedures for calculating the two variables. It could well be that a person who was the leader of a large population subgroup, well-known and trusted by them and, consequently, having a large clientele (for example, a labor leader) would have a high index of dissimilarity.[5]

Turning to column 2 of Table 11.6, we see that only two of the eight resources are significantly associated with the index of clientele bias. Happily, both are correctly predicted from our theory. Money is associated with low indices of dissimilarity (or greater representativeness), and influence over subgroups is associated with higher indices of dissimilarity (or less representativeness). While all the other correlations fail to achieve the conventional level of statistical significance due to the small sample size, two are worth looking at a bit more closely if one relaxes the required level of significance to $p < .10$. Public mobilization is, as predicted, associated with higher representativeness ($p < .066$, one-tailed), while expert knowledge is, as predicted, associated with lower representativeness of the clientele ($p < .075$, one-tailed). The direction of the association with honorable broker is correctly predicted although it is much too low to be taken as reliable. Only "good connections" and "land and jobs" run counter to our expectations at least so far as the

---

[5] The index of dissimilarity seems to be a reasonable means of operationalizing the concept of a clientele's biases in composition on grounds of face validity alone. Before taking this measure seriously in our analysis of types of resources, however, it would be reassuring if we could demonstrate that the index of clientele bias is distributed among our elite members in a manner that is consistent with other information available about them. First, with respect to its distribution among the primary institutional sectors, we can show that the economic elite has, as we might have expected, the lowest average index (least bias) (17.7), followed by the political elite (21.5) and the two oppositional groupings in the elite located in the pattern-maintenance sector, the *Altbürger*, Catholic-oriented religious and educational leaders (32.3) and the *Neubürger*, Protestant-oriented science personnel (34.8) ($p < .05$). Second, with respect to the elite's division into several socially organized coalitions, we can show that the extended dominant CDU coalition has the lowest average index (23.3), followed by the social isolates (26.7) (who belong to no coalition and represent somewhat specialized claims on the polity) and, finally, by the challenging opposition coalition of the SPD elite members who have the most extreme average index (38.3) ($p < .05$). The SPD coalition, thus, has the most concentrated and unrepresentative popular base for their influence attempts. It is also worth noting in passing that the index of clientele bias is not significantly associated (.170) with reputed influence rank in the elite, while popular trust and esteem is correlated positively with influence rank (.487, $p < .006$).

direction of the correlation is concerned, although both correlations are also much too low to be reliable even under the more liberal standard of significance. A final disappointment is the lack of association between number of resources and clientele bias where we hypothesized a negative association.

THE RELATIVE EFFICACY OF INFLUENCE RESOURCES

Thus far, we have confined our attention to the differential distribution of resources among the elite. An obvious question, however, must be raised: so what? More concretely, what are the consequences of possessing different types of resources? On what resources does general reputed influence in the elite especially depend? Can certain features of the network structures that organize the elite be used to predict the different types of resources controlled by elite members? Is the differential activation of elite members on different community issues a function of the types of resources they possess? Table 11.7 has been constructed to answer these and other questions regarding the relative efficacy of influence resources.

Reputed General Influence and Types of Resources

Relative rank in the hierarchy of reputed influence among the elite has often been used to get some handle on the structure of community influence. Such a strategy suffers from many limitations, both methodological and theoretical (see, for example, Kaufman and Jones, 1954; Wolfinger, 1960). Perhaps the most important limitation is that it projects a unidimensional picture of an influence structure even when a pluralistic, multidimensional structure would be more appropriate. Moreover, as a global measure of influence, it suppresses most of the more interesting questions in the study of influence—namely, the grounds on which people are making their very complex judgments regarding relative influence among elite members. Our theoretical stance has stressed the necessity of recognizing that influence is relative to particular decision situations and rests on different types of resources. Particular influence resources may simply not be relevant to a particular influence transaction. Obviously, the more types of resources one possesses, the more likely it is that one will have a resource appropriate to a given influence transaction. In addition, types of resources are hypothesized to vary in their scope, generality, or convertibility (see Table 11.1), thus

TABLE 11.7

Zero-Order and Multiple Correlations of Eight Influence Resources with General Influence Rank, Reachability in the Elite Network of Social Relations, and Activation of Participation in Resolution of Five Community Issues

Influence resources	General influence rank[a] (1)	Reachability			Activation of influentials				
		Business-professional[a] (2)	Social[a] (3)	Community affairs[a] (4)	Industrial resettlement[a] (5)	City hall[a] (6)	Community incorporation[a] (7)	Pop festival[a] (8)	School[a] (9)
Authority	.562[bc]	.273[b]	.181	.174	.130	.403[b]	.356[b]	.159	.407[b]
Public mobilizer	.324[b]	−.037	.120	.176	.017	.327[b]	.200	.335[b]	.315[b]
Good connections	.487[bc]	.331[b]	.274[b]	.303[b]	−.030	.461[bc]	.556[bc]	.267[b]	.258[b]
Influence over subgroups	.475[bc]	−.179	.017	.248	.282[b]	.172	.310[b]	.191	.428[b]
Special expert knowledge	.400[b]	.120	.152	.073	.150	.334[b]	.062	.203	.533[bc]
Honorable broker	.501[c]	.257	.493[bc]	.360[bc]	−.057	.274[b]	.097	.289[b]	.120
Control over money and credit	−.025	.131	−.043	−.114	.134	−.129	−.137	.112	.186
Control over land and jobs	.043	.116	−.113	−.135	.056	−.151	−.160	−.119	.217
Number of resources[d]	.763[b]	.247	.300[b]	.326[b]	.199	.505[b]	.398[b]	.386[b]	.529[b]
Multiple R	.805[b]	.545	.561	.494	.412	.615[b]	.657[b]	.474	.626[b]
N	49	39	43	43	49	49	49	49	49

[a] Excludes the most influential man in the elite because he is an extreme outlier on this variable.
[b] Significant at the .05 level.
[c] Coefficients remained significant at the .05 level in the multiple regression equation.
[d] This variable was omitted in the multiple regression equation.

affording different possibilities for use in a variety of influence situations. Informed judgements of general reputed influence may thus be seen as a function of the number and the types of resources possessed. We also agree with Gamson, however, (1966b: 122) that: "Reputation is not simply the manifestation of the possession of large amounts of resources but is, itself, a resource in the same sense that money, wealth, or authority might be." More generally, he argues that reputation for influence is significant because it is a stable and generalized persuasion resource. In our terms, it is a resource located in the "personal locus of influence, generalized scope" cell of Table 11.1. For our purposes here, however, we shall examine the factors that can be seen as contributing to or generating general reputation for influence.

Column 1 of Table 11.7 presents the zero-order correlations of the types of resources and number of resources with the rank order of the influentials according to their reputed influence.[6] The multiple R (based only on the eight resources and excluding the number of resources possessed by each individual) is quite high (.805). At the zero-order level, six of the eight resources contribute positively to a man's rank in the influence hierarchy. Only the two economic resources appear to play no role in determining general influence rank. We will discover that this finding of the relative lack of efficacy of adaptive resources in generating community influence is consistently supported in the analyses that follow. On the basis of the multiple regression analysis, authority, good connections, influence over subgroups, and honorable broker seem to be especially powerful predictors, suggesting that these resources are the most easily converted into general repute for influence. As predicted, the number of resources that an elite member has is an especially powerful predictor of general influence—the zero-order correlation is almost as large as the multiple R for the eight resources.

Connectedness and Types of Resources

Another way of looking at community-level influence is to identify those people in the elite who are especially well-connected with others in the sense that they have short communication and interaction links (channels) to a high proportion of their fellow elite members. If they

---

[6] See Chapter 5, pp. 98–100, for a description of our measure of an elite member's influence rank.

As mentioned in Footnote 4, the most influential man is an extreme outlier in all variables discussed in Table 11.7, except the index of clientele bias. Since he would have unwarranted impact on these correlation coefficients, we have excluded him from the correlational analysis of the relevant variables.

wanted to get something done, they would presumably have better access to a larger range of relevant actors along with their associated resources than those who were less well-connected. Their roles in the elite would be those of coordinators and integrators (cf. Lawrence and Lorsch, 1967). In this case, we argue that causality runs in the opposite direction from that hypothesized for reputed influence—that is, a man's connectedness in the elite network generates certain types of resources. Two resources seem to be especially linked to an elite member's connectedness: good connections and reputation as an honorable broker. Public authority also seems to be linked to connectedness but, in this case, given the formal methods prescribed for moving into positions of authority, more as a cause of connectedness than as a result. That is, other actors orient themselves with respect to persons with decision-making authority and attempt to establish channels of access to and communication with such persons. The other resources seem to depend on links to more specialized institutional sources, such as the economic subsystem, as in the case of adaptive resources, or special interest groups in the general population. Consequently, these other resources should not be related to connectedness within the elite.

Using the graph theoretic approach discussed in Chapter 6 (pp. 102–105), we first computed the reachability of each elite member in each of the three elite networks of business–professional, social, and community affairs relations (cf. Harary et al., 1965: 159–193). For each elite member, we then calculated the proportion of the elite that he could reach in two or fewer steps along directed paths in each of the three networks. For instance, Herr Koenig, who had, not surprisingly, the highest reachability, could reach 91% of the elite in the community affairs network in two or fewer steps, while the man with the lowest reachability could reach only 20% of the elite. Columns 2, 3, and 4 present the zero-order correlations for abilities to reach others in each of the three networks and types of resources. As hypothesized, good connections is consistently correlated with reachability, and reputation as an honorable broker shows results reasonably consistent with our expectations. Thus, we have some support for our suggestion that good connections and reputation as an honorable broker are peculiarly integrative or coordinative resources that derive from the relational patterns in the elite.[7] Note that these are both *personal* resources (see Table 11.1) that are not easily transferred from one individual to another. Authority, contrary to our

---

[7] In addition, we calculated the multiple regression of each resource on the three types of reachability. Only the multiple Rs for good connections and honorable broker, .421 and .420, respectively, were signicant at the .05 level.

expectations, is correlated only with reachability in the business–professional network. We have no ready explanation for this lack of support for our speculations. All the other resources have nonsignificant correlations with reachabilities, as hypothesized. It is also worth noting here that the more resources a man controls, the higher is his reachability in the social and community affairs networks. That is, well-connected people tend to have more resources than poorly connected people.

The Activation of Influentials and Types of Resources

As a final effort to examine the relative efficacy of different types of resources in the community decision-making process, we turn to a consideration of their differential mobilization in the activation of specific influentials who were especially prominent in resolving specific community controversies. A persistent theme throughout our discussion has been the contention that different types of community issues require the mobilization of different types of resources for their resolution. This proposition implies that influentials possessing relevant influence resources in a given decision situation are more likely to become active in its resolution than those possessing less relevant resources. Chapter 9 discusses the rationale for selecting community issues for study according to their relevance to the four functional subsystems of the community and a description of the five issues selected for intensive study in Altneustadt.

The basic hypothesis guiding the following analysis is that, while authority must ultimately be brought to bear to implement a decision once it is made (and, thus, is likely to become activated regardless of the issue), an issue's functional locus will require the mobilization of resources appropriate to its functional sector (see Figure 11.1 schematization of hypothetical model). Thus, the mobilization of adaptive resources is especially likely in an economic issue since its resolution tends to have important implications for their subsequent distribution in the community. Persuasion resources *internal* to the elite, including good connections and honorable broker (see the earlier discussion regarding reachability in the elite and these resources), should be especially relevant to goal-attainment and integrative issues since they deal with the implementation and coordination of conflicting technical requirements and decisions. Moreover, special expert knowledge may need to be activated in executing specific policy decisions. Finally, pattern-maintenance issues are especially likely to arouse large populations groups outside the elite (e.g., Protestants versus Catholics, *Altbürger* versus *Neubürger*), as well as specialists having a particular stake in the issue outcome (e.g., educators on educational issues), over their "satisfactory" resolution (that is, in favor of a preferred value). In these issues, we would expect influence resources to be mobilized which filter external demands—specifically, the resources of the public mobilizer and influence over subgroups.

Before examining the evidence bearing on this guiding hypothesis, we must first describe the means by which we identified those influentials who actively participated in a given community controversy. Each respondent was asked at the beginning of the interview a series of questions about each issue, probing such matters as the individuals and groups he perceived to be most strongly in favor of or opposed to the issue, his own position on the issue and his degree of actual or likely participation in the decision process on the issue, and his estimate of the level of conflict over the issue and whether the conflict would be public or confined to the "inner circle" of community influentials. The names of the active participants, pro and con, were spontaneously generated by the respondents—the list of influentials we had identified was not presented until much later in the interview. In order to designate an influential as "activated on an issue," at least two respondents had to have spontaneously mentioned him as either an active proponent or opponent. This is a somewhat conservative rule (as compared to simply using self-reported activation on an issue), but we thought that it measured more accurately the underlying concept of elite activation.

Columns 5–9 of Table 11.7 provide the data relevant to examining our basic hypothesis. Note, first, that the hypothetical issues (Columns 5 and 9) reveal less pattern than the actual issues do (their multiple R's are insignificant too). This might well arise from the fact that the respondents had to "project" the probable behavior of their peers and, like social scientists, are not especially good at doing this. In both hypothetical issues, authority is not significantly activated (perhaps because neither issue came to an actual decision). In all of the issues that led to an actual collective decision, however, authority plays a very definite role, just as we hypothesized. Consistent with the pattern already noted in the other columns of the table, adaptive resources are not significantly activated on any issue—even in the case of the economic issue, industrial resettlement. Influence over subgroups, however, which obviously involved economic group claims on the polity in the economic issue, is significantly activated.

With respect to the goal-attainment and integrative issues (both of which were perceived by the elite as a whole as being nonpublic controversies confined to the elite itself), good connections, a persuasion resource within the elite, is activated in both cases, as hypothesized. The honorable broker plays a role only in the city hall issue, being unactivated in the community incorporation issue. Influence over subgroups was activated for the later issue probably because the CDU county leaders were basically opposed to the move as being inimical to their long-term power interests—they were losing a large chunk of their most reliable CDU voting bloc by the incorporation of a number of small villages into the city administrative unit. Needless to say, this was the principal reason why the dominant CDU city coalition was so anxious to arrange the incorporation. Special expert knowledge was involved in the city hall controversy because of some technical arguments about where to build the new city hall and its architectural design. In the case of the school issue (pattern maintenance), the two "filtering" resources (public mobilizer, influence over subgroups) and expert knowledge were significantly activated, as was the resource of public mobilizer in the case of the pop festival. We have no satisfactory explanation for why good connections, in both issues, and honorable broker, in the pop festival issue, were activated.

In fact, the good connections resource was activated in four of the five issues as well as being highly relevant to general reputation for influence, reachability in the three networks, and popular trust and esteem. This consistent pattern suggests that this integrative resource, contrary to our rationale for Table 11.1, is a highly generalized resource that is usefully employed in a wide range of contexts.

CONCLUSION

There are obvious limitations to the preceeding empirical analysis with respect to its bearing on the hypothetical model developed in the chapter's introduction. The most important limitation arises from the fact that all the data were gathered at one point in time (that is, the data support only a synchronic analysis); whereas the model itself contemplates a dynamic process in which a system of variables continuously *interact* with one another over time, often with lagged consequences (cf. Lieberson and O'Connor, 1972). It is true that the issues either were contested at different points in time over a 3–5 year period in a particular sequence (which in itself may have implications for how specific issues were resolved) or refer to hypothetical matters that have no time reference at all or, at best, refer to a future state of the system about which people may only speculate. Judgments regarding control over particular resources reflect cumulative historical judgments at one point in time and are subject to change, given the possibility that new issues might arise to modify them. Judgments concerning personal resources are especially subject to revision on the basis of experience with elite members' changing successes and failures. For instance, informal leaders of coalitions that enjoy a spectacular success or suffer a major defeat are likely to be evaluated differently regarding their personal resources. What is clearly needed to validate the process model are careful case studies of issues over time that take into account the temporal ordering of events and changing states of the resource positions of the relevant actors. Moreover, an explicit theory of the activation of elite members on an issue and the timing of their entry into an issue arena is needed. Despite these problems with the evidence in hand, we believe that the results do suggest the model's utility as an analytic framework.

12

The Interface between
Community and Elite*

SOME PRELIMINARY REMARKS

A central task of democratic political theory as a normative guideline
has been to specify a collective decision-making system that adequately
and responsively represents and articulates the wishes of the majority
of the community at the same time that it does not unduly neglect
minority rights and interests (cf. Lipset, 1959; Arrow, 1963; Dahl, 1956;
Olson, 1965; Cnudde and Neubauer, 1969). Utilizing these normative
prescriptions to evaluate the actual decision-making processes and outcomes in various societies, communities, and organizations, empirical research has revealed a number of obstacles to the realization of an ideal
democratic polity, however defined. Some investigators have stressed
obstacles rooted in the nature of mass publics themselves. For instance,
mass publics, being extensively differentiated with regard to awareness
of their short- and long-term "best interests," vary greatly in their
political knowledge and in their organizational competence to communi-

* This chapter has benefited from the helpful criticism of many colleagues at the
University of Chicago, including Morris Janowitz, William Wilson, Terry Clark,
Charles Bidwell, and James S. Coleman, as well as students, including Peter
Marsden, Michael Burowoy, and Terrence Halliday. Participants of the *Fakultäts-
seminar* (winter, 1974–1975) of the social science department of the Universität
Mannheim have also provided very useful critiques.

cate their demands to the "core" decision-making system (cf. Michels, 1959; Almond and Verba, 1963; Lipset *et al.*, 1956). Other writers have stressed the structural arrangements of the decision-making system itself that make it more or less responsive to the varied conflicting interests of the public at large (cf. Mills, 1959; Hunter, 1953; Parsons, 1960; Kornhauser, 1959; Clark, 1968a). Still others have debated the proper role of elected representatives responsible for making collective decisions with respect to how they should act in response to the demands of their electoral constituencies (cf. Chapman, 1967).

Whether explicitly acknowledged or not, every research problem has a corresponding set of theoretical assumptions. If one assumes, for example, that elite systems are essentially determined by social structural givens, as a crude Marxist model would have it, then studying the connections between population groups and elite members would appear to be quite unimportant when compared to the problem of identifying the interest and power differentiation derived from the "objective" social structure. Similarly, if one assumes that the one-sided manipulative capacity of the elite itself is the key factor in accounting for policy outcomes, as in a simple Pareto–Mosca-like model of the circulation of elites, then the question of the interface of the elite and the population under its control is again of minor concern. The linkage problem arises only if one is prepared to impute autonomous internal dynamics to both the population and its elite subsystems and, further, to postulate some sort of reciprocal or mutual interdependence of both subsystems in accounting for collective decision outcomes (cf. Aron, 1950). As an empirically grounded perspective, democratic political theory (cf. Cnudde and Neubauer, 1969) clearly implies the last set of assumptions.

Unfortunately, this perspective has not been sufficiently developed to permit the formulation of many interesting, empirically testable propositions concerning the elite–population interface. As a result, biases in the elite system in articulating, coordinating, and implementing the population's manifest and latent demands for collective action cannot be assessed empirically. (For a notable exception, see Miller and Stokes, 1961.) Lacking an empirical basis for determining elite biases in decision making with respect to community preferences, many investigators have turned to their own, often unspecified, normative preferences in evaluating collective decisions (e.g., Hunter, 1953; Mills, 1959). In this final empirically based chapter, we, therefore, have relatively little theoretical guidance to help us in exploring some of these issues and must, as a result, be even more eclectic and exploratory in our approach than before, taking hints wherever we may find them.

As sources for these hints, we have already turned to both functional and conflict theorists to help us specify the structural bases of the community differentiation of interests in collective action. The so-called conflict theorists, usually Marxian in inspiration, have stressed economic relationships and transactions as the ultimate sources of conflicting interests (cf. Giddens, 1973). Functionalists, on the other hand, while not denying the significance of economically based interests, have stressed, in addition, other sources of differences in basic value commitments in the population that arise out of occupational, religious, ethnic, racial, or even generational group differences. What we have learned in Part I has hopefully clarified the social structural and value differentiation of the community at large in a manner that borrows from both schools of thought. The close analysis of the elite decision-making system in Part II should have given us some notion of the internal structure and functioning of this subsystem. It now remains for us to juxtapose these two levels of analysis to discover what they may illuminate about the structure of their interface. While the discussion will again be couched in terms of Altneustadt's interface, we will, of course, be following our now familiar strategy of using the case study to illustrate theoretical and methodological propositions of more general applicability.

The reader, however, should be alerted to several important limitations in the following analysis. First, remember that the community and elite subsystems are at quite disparate levels of analysis, the macrostructural and microstructural levels, respectively. Our characterizations of the community's social and value structures rest on sample data that have been statistically manipulated to estimate differential likelihoods of members of various *population subgroups* being associated with one another in bonds of friendship and intimacy or having similar or discrepant profiles of value preferences. The elite structures, in contrast, are based on enumerations of the linkages among almost all members of the elite population universe. The criterion of inclusion for the community sample is random selection from the population of eligible voters in a defined territory, while the criteria for inclusion in the elite population is a complex amalgam of incumbency in top-level authority positions of consequential corporate actors and reputations for influence in community decision making, yielding an enumeration of the entire population universe. Not surprisingly, the organizing principles of structural differentiation in the two subsystems, while remarkably alike in some aspects, do differ in fundamental respects. In the community structure, for example, class–prestige and residence–religion appear to channel friendship choices and value similarities among population subgroups. On the other hand, linkages among elite members are formed more in accordance with the elite's differing functional responsibilities as leaders in various community sectors or as mediators between them. (Recall our earlier discussion of the principles of integrative centrality and sectoral differentiation in the elite subsystem.)

Perhaps more important, one should remember that, properly speaking, the interface between community and elite is in a continuous process of adaptation and change. Elite members can "move" closer to or farther apart from given population subgroups as a result of their behavior in critical issue episodes which make them more or less visible to the population at large. Moreover, hotly contested public controversies may engender greater "group consciousness" among population subgroups regarding their preferred outcomes, thus inducing them to be more attracted or repulsed by elite members who publicly express acceptable or unacceptable views. Our data, being gathered at one point in time, necessarily arrest this process in mid-career and can, therefore, be used only as a crude estimate of the precipitate of a highly idiosyncratic historical process of unknown duration that is compounded of a sequence of collective events (i.e., community–elite transactions) in the more or less recent past. In other words, we do not know how long a critical community controversy can remain as a formative base for structuring the interface. Nor do we know the extent to which the occurrence of a new community controversy, with all of its attendant particularities of community and elite mobilization and polarization, will induce fundamental transformations of the interface.

Our predicament in studying the interface, however, may not be as awkward as these remarks imply. To the extent that the community has been subjected to a stable agenda of recurrent conflicts and resolutions, we should expect to find some stability in the relative attractions and repulsions of elite members and population subgroups. The more these recurrent conflicts and "definitive resolutions" are rooted in the basic structural differentiation of the community at large, the more we can expect leadership to have crystalized around the contending poles of the axes of cleavage, and the more perdurable or stable the structure of the resulting interface will be over time. From what we know about Altneustadt's history of community controversy over the past 10 to 15 years, it seems reasonable to assume that the interface we shall be depicting for the recent past reflects a pattern that would not differ appreciably from a "snapshot" of the interface made some years earlier (if it were available). The reasonableness of this assumption will, we hope, be justified in the following analysis.

THE SOCIAL STRUCTURE OF THE
COMMUNITY–ELITE INTERFACE

An Analytic Rationale: The Bases of Elite
Attractiveness to Population Subgroups

Our general objective is to represent *both* elite members *and* population subgroups in the *same social space* such that the relative distances among individuals and groups will be a monotonic function of the relative degree of popular trust and support accorded individual elite members by specific population subgroups. Note that, in contrast to our previous structural analyses of the community and elite social spaces that assumed a fundamental symmetry or mutuality in choice behavior, we shall be viewing the interface structure asymmetrically—that is, from the vantage point of population subgroups' "approach" or "avoidance" orientations toward individual elite members. We must do this because the source of our data is the community sample's reports of whom they trust and turn to for advice from a list of the top 27 influentials in the community (see Chapter 11, pp. 203–204, for the questions used). An equally interesting question would also view the interface structure asymmetrically, but from the vantage point of individual elite members, indicating those population elements toward which they feel a special sympathy, attachment, and responsibility or from which they expect electoral support. Unfortunately, we have no adequate data to undertake this latter enterprise systematically even though we will be able to make some fairly strong inferences about elite members' probable orientations to specific population subgroups. For the purposes of this chapter we shall confine the analysis to treating individual elite members as complex stimuli that holistically serve to attract or repulse tenders of trust and popular support from specific population subgroups.

Before the discussion becomes too abstract, let us introduce the specific procedures employed to generate our model of the interface structure, together with their concrete application in Altneustadt. We can then return to the more general discussion with a concrete model in mind.

The original data for this analysis consisted of a 9-by-27 matrix of choices of 27 elite members made by 9 population subgroups in the cross-section sample. Cell entries represented sums of mentions of elite members made by respondents in answers to three questions intended to discover those members of the elite to whom people would turn for aid and advice in dealing with a personal or community-related problem. Since we were not concerned either with the fact that individual elite members differed in their popularity (i.e., some were chosen by many people in the population while others were infrequently chosen) or that the nine population subgroups differed considerably in size, but only in the "relative proximity" of each member of the elite to each of the subgroups, we eliminated these row and column effects by the following procedure.[1]

Since natural logarithms were to be used in adjusting the cell frequencies, zero cells were first eliminated by adding a constant (0.5) to all cell entries. The adjusted cell entries, d_{ij}, were then computed according to the following formula:

$$d_{ij} = ln_{ij} - ln_{i.} - ln_{.j} + ln_{..},$$

where ln_{ij} is the natural log of the original cell entry (plus the constant), $ln_{i.}$ and $ln_{.j}$ are the averages of the row and column logs, and $ln_{..}$ is the average of logs in the entire table.

These adjusted cell entries, which may be taken to estimate the relative "attraction" or "avoidance" in a given elite member–population subgroup combination, were the basic data submitted to a smallest space analysis–partitioned (monotone distance analysis–partitioned unconditional) computer routine developed by Louis Guttman and James C. Lingoes (cf. Lingoes, 1969; 1972: 57, 59–60; 1973, especially Sections 2.0 and 6.0). This procedure is designed to analyze matrices partitioned into two sets of components (objects and attributes or, in our case, population subgroups and elite members), given intraclass relationships among subgroups and elite members, and interclass relationships between subgroups and elite members. These three sets of relations need not be in similar units; the procedure seeks to maintain order only within each of the three sets of relations in placing the subgroups and elite members in a joint space.

Imagine a 36-by-36 matrix in which the 27 elite members and 9 population subgroups are arranged along the rows and columns, as shown in Figure 12.1. Initially we use our adjusted 9-by-27 basic data matrix for the off-diagonal rectangular submatrix. We must now estimate the entries for the elite members' and population subgroups' triangular submatrices. There are several ways in which this may be done. One way is to use the information about the informal social relations among the elite members (see Chapter 6, pp. 105–118) in order to estimate their proximities to one another and, in turn, to use information on how members of the population subgroups chose friends across the subgroups (see

[1] We are indebted to Professor Shelby J. Haberman, Department of Statistics, University of Chicago, for his advice in designing this procedure for constructing the input data matrix. Peter Marsden, our research assistant, was responsible for executing the analysis.

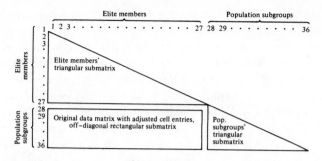

Figure 12.1 The input matrix for the structure of the interface.

Chapter 3) to estimate the group proximities. While this tactic brings three highly disparate sets of information into one system of analysis, comparable units between the three submatrices are unnecessary since the scaling procedure compares entries within submatrices only.

An alternative procedure, which we adopted, is to regard groups as proximate to the extent that they approach similar sets of elite members and to regard elite members as proximate to the extent that they are approached by similar sets of "client" subgroups. This involves estimating the entries for the two triangular submatrices by calculating association coefficients, first, for all pairs of individuals across the nine population subgroups to obtain entries for the elite members' submatrix, and, second, for all pairs of population subgroups across elite individuals to obtain entries for the population subgroups' submatrix. In other words, the entries for the two submatrices are estimated from information contained in the off-diagonal rectangular submatrix. The computer then places the objects and attributes (population subgroups and elite members) in a joint Euclidean space in which all scaled proximities are in a common metric. In estimating goodness of fit to the original rank ordering, however, only comparisons within submatrices are made. We obtain measures for goodness of fit within each of the submatrices as well as an overall coefficient of alienation.

It is desirable, for both procedural and substantive purposes, that the final solution be one in which subgroups and individuals are intermingled in the space, rather than separated from one another. Solutions in which the objects and attributes are separated are regarded as degenerate by Lingoes (1969). Our original attempt to use the routine, using the adjusted basic data matrix for the off-diagonal rectangular submatrix and product–moment correlations as the association coefficients in the triangular submatrices, resulted in such a degenerate solution. That is, the elite members were tightly clustered in a small central region of the space, while the population subgroups were scattered along the periphery of the space at considerable distances from the central region. Consequently, it was necessary to simplify the input data to allow somewhat more freedom in rescaling the entries by the program. This was done as follows: Within the off-diagonal submatrix, all entries greater than the mean were regarded as "approaches" to an elite member and given value "1," while all entries less than the mean were given value "0," signifying "avoidances." In addition, normalized agreement scores (common element product–moment correlation coefficients) were used as the association coefficients in the triangular submatrices. Lingoes (1969) shows that this coefficient is the one for which nondegenerate solutions are most frequently attained. These modifications in the data matrices do involve some loss of precision in input figures but have the advantage of producing the desired interspersing of population subgroups among the elite members.

Table 12.1 summarizes the results of fitting the latter data matrix into two- and three-dimensional solutions. It is clear that the three-dimensional solution, portrayed in Figure 12.2 fits the input data much better than the two-dimensional one does. It will, therefore, be used as our estimated model of the structure of the interface.

To facilitate reading the figure, we have underlined the population subgroups. We shall consider the relative distances of the elite members from each of these "fixed points." The names of individual elite members should, of course, be familiar to all of us by now. Elite individuals who were overchosen by a given population subgroup will be located relatively closer to that group than elite individuals who were underchosen

Table 12.1

Measures of Goodness of Fit for the Two- and Three-Dimensional Solutions for the Structure of the Interface

Guttman–Lingoes K values	Number of dimensions[a]	
	Two	Three
Between groups and individuals	.156	.067
Within groups	.173	.084
Within individuals	.195	.099
Overall coefficient of alienation	.176	.087

[a] The overall coefficient of alienation for the one-dimensional solution was .343, placing it clearly outside the range of acceptable solutions.

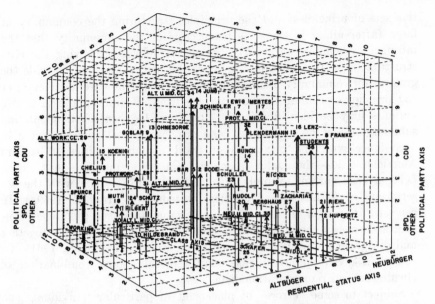

Figure 12.2 Three-dimensional representation of the community–elite interface, based on a monotone distance analysis, partitioned unconditional, coefficient of alienation = .087.

(or avoided) by that group, subject to the constraints simultaneously imposed by the pattern of choices of all the other groups. Persons over-chosen by all groups—that is, individuals who are universally trusted and esteemed—will tend to be located toward the center of the space. In fact, this pattern apparently did not occur in Altneustadt since there are no persons falling in the central region of the space. Working in a three-dimensional space is never an especially easy task, but the reader is urged to take a moment to familiarize himself with the overall structure because it will considerably ease following the discussion. In visualizing the space, it may help to think of a fat horseshoe with the *Neubürger* upper middle class at one of the open ends, the curved extreme, the hank of the horseshoe, passing through the *Altbürger* working class, and the *Altbürger* upper middle class at the other open end of the horseshoe.

What, however, are the organizing principles that determine (or may be used to interpret) the structure of the interface between community and elite? The fact that both the elite and the community are themselves highly differentiated internally in no way implies that there should be a high correspondence between their respective structures in the interface, especially in view of their different principles of organization. The structure of the interface may be organized according to at least three alternative sets of principles: *(1)* the principles structuring the community at large (after all, it is from the perspective of the community that the interface is being constructed); *(2)* the principles organizing the elite structure (since the functional organization of the elite may provide the grounds for community members targeting on specific elite members); or *(3)* principles peculiar to the interface itself. Regarding the last, two variants may be identified in the literature. In *clientelism,* population subgroups target on individuals who dispense special private favors in accordance with the principles of ward machine politics in certain American cities—the Daley Regular Democratic machine in Chicago being a good current example (cf. O'Connor, 1975) along with the descriptions of African urban political systems (cf. Mitchell, 1969a). In *representationalism,* on the other hand, value and issue preference congruence bring a population subgroup and its elite representatives together and disagreement pushes them apart (cf. Miller and Stokes, 1961). Of course, a given empirical case may represent some combination of clientelism and representationalism.

Subject to some "errors" of placement of particular individuals and groups, the space is organized around three broad axes. The first axis rather neatly divides the points between *Altbürger* and *Neubürger* regions, while the second axis, running at an oblique angle to the first, appears to be a socioeconomic class axis. (Recall that length of residence and class status are, in fact, correlated in this community, which may account for the fact that the two axes are obliquely rather than orthogonally related.) The third axis divides the points according to political party preference, with CDU-oriented persons and groups being in the upper region and SPD-oriented persons and groups tending toward the lower regions of the space. Subsequent sections will adduce more systematic evidence in support of this interpretation of the dimensional structure of the space.

The general strategy for the following analysis derives, in part, from the one employed in Chapter 8, where the unit of analysis was the interpoint distances among elite members and we proposed a causal model accounting for the relative locations of persons in the elite community affairs influence structure. Here, however, due to the asymmetric nature of the original data, we shall attempt to predict the relative distances of individual elite members from each of the nine population subgroups on the basis of two distinctive but complementary "theories" of the bases of elite attractiveness to population subgroups. The first theory takes into account certain personal attributes of individual elite members, such as their functional positions in the elite, value preferences, and memberships in particular population subgroups, while the second theory considers issue preference congruence, which provides a more proximate basis of elite attractiveness to population subgroups.

Our strategy will generate two sets of nine multiple regression equations, each set referring to a particular theory and each equation to a particular population subgroup. Two kinds of questions may be answered with these sets of "structural equations." First, examining each set of equations, we can ascertain their bearing on one or another of the organizing principles that account for the structure of the interface. Second, focusing more closely on the equations for specific population subgroups, we can ask if the groups differ in the degree to which they manifest different mechanisms (i.e., organizing principles) for structuring their approach to leadership personnel. For example, do relatively unassimilated population subgroups (that is, out-groups) manifest special sensitivity to elite members most like themselves in social structural locations, value preferences, and issue positions? Or, do more assimilated or integrated groups follow less special interest group- or issue-oriented mechanisms and express more generalized or undifferentiated confidence or trust in the leadership group as a whole (and, consequently, manifest low coefficients of determination for predicting interface distances from such variables)?

While we cannot empirically evaluate the following comprehensive model with the data in hand, Figure 12.3 causally specifies the formative process of the community—elite interface, representing a synthetic model of the bases of elite attractiveness to population subgroups and, conversely, the bases of population subgroup attractiveness to individual elite members (cf. Miller and Stokes, 1961, for a less elaborated view of the underlying process). A complete model would specify two analytically distinguishable submodels. Model a' is what we can evaluate with our data—it predicts elite members' distance from population subgroups using information about elite members' structural location in the elite, value orientations, and issue preferences. Looking at it from the vantage point of individual elite members, model b' would attempt to account for

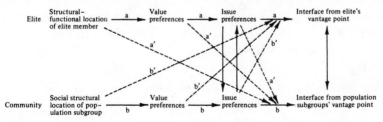

Figure 12.3 A causal model of the process of formation of the community–elite interface.

the population subgroups' distances from given elite members. (Note that, in our case, this would have involved 27 equations based on 9 population subgroups.) There is no a priori reason to assume that the interface distances would be identical or even approximately equivalent when estimated from these two disparate perspectives on the interface. One might, of course, propose a number of theoretical reasons to expect them to converge over time.

To be sure, the two submodels are not of equal substantive or normative importance. In a democratic polity, it is model a', in which popular support is mobilized around specific elite members who will attempt to implement or at least articulate subgroup preferences that is normatively important, rather than model b's concern with the extent to which elite members can mobilize population subgroups for their own purposes.

Here it is worth making a final observation about Figure 12.3. While one might expect, following Converse (1964), the elite model a (social structural location → value preference → issue position) (see Chapter 8) to have a higher predictiveness (coefficient of determination) than the community's model b (see Chapter 4) because of the elite's presumptively stronger constraints on their ideological belief systems and higher levels of measurement reliability, neither submodel differs in its basic causal mechanism. In other words, both the community and the elite subsystems are assumed to be parts of the same social system at least insofar as the mechanisms for translating structural locations into preferred issue outcomes are concerned. The causal mechanisms coming into play at the level of issue preferences, however, can be expected to differ between the elite and the community at large. Elite members attempt to influence the issue positions of population subgroups and other elite members and, in turn, are influenced by their perceptions of majority opinion in their support groups (cf. Miller and Stokes, 1961; Cnudde and Mc-Crone, 1966), as well as by the behavior of their fellow elite members. Population groups become attracted or repulsed by public acts of elite members. One should not forget, however, that a member of a population subgroup who becomes sufficiently aroused over an issue to attempt to influence its outcome by personal acts of leadership, such as by deciding to run for the school board, has moved, by definition, across the fluid line dividing the population from its elite.

Social Structural and Value Bases of Elite
Attractiveness to Population Subgroups

Turning first to a consideration of our theory of the social structural and value bases of elite attractiveness to population subgroups, we are faced with an embarrassment of riches. We possess an enormous amount of information about each influential from which we must select only those pieces of information that best represent our theoretical variables. The relatively small case base of 27 individuals imposes severe limits on the degrees of freedom in the multiple regression equations and generates considerable unreliability in estimating correlations among variables. Consequently, a "data-dredging" operation in which we search through all the possible indicators, or even a limited number of possible indicators, of an influential's social structural positions or value preferences to find the "best" ones (i.e., those that best predict interface distances) is inappropriate because it is likely to generate purely artifactual results by capitalizing on "chance" relationships. We have, therefore, followed the more scientifically defensible strategy of picking variables for which there is reasonably strong a priori theoretical justification, without regard to their observed correlations in the case study. The results reported later are, thus, likely to be conservative in providing support for the proposed theory.

With regard to indicators of functional position in the elite collective decision-making system, we decided to use two measures: incumbency in a top civil authority post and SPD party preference (both coded as dichotomous variables). Many observers of the German scene (e.g., Almond and Verba, 1963; Dahrendorf, 1967) have commented that the Germans place considerable trust and confidence in civil bureaucracies and their functionaries to resolve fairly and expeditiously their complaints and dissatisfactions with community affairs, as compared to people in other countries. Americans, for example, seem to believe that, at least on local matters, some extrabureaucratic clout is necessary to resolve issues to their satisfaction. This observation, if true, would imply that Germans, especially those of the lower classes who possess few other alternatives, would "target" on persons with public authority to solve many communal problems. As our other indicator of functional position in the elite, SPD party preference identifies the rival coalition in the elite that is most likely to be especially responsive to the needs of relatively unassimilated population subgroups and, thus, likely to intercede on their behalf.[2] Moreover, it determines the valence or direction of preferred outcomes by elite members on a whole complex of issues in which the population at large is also likely to have varying degrees of vested interest.

[2] Leadership positions in economic and pattern-maintenance organizations were other possible functional bases for attracting popular support. We could not examine all these variables simultaneously because of the technical limitations of the aforementioned data base. In an analysis not reported here that included these variables in place of the authority and party measure, however, we found no evidence of their substantial involvement in structuring the interface.

The crucial variable in the proposed model, however, is perhaps the relative social distances between the population subgroup to which a given influential belongs and the other population subgroups in the community. For a variety of reasons, one would expect the relative proximity of an influential's population subgroup to others to affect his relative attractiveness and accessibility. Certainly his own group should feel attracted to him on the grounds of shared social characteristics and, in addition, should enjoy the competitive advantage of being able to use relatively short channels (paths) of the informal social network to approach him, when compared to other groups. (Recall that we partially defined population subgroups in Part I in terms of their higher frequencies of group self-selection in informal relations.) Conversely, as population subgroups become less and less accessible to one another through informal ties, following the distance-generating mechanisms postulated in Part I, individuals in the respective groups should become less and less accessible to one another via informal social networks and shared social characteristics.

Social distance between groups was measured by referring to the results portrayed in Figure 3.2 of Chapter 3, which presented the social structure of 38 religiously and class-defined subgroups. Since only nine subgroups are of concern here, the groups' interpoint distances were recomputed for the collapsed set of groups. Each influential was then assigned to one of the nine subgroups, and the distance of his membership group to all the others was then calculated. Note that an influential's social structural location is simultaneously defined in terms of his religious preference and his occupational class, reflecting the basic axes of structural differentiation in the community at large.

Finally, we were interested in determining elite members' general value orientations because they presumably provide broad guidelines for participation in community affairs. The correlations between a man's social structural location and his value preferences are modest at best because there are so many factors, rooted in both social and personal history, that are involved in the formation of a person's position. To the extent that an influential's involvement in community affairs reflects value positions actually shared with particular population subgroups, regardless of their objective social distance from him, members of these groups can be expected to be attracted to him. One need only think of an influential from an upper-class group, who identifies, for whatever reasons, with the needs and aspirations of the working class and works to further these interests, to see the possibilities of values being an independent basis of attraction of group support.

A recurrent theme throughout the book has been the two principal axes of cleavage in the community, including differences in pattern-maintenance values and differences in socioeconomic class values. To determine these differences in value orientations, we selected an indicator of a man's commitment to traditional family values and a measure of his economic ideology, specifically, his support or opposition to co-determination of workers in management decision making in economic organizations. The traditionalism measures that we used were identical in both the community and elite surveys, while the measures of economic ideology contain items that differ between the two surveys. We had not asked the general population about their views on co-determination, but we had assessed their positive attitudes toward unions and employers. These latter attitudes are known to be fairly highly correlated with views on co-determination.

Table 12.2 presents the results of our effort to predict the relative proximities of elite members to particular population subgroups from information on the elite members. In order to provide a basis for predicting at least the direction (i.e., sign of the coefficient) of relationships between the predictor variables and the dependent variable of interface distance, we have provided, in Panel A of Table 12.2, comparative information on the political and value preferences of the population subgroups and the population as a whole (see Chapter 4 also). To illustrate its use, consider the first row of Panel A. The Protestant and *Altbürger* working class, Protestant lower middle class, *Neubürger* middle and upper middle class, and the students were disproportionately likely to vote for the SPD in the last city election in comparison to the population at large and the other groups. We should, therefore, expect these groups to be positively associated (i.e., closer or more attracted) to SPD members of the elite than the other groups which, on the contrary, should manifest negative associations with (or greater distance from) SPD influentials. Similar predictions can be extrapolated from the other rows in the panel. Social closeness (i.e., objective social distance between an influential's membership group and the other population subgroups) should be positively associated with interface distance for every group.

Panel B gives the zero-order, product–moment correlations of the elite's characteristics with interface distances to the respective groups, while Panel C presents the beta coefficients in the multiple regression equations for the respective groups, including the five independent variables simultaneously. The beta coefficients provide a rough estimate of the relative importance of each predictor variable in predicting interface distance, net of the effects of the other four variables.

What criteria, however, should be used to evaluate the substantive and statistical significance of these coefficients? Conventional tests of statis-

TABLE 12.2

Predicting Proximities of Population Groups and Elite Members According to their Structural Positions and General Value Orientations

Population attribute (A) or elite characteristic (B,C)	Prot. work. cl.	Alt. work. cl.	Alt. lo. mid.	Alt. mid. mid.	Prot. mid. mid.	Neu. mid. mid.	Alt. up. mid.	Neu. up. mid.	Students	Total population
A. Percentage SPD vote in last city election and mean value orientations of population groups										
Percentage SPD vote	62	57	46	22	52	65	24	62	67	49
Economic ideology favoring unions[a]	.66	.42	−.06	−1.12	.16	.56	−2.63	1.52	1.68	.10
Family traditionalism[b]	1.80	.88	−.64	.64	−.98	−2.09	−1.62	−4.15	−6.73	−.59
B. Characteristics of elite members predicting proximity to a population group (zero-order correlation)										
Authority[c]	+.32	+.20	−.02	−.05	+.05	−.34	+.29	−.27	−.07	Inapp.
SPD party member[d]	+.02	−.31	−.11	−.35	+.05	+.01	−.48**	+.52**	−.31	Inapp.
Social closeness[e]	+.07	+.67**	+.38*	+.61**	−.34	+.25	+.47**	+.74**	+.35	Inapp.
For co-determination[f]	−.18	−.36	+.03	−.19	−.18	+.36	−.57**	+.54**	−.12	Inapp.
Family traditionalism[g]	−.34	−.32	−.26	−.12	+.16	+.29	−.21	+.27	+.20	Inapp.

*p < .05; **p < .01, two-tailed test

C. Characteristics of elite members predicting proximity to a population group (beta weights)

Authority[c]	+.17	+.02	−.12	−.16	+.11	−.23	+.04	−.13	−.07	Inapp.
SPD party member[d]	+.46	−.01	−.09	−.18	+.28	−.48	+.16	+.24	−.34	Inapp.
Social closeness[e]	−.04	+.60*	+.43	+.62*	−.39	+.22	+.35	+.62*	+.32	Inapp.
For co-determination[f]	−.33	−.08	+.38	+.18	−.53	+.56	−.55	+.05	+.08	Inapp.
Family traditionalism[g]	−.33	−.14	−.32	−.03	+.22	+.22	+.08	−.01	+.40	Inapp.
Multiple R^2	.23	.48*	.27	.41	.28	.40	.40	.65*	.29	Inapp.

$*p < .05$, two-tailed test

a See Chapter 4, pp. 77–79.

b See Chapter 4, pp. 77–79.

c Elite members with authority are defined as incumbents of the highest, full-time public administrative positions.

d SPD party members includes only those elite members who stated that they were members of the Social Democratic Party.

e A social distance space for the cross-section sample was calculated, considering occupational and religious characteristics simultaneously. (See Chapter 3, pp. 64–69, for the rationale for this procedure and the results of the analysis.) Elite members were assigned to group locations in this space according to their occupation and religious preference. The social closeness measure used here indicates the distances of the 27 elite members' group locations from a given "target" population group. For example, let us consider the *Altbürger* upper middle class as the target group. Herr Koenig is a member of the *Altbürger* upper middle class; consequently, his distance from that group is "0." Herr Dr. Zacharias, a scientist at the Natural Science Research Center, is in the *Neubürger* upper middle class. His distance from the *Altbürger* upper middle class is equal to the distance of his population group from the *Altbürger* upper middle class—in this case, a considerable distance.

f See S24, Appendix C.

g See Chapter 6, p. 120.

tical significance are clearly inappropriate here because complex interdependencies within the interface distance measure itself violate a key assumption in regression analysis (see also Footnote 4, Chapter 8). In addition, we must be cautious in comparing coefficients because of the small case base and the correspondingly limited degrees of freedom in fitting the data to the regression model. Our interest in this exploratory investigation, however, does not involve making unbiased estimates of the values of specific coefficients. Rather, we want to detect theoretically interesting overall patterns in the results. To avoid short-circuiting the analysis with overly stringent requirements at this preliminary stage, we propose to use the relatively arbitrary cut-off point of .30 as the minimum value of a coefficient as being of substantive interest. (Note that this cut-off point is fairly close to the minimum zero-order correlation for passing a two-tailed test at the .05 level of significance.) We have drawn boxes around the coefficients in Panel C that meet this criterion of substantive significance and are consistent with the direction (sign) of the relationship predicted from Panel A. Italicized coefficients meet the criterion but are *inconsistent* with the predicted sign of the relationship—that is, they are inconsistent with our theoretical expectations.

Having completed these preliminaries, what can we learn from Table 12.2? First, it is readily apparent that social closeness in both panels B and C is overwhelmingly the "best" predictor of the relative proximities of elite members to the population groups. Only one group, the Protestant lower middle class, has a coefficient inconsistent with our theoretical expectations, in the sense that its members appear to be targeting on elite members who are most distant to them in the objective social structure of the community and to be avoiding elite members recruited from more proximate groups.

Let us consider the inconsistent and nonsignificant coefficients more closely. The Protestant working class and the *Neubürger* middle middle class show no consistent patterning with respect to social closeness (i.e., their coefficients fail to meet our criterion of substantive significance). Recall that no elite member comes from either of these groups, nor, for that matter, from the Protestant lower middle class. Consequently, they must necessarily rely on leaders recruited from groups structurally distant from them to represent their interests in collective elite decision making, if, indeed, their interests are to be represented at all in such deliberations. They are also precisely those groups most marginally integrated into the community social structure. In fact, most of the coefficients that are inconsistent with our theoretical expectations deal with these groups and the students, the other marginally integrated group in the community. In other words, these groups are the most likely to target on precisely those elite members who are most apt to diverge from the groups' preferred value and political stances. What better indication of their structural marginality to—indeed alienation from—the collective decision-making processes of the community could we find? Here we have a clue to the misrepresentation and aggregation biases against certain popular interests in the elite system at a particular point of time. These are the "stress points" in the interface structure (cf. Merton, 1957) where we would expect the greatest sources of popular strain and dissatisfaction with how community affairs are handled and the greatest likelihood of equilibrating readjustments or realignments of the elite–population subgroup interface distances over time to achieve a structure more consistent with the groups' preferred outcomes.

In short, we are arguing that our theoretical model can be used to identify some of the conditions for a stable interface and, where they are systematically violated (as they are in the case of these groups), the directions in which re-equilibration is likely to proceed. Of course, if the groups in question are of such small size that they can play no significant electoral role and/or lack other resources with which to reward or punish the elite leadership, such structural inconsistencies may persist indefinitely. Members of the excluded groups may, of course, exercise other response options, including generalized political apathy and indifference to community affairs and low subjective identification with the community. We shall return to a discussion of these alternative responses later.

Rather surprisingly, authority plays no significant role in structuring the interface. It is true that the two working-class groups show some tendency toward targeting on top civil authority figures in Panel B, but the beta coefficients in Panel C indicate that, once the effects of the other variables are controlled, there is no significant structuring effect. Even more surprising, given the many reasons one could adduce for expecting party preference to provide important cues to population groups in their selection of "appropriate" elite leaders, there is only one consistent coefficient for the Protestant working class, but two inconsistent ones for the *Neubürger* middle middle class and the students, with the rest indicating no structuring effect worthy of consideration.

The two value measures do appear to have some explanatory power in accounting for the interface structure, but somewhat more often in directions that are inconsistent with our theoretical expectations. Class values have somewhat stronger structuring effects than pattern-maintenance values, but we should hasten to add that their relative strength may depend significantly on the particular value indicators we happened to select for analysis. More generally, we again have evidence that our marginal groups are poorly served by their selection of elite members in whom to place their trust and esteem.

On a more speculative level, let us turn for a moment to a comparison of the population groups' responsiveness to differences in elite members' value stances. The groups obviously differ considerably among themselves regarding their commitments to the SPD, conservative economic ideology, and family traditionalism. Another strategy immediately suggests itself for assessing the degree to which relative levels of popular commitment to a particular party or value stance predict the patterning of the community–elite interface. Our reasoning here is that the more a particular group expresses support for a given political party, for example, the more strongly it should orient itself toward elite members sharing that party preference. Conversely, the more the group eschews such party affiliation, the more it should avoid elite members holding that preference. Accordingly, we can calculate the rank-order correlation (Spearman's *rho*) between the row entries in Panel A concerning population groups with the corresponding row entries in Panel B concerning the interface correlations. The following *rho*s were obtained: *(1)* .46 (n.s.) between the percentage SPD vote among population groups and the correlation of elite SPD membership and interface distance; *(2)* .61 ($p < .05$) between the mean economic ideology favoring unions and the correlation of elite support for co-determination and interface distance; and *(3)* −.85 ($p < .01$) between the mean family traditionalism and interface distance. Although the first two *rho*s are in the expected direction, the last *rho*, while statistically significant, is exactly contrary to our expectations. This means that population groups low on family traditionalism are overselecting elite members who express strong support for traditional family values. What can we make of these conflicting results?

In modern societies, personal values regarding family life are usually seen as peculiarly "private" ones, outside the legitimate limits of public comment and sanction. How a man would ideally prefer to deal with his wife is not a matter of high public visibility. A man's economic ideology, especially if he is a member of the elite, is much more likely to become politically salient and relevant in various public controversies. The population's failure to target on leaders sharing their family values is, perhaps, to be explained in terms of the low public communication and politicalization normally associated with such values. But these values do, in fact, play a highly significant role in certain public controversies surrounding pattern-maintenance values. For instance, they are highly associated with preferred outcomes on the pop festival issue. When such relatively novel and nonrecurrent issues arise, the elite–community interface appears to be especially out of joint, and they are likely to lead to popular dissatisfaction with "their" leadership personnel who have suddenly shown "their true colors." The malaise will be general as the "liberated" upper middle class will regard "their" leaders as too conservative on the issue, while the more conservative lower classes will find "their" leaders to be too liberated for their tastes. It is under such circumstances of considerable popular agitation and concern about a pattern-maintenance issue that we might expect extensive reorganization of the elite–community interface. In our case study, for example, these two value stances of economic ideology and family values are negatively associated among the population groups but positively associated among individual elite members. Consequently, the community "picks" the "right" elite people on class-based issues but the "wrong" elite people on pattern-maintenance issues. This is the structural base for the inherent dynamism (or structural contradiction, in Marxian terms) of the elite–community interface—it is on these grounds that we find uneasy alliances and strange bedfellows.

In short, it may be useful to postulate the existence of a multiplicity of "latent" values that distinguish population groups and elite members and that have only potential and episodic relevance in structuring the interface. The degree of social coherence on a multidimensional set of values, both within individuals and among groups, is remarkably low for a variety of reasons (cf. Converse, 1964), and specific issues may serve to activate only one or another of these dimensions sequentially. Such a model implies that what would be a perfectly appropriate set of influentials for a population group to favor, given the value and interest-based nature of recent community controversies, may suddenly become highly inappropriate and ineffective when an issue arises that appeals to an entirely different basis in the "latent" value structures of the community and elite subsystems. If the community confronts an agenda of issues that activate different positions on economic ideology in a stable and recurrent pattern, its interface with the elite should eventually reflect rather faithfully the corresponding differentiation of elite and community. The interface's stability, however, is more apparent than real, making the potential volatility occasioned by a new issue that does not map onto the "old" understanding.

Turning from these frankly speculative remarks to a consideration of the overall pattern of results, we tentatively conclude that the organizing principles structuring the interface in our case study derive essentially from those that serve to organize the community social structure and not from those functional principles that organize the elite community affairs structure. This conclusion rests on the superior and consistent performance of our measure of social closeness in structuring the interface (as well as the somewhat less consistent patterns observed for the value-based measures) versus the virtual absence of any patterning derived from our two indicators of elite members' functional positions in the elite structure.

Issue Similarity as a Basis of Elite Attractiveness to Population Subgroups

Let us now examine a model that considers a more proximate or contemporary basis for relative elite attractiveness to population subgroups—that is, for the case in hand, the elite's advocacy or implicit support for particular issue outcomes on five recent community controversies. This model and the one considered in the previous section are not alternative explanations for elite attractiveness to population subgroups. Nor should they be seen as inherently incompatible with one another—indeed they really should be regarded as complementing one another. It is merely the constraints of the data base (i.e., the limited degrees of freedom) that prevent us from considering the two sets of variables in the respective models simultaneously in a "complete" model.

Our initial assumption throughout the study has been that a primary function of the community influence system is to resolve (i.e., generate binding decisions) controversial community issues that may or may not be in the public limelight. In their leadership capacity, elite members are activated on one or another side of an issue. This participation may become a matter of public visibility and concern. Predicting an elite member's attractiveness to a population subgroup should, therefore, depend upon the degree to which the issue was a matter of actual or potential public concern and popular mobilization. Technically grounded, intra-elite issues, which tend to be resolved quietly within the precincts of elite deliberations, should not provide a basis for moving an elite member toward or away from a population group simply because of the nonpublic nature of such deliberations. On the other hand, in the context of public mobilization or concern over an issue, individual elite members should become, as a result of their public stances, more or less attractive to different groups on the basis of the group's preferred outcomes and be ordered, accordingly, in terms of their proximities to the groups in the interface.

In short, a representational model of the interface (cf. Miller and Stokes, 1961) would lead us to expect positive correlations of population group positions and proximity to elite members of similar persuasion. Given our methodology, however, we can only assess for one point in time the resultant of an historical process. This process is intrinsically idiosyncratic in that it involves the sequential handling of a set of issues that comprised the community's issue agenda in the recent past and only some of which provoked sufficient popular controversy and awareness to provide relevant bases for structuring the interface. Following the same format as Table 12.2, Table 12.3 presents the results of our analysis.

Although all the issues split the elite around varying cleavage axes (see Chapter 9), it is apparent from Panel A of Table 12.3 that, except for the hypothetical pop festival issue, the level of disagreement across groups is very small indeed—with very substantial majorities favoring the issue outcome that actually prevailed. Two factors, however, may account for this quite misleading impression of massive popular consensus. First, as has often been noted in studies of popular opinion regarding public issues and voting behavior, there is a general tendency for cross-section samples to express support for what is already established policy or an accomplished fact and to favor the winning side of an issue, even if there was substantial opposition to the policy at the time of decision. In the case of the school issue, for example, we know from newspaper accounts at the time and the nearly unanimous report of our elite respondents that it was an issue that caused great popular outcry and mobilization into competing factions. With more technically circumscribed controversies handled by the elite among themselves, there is simply an absence of public awareness and knowledge of what issues were at stake at the time of the decision and no public discussion of what interests might have been advanced or harmed by the particular decision made. Thus we think it is reasonable to proceed with the assumption that, at the very least, we can rank the relative support of the groups for a given side of the issue, despite the apparent lack of popular disagreement with the winning policy.

Compared to the social structural model (see Table 12.2), Table 12.3 reveals almost the same "goodness of fit" in the sense of approximately similar levels of interface distance variance explained (i.e., compare the multiple R^2s in the two tables) across the population subgroups.[3] These

---

[3] Peoples' opinions on the issue of community incorporation were not solicited because we were informed, before we entered the field, that the issue aroused no popular interest due to the peculiar way in which the matter was arranged. Legally, a ministry at the state level of government is responsible for establishing city boundaries according to complex rules for taking into account urban growth and designing urban development regions and tax cachement areas. Although city and county leaders were extensively and decisively involved in the development of the particular plan of incorporation in question, the locus of the decision was the state capital. Only after its formal promulgation at Düsseldorf were citizens apprised of the decision. City residents were essentially unaffected by the decision so far as

relatively good fits occur despite the very restricted variation in population subgroup differentiation on the four issues. Prediction is again poorest for the same three groups as in Table 12.3, which is consistent with our argument concerning their relative structural alienation from the two dominant rival groups in town, the *Altbürger*—traditionally oriented, upper middle-class Catholics—and the *Neubürger*—more secularly oriented scientists and professionals associated with the Natural Science Research Center.

Using once again our arbitrary criterion of .30 to identify substantively interesting coefficients, 10 of the 15 coefficients meeting the criterion are in the direction predicted by the population subgroups' relative preferences for a particular side of an issue. Moreover, three of these five "inconsistencies" occur for the *Altbürger* lower middle class, which was distributed almost precisely along the total population split for the issues in question, suggesting the possibility that chance factors alone determined which side of an issue this class favored. The pattern-maintenance issue over the pop festival and over what we have regarded as an instrumental, intra-elite issue concerning the city hall yielded the largest coefficients consistent with population subgroup orientations. While the pop festival pattern is in accord with our hypothesis, the apparently strong structuring effect of the city hall issue requires comment. This issue did, in fact, raise moderate public controversy (as our elite informants told us) because the voluntary associations, especially the carnival clubs, which draw their membership heavily from the *Altbürger* lower middle and working classes, were strongly in favor of designing a civic center where they could hold their meetings. They found themselves in opposition to members of the upper middle classes who were less interested in such a facility and argued that there were more important things on which to spend the money—for example, on expanding kindergarten facilities for preschool children. Herr Koenig, the most in-

---

local tax rates and administrative matters were concerned, but people living in the newly incorporated areas (who were not included in our sample) were potentially adversely affected because of possible changes in their tax rate. The leaders of the CDU used the plan of incorporation as a self-consciously designed strategy to enhance their electoral support base by including a number of rural hamlets that are composed almost exclusively of CDU voters. The deed was accomplished (due to the CDU's control of the relevant city, county, and state government administrative offices) before the SPD leaders were able to intervene, even if they had wanted to do so. In fact, the SPD leadership could not intervene effectively, first, because of their general commitment to the cause of expanding city control over the development of the local region and, more specifically, because the newly incorporated area brought the entire natural science research facility under city responsibility for local administration and provision of services.

TABLE 12.3

Predicting Proximities of Population Groups and Elite Members According to their Preferences on Four Community Issues

Issue	Prot. work cl.	Alt. work cl.	Alt. lo. mid.	Alt. mid. mid.	Prot. lo. mid.	Neu. mid. mid.	Alt. Up. mid.	Neu. Up. mid.	Students	Total population
A. Percentage in favor of issue among those interested, by nine population groups										
School	98	84	86	80	86	93	69	100	96	87
Pop festival	46	44	46	37	48	67	30	81	88	50
City hall	95	87	84	86	91	89	79	75	81	85
Industrial resettlement	93	97	94	91	93	95	89	87	93	93
B. Issue positions of elite members[a] predicting proximity to a population group (zero-order correlation)										
School	−.09	−.30	−.08	−.29	.14	.14	−.33	.36	−.16	Inapp.
Pop festival	−.18	−.40[b]	.06	−.22	−.09	.39[b]	−.59[c]	.56[c]	−.15	Inapp.
City hall	.32	.59[c]	.53[c]	.47[b]	−.24	−.34	.17	−.48[b]	−.22	Inapp.
Industrial resettlement	−.13	−.51[b]	−.36	−.45[b]	.28	.12	−.28	.53[c]	.05	Inapp.
C. Issue positions of elite members[a] predicting proximity to a population group (beta weights)										
School	.08	−.09	−.03	−.26	.29	−.19	−.09	.12	−.22	Inapp.
Pop festival	−.09	−.10	.39	.14	−.40	.39	−.54[b]	.31	−.18	Inapp.
City hall	.31	.48[b]	.62[b]	.38	−.24	−.27	−.09	−.28	−.38	Inapp.
Industrial resettlement	−.08	−.46[b]	−.38	−.46[b]	.35	.02	−.21	.47[b]	.03	Inapp.
Multiple R^2	.12	.58[b]	.49[c]	.43[b]	.23	.22	.39	.60[c]	.14	Inapp.

[a] The issue positions of an elite member were determined for most elite members on the grounds that at least two other elite members had reported him as being active on a given side of an issue. For those few cases who were not attributed a position by other elite members on an issue, we used their self-reported position. This procedure of attributed positions seemed most consistent with our objective of examining the public visibility and consequent attraction (or repulsion) of population groups for various leaders.

[b] $p < .05$.

[c] $p < .01$.

241

fluential man in town, personally quite active in the carnival association, president of the largest soccer club in town, and, as shown in Figure
12.1, in close proximity to the *Altbürger* working class, was strongly in
favor of a large civic center. In fact, he was accused by his political opponents, both within and outside the dominant CDU coalition, of want-
ing to build a monument to himself as his legacy to the city for his years
of public service. Many of his elite allies in the upper middle class were
less than enthusiastic about his plans on grounds of cost and need, but
he, almost single-handedly within the elite group but with substantial
popular support, had his way.[4]

The controversy over industrial resettlement yielded the most inconsistent pattern of coefficients of the four issues considered. Chapter 6 already indicated that this issue, a hypothetical one, would probably have
caused considerable trouble within the CDU dominant coalition because
it aroused conflicting economic interests among its members. For the interface structure as well, we can see potential difficulties. The group least
in favor of industrial resettlement (the *Neubürger* upper middle class)
is linked most closely to the elite members most in favor of it: Conversely, the population group most in favor of it (the *Altbürger* working
class) is linked closely to elite members most against it. Although the
elite structural analysis suggested that the CDU coalition would have
the most internal difficulties with the issue, the interface analysis suggests
that the SPD coalition would be in serious difficulty too as its popular
support base is relatively against its position.

These inconsistencies suggest the need for a longitudinal study of issues to determine the interactions between the elite system and the community at large to see whether, when there are interface inconsistencies,
there are moves toward consistency of population groups and elite elements favoring their views. Alternatively, it may well be that these inconsistencies represent inherent structural strains and sources of tension
and disequilibrium that are irresolvable, given the existing coalition system that combines highly heterogeneous population elements into a common alliance. This is particularly true for the SPD elite–community interface which generally shows, save for the *Neubürger* upper middle class,
poor articulation between the SPD leadership elements and their puta-

---

[4] Following the strategy employed in our discussion of Table 12.2 that examined the
rank-order correlations between population preferences in Panel A and correlation
coefficients between elite members' issue preferences and interface distances, we
obtained significant *rho*s of .72 and .78 for the two pattern-maintenance issues and
nonsignificant *rho*s for the other issues. This provides additional supporting evidence for our contention that pattern-maintenance issues should be more directly
involved in structuring the community–elite interface than the other types of issues.

tive popular bases of support. The "marriage" of the *Altbürger* leadership with its support groups in the community reflects a much better articulation and congruence of orientations and interests between community elements and the elite subsystem, suggesting that it may be fairly durable and resistive to change. Given a more dynamic perspective of the interface over time, we might hypothesize the appearance of an oscillatory movement between consensus (consistency) and dissensus (inconsistency) of selected elements of the community—elite interface as a function of the occurrence of controversial events that structurally crystalize around one or another principle for selecting particular leadership personnel in which given population subgroups place their confidence, loyalty, and support.

As we have already remarked, the foregoing analysis does not permit us to assess the relative efficacy of the variables used in the social structural and issue preference models to account for the structuring of the interface. It is quite clear, however, that the results for the two models closely parallel one another and, in no instance, provide contradictory evidence to our interpretive remarks. We should, of course, not be surprised by this happy state of affairs, nor should we overestimate the mutually confirmatory nature of the two sets of results since the social structural variables are, in fact, systematically related to individual- and group-level issue preferences.

The Differential Access of Population Subgroups to Elite Possessors of Influence Resources

To this point in the discussion, we have dealt with the bases of elite attraction or repulsion to the community at large assuming that the population at large, by some unspecified processes, perceive more or less attractive features of elite members and are more or less favorably located in social networks that lead to specific individuals in the elite. Now we want to turn to an even more speculative consideration of the ways in which different population groups may enjoy more or less favorable access to specific influence resources controlled by different elite members. Note that we shall now be speaking of salient characteristics of the elite system that have no counterpart in the community subsystem but are especially relevant to the resolution of binding collective decisions among competing alternatives. In a sense, we are concerned with characterizing the competitive advantages of different population groups in having their preferences prevail in community controversies as a result of their relative access to relevant elite influence resources—in other words, the competitive advantages of different groups in the community market of political choice.

Throughout this discussion, the reader should keep in mind the preceding chapter's discussion of the nature of influence resources and the mechanisms by which they are converted into authoritative decisions. In the present context, the earlier discussion has the following noteworthy implications: *(1)* According to the influence resource-conversion model, "good connections" and "honorable brokerage," while playing critical roles in the elite decision-making process, are nevertheless peculiarly intra-elite resources with little bearing on or visibility to the community's population at large. In addition, "fluid capital" and "fixed capital" are functionally specialized around economic functions and require, according to the model, conversion into more relevant influence resources for their efficacy in the community decision-making system. The groups' differential access to these resources should, therefore, be of little direct or immediate benefit in determining community decision outcomes. *(2)* On the other hand, the resources of "influence over subgroups" (the obverse of the population subgroup's "representation" in the councils of the elite) and "public mobilizer" are peculiarly relevant to the dynamics and moblization of the pattern-maintenance sector and should be highly differentially distributed among the population groups. "Expertise" is a special case of a pattern-maintenance resource that has little direct bearing on popular concerns. *(3)* Since incumbents of the top bureaucratic posts in the civil administrative apparatus are normatively constrained at least to appear impartial and universalistic in their functioning, direct access to such positions should be roughly equal among all groups. Elected legislative officials (e.g., the city or county council members) will presumably vary in their proximities to groups as a function of their group-based electoral support. But since we shall be disregarding party or coalition labels of elected officials in the following analysis, group proximities to all elected officials will tend to average out to roughly equal means, although there may well be some bias in access to authority positions for those groups who supported authority holders in the more numerous dominant political coalition.

Table 12.4 presents the average distances of groups from elite possessors of specified influence resources. The table entries were calculated according to the following procedure. First, all the elite members with a given influence resource were identified (see Chapter 11 for the procedure used to identify such resource holders). Then, for each group, we summed the distances (in Figure 12.1) between the elite members with the resource in question and the particular group and then computed the average distance to the group. To facilitate comparing entries within rows, we have also calculated the mean of the average distances in the row and its standard deviation. To illustrate what can be learned from this table, consider the first row, "authority." The *Altbürger* lower middle class would appear to enjoy the greatest access to authority holders (i.e., it has the lowest average distance to such persons), while the *Neubürger* middle middle class is farthest away from incumbents of authority positions. Also note, however, that the standard deviation for the mean of all the groups' average distances (the last column) is the lowest for all eight resources, suggesting that the groups do not differ among themselves with respect to distance from authority holders as much as they do for other types of resources such as public mobilizer or honorable broker; all the groups enjoy roughly equal access to holders of authority.

In order to regard this table as mapping the groups' competitive advantages in elite resource mobilization in the market of political choice, we must accept a critical, but debatable, assumption that a group's relative proximity to certain resource holders provides it with a competitive advantage in mobilizing that type of resource in the elite decision-making system. This assumption is acceptable only insofar as the interface between community and elite is approximately symmetric—that is, the distances are about the same whether viewed from the vantage point of the community's population subgroups or from the vantage point of the elite members. To the extent that a population subgroup targets on elite members who do not share their preferences, it makes no sense to assume that the subgroup can mobilize these elite members' resources in its behalf. The preceding two sections' discussion of the social structural and issue preference models indicates that the structuring of the interface reflects a general consistency between popular and elite member preferences, but that there is also evidence of systematic discrepancies for certain groups whose interface structures are simply inappropriate, indeed at points diametrically opposed, to their own conception of their best interests and preferred outcomes.

Taking the standard deviations of average distances across the groups as a measure of the differentiation of group access to specific resources (or, in other words, as a measure of the differentiation of group competitive advantage across different types of resources), we tentatively conclude that, as we expected, "authority" is the least group differentiated resource while "public mobilizer" and "honorable brokerage" are the most differentiated resources. The groups seem reasonably equal in access to elite members reputed to be "influential over subgroups," but one should recall here that the relative size of a group would be expected to be crucial determinant of this resource's relative importance in resolving specific community controversies.

TABLE 12.4

Average Distance of Groups from Possessors of Influence Resources

Type of resource	Prot. work. cl.	Alt. work. cl.	Alt. lo. mid.	Alt. mid. mid.	Neu. lo. mid.	Neu. mid. mid.	Alt. up. mid.	Neu. up. mid.	Students	Mean[a]	Dev.[b]
Authority	131.9	133.3	118.1	125.2	136.8	136.0	127.6	128.3	126.5	129.3	5.6
Fluid capital	108.7	110.6	115.2	118.3	141.1	146.5	117.3	159.1	134.2	127.9	16.9
Fixed capital	116.4	132.0	127.1	135.8	115.9	137.3	109.8	140.8	134.8	127.8	10.5
Expert knowledge	127.3	134.9	114.9	127.6	137.3	139.7	140.2	117.6	138.7	130.9	8.5
Good connections	122.8	133.9	119.2	129.7	137.4	142.4	123.5	128.1	127.4	129.4	7.0
Public mobilizer	143.7	85.7	97.9	75.3	155.7	139.9	88.4	171.6	109.4	118.6	32.7
Honorable broker	146.3	104.7	121.0	89.4	146.6	135.3	88.5	167.5	101.6	122.3	26.5

Subgroup influence	142.2	137.6	122.1	125.7	131.5	133.6	124.6	126.0	118.7	129.1	7.2
Average distance[c]	136.9	137.5	122.3	126.7	132.3	131.3	124.7	129.6	120.4	—	—
Relative influence of group[d]	4.12	3.81	4.41	4.21	3.56	3.37	8.87	4.14	4.63		

[a] The mean refers to the unweighted average of the row entries.
[b] "Dev." is the standard deviation of the row mean.
[c] These are the average distances of the groups from the 27 elite members.
[d] The relative influence of a group is a summary measure calculated according to the following formula:

$$RI_g = \sum_{j=1}^{27} \frac{V_j}{D_{(g,\,j)}}$$

where V_j is the number of votes for influence individual j received from the elite population (see Q25, Appendix B) and $D_{(g,\,j)}$ is the distance between individual j and group g. In other words, a given group's influence score is the sum of the elite's influence scores discounted by their distances from that group.

Turning to a more direct comparison among the groups in their relative access to specific resources, we note, first, that there is strong differentiation between *Altbürger* and *Neubürger* (irrespective of class) with respect to access to economic resources and, more importantly so far as popular influence is concerned, with respect to access to public mobilizers. Of the three structurally marginal groups we have identified in the two preceding sections, two of them (the Protestant working class and the Protestant lower middle class) are very far indeed from public mobilizers and people who represent them as special interest groups in elite deliberations. The students, however, are well within the overall average distances to such resources. Finally, it should come as a surprise to no one that the *Altbürger* lower middle class and *Altbürger* upper middle class enjoy the greatest competitive advantages of all since they have below average distances and, presumably thereby, greatest access to all (or nearly all) types of resource controllers.

As a final summary measure of the relative influence of the groups as a function of their relative proximity or access to elite influentials who control different influence resources, we computed the group's influence score as a function of the sum of the elite member's total number of elite votes for repute as a community influential, discounted by the elite member's distance from the group in question. (See footnote *d*, Table 12.4, for the details of the computation and the last row of Table 12.4 for the computed scores.) Since we demonstrated in the preceding chapter that there is a very high correlation (viz., .805) between a man's total number of votes for repute as a community influential and the total number of influence resources he is reputed to control, this seems to be a meaningful way of bringing into focus the more differentiated picture provided by our analysis of the specific resources. Again we see a pattern of differentiation of influence among the groups that is quite consistent with what we have come to expect from our previous discussion. The *Altbürger* upper middle class is far and away the most influential group in the community, despite its small size. The other groups show a much more restricted range of scores, but the *Neubürger* groups in general tend to have lower scores. The major departure from this generalization is the students, who have a much higher group influence score than we would have anticipated. This occurs because they happened to select disproportionately high status *Altbürger* influentials in the religious and educational sector instead of members of the SPD coalition recruited from the Natural Science Research Center who would have shared their political and value concerns. Remember that the students picked the wrong people for their elite interface, given their value and issue preferences. Thus, it is very unlikely that the students could, in fact, mobilize, in support of their own interests, the elite persons to whom they felt most attracted. As we pointed out earlier, to the extent that our assumption about the symmetry of the interface from the elite's and population subgroups' points of view is in error, we must expect such inconsistencies to occur. In fact, our general model provides the grounds for predicting, or at least explaining, the "errors" as well as the consistent results.

Thus far in the argument, we have used the groups' differential access to possessors of influence resources as an indicator of their competitive advantages in the marketplace of political choice. These relative advantages can be interpreted in part as an outcome of past political conflicts in which group-specific policy preferences were advocated by particular elite members, the result being that they are now trusted to a greater or lesser degree by the different groups. At the same time, the influence resources possessed by the most trusted elite people should signify the potential means at the disposal of a group in attempting to influence the outcomes of future political battles. We can now close the circle of our argument in terms of the general feedback model of community–elite interaction described in Chapter 1 by contending that a group's relative competitive advantages in the mobilization of influence resources or, more generally, the nature of its access to community influentials should affect its relative level of satisfaction with the community as a whole and political participation in its affairs.

More specifically, our hypothesis is that the better the access to influence resources and, thus, the better the competitive advantage of a group, the more satisfied it will be with regard to living in the community and the more likely that it will find political participation in community affairs to be rewarding (i.e., successful in leading to group-preferred outcomes). The processes forming the interface between community and elite will, thus, finally have a feedback to the community at large (cf. Parsons, 1960). Our discussion of influence resources in the preceding chapter, however, clearly indicates that we should not expect all eight resources to be equally efficacious in resolving popularly based community issues—that is, they could not simply be substituted for one another. The discussion does provide a basis for specifying which resources will be especially relevant to the feedback process suggested by the hypothesis under consideration. Following the functional logic of our resource model, access to the resources "public mobilizer" and "influence over subgroup" is most likely to have favorable feedback results.

Table 12.5 presents the rank-order correlations between the groups' relative access to given influence resources and overall influence and their mean community satisfaction and percentage nonvoters in the last city election, our indicator of community political participation. Since we have only nine data points for each *rho*, it is hardly surprising that many fail to reach a conventional level of significance. It is noteworthy that only three of the 18 *rhos* have negative signs (and 2 of these are quite small ones of −.03), which are clearly contrary to our general expectation of a positive association between competitive advantage and community satisfaction and political participation. (If chance alone were generating the results, we could expect a 50–50 split in the signs of the coefficients.)

With regard to community satisfaction, we encounter several surprises, as well as only modest support for our speculations. First, the significant *rho* for fluid capital was not anticipated and is probably spurious, for the following reasons. Possessors of fluid capital are in fact local businesspeople (bankers, merchants, wealthy industrialists). *Altbürger*, being more fully integrated into the economic life of the community than *Neubürger* because of their long residence, naturally turn to these people for advice and assistance on personal economic matters, one of the component indicators of popular trust. Newcomers are less economically integrated into the local community. They often retain a cosmopolitan orientation and life style that leads them to use the economic facilities of neighboring large cities, three of which (Cologne, Düsseldorf, and

TABLE 12.5

Rank-order Correlations of Access to Influence Resources and Relative Influence of Groups with Community Satisfaction and Percentage Nonvoters across Population Groups

Influence resource	Mean community satisfaction[a]	Percentage nonvoters[b]
Authority	.33	.35
Fluid capital	.62[c]	−.03
Fixed capital	.35	.18
Expert knowledge	−.17	.03
Good connections	.15	.12
Public mobilizers	.87[d]	.35
Honorable broker	.72[c]	.28
Subgroup influence	−.03	.33
Relative influence of group	.25	.22

[a] The index of community satisfaction is a simple sum of the scores of Q1, Q2, and the reflected scores of Q5 (see Appendix B, Part II).
[b] Percentage nonvoters in last city election in 1969.
[c] $p < .05$.
[d] $p < .01$.

Aachen) are only 45 minutes away by car. Since *Altbürger,* irrespective of class, are more satisfied on the average with the local community than the newcomers, the correlation was probably generated by this differential use of local business facilities. Second, the *rho* for public mobilizer was statistically significant, conforming to our expectations; the other hypothetical expectation of a positive association between community satisfaction and access to the resource of influence over subgroups was not supported. Finally, another unanticipated result was that access to honorable brokers was significantly associated with community satisfactions. There is no ready reason at hand to regard this result as especially implausible or spurious—indeed, it makes good sense after the fact. It is true, however, that this resource was attributed exclusively to highly respected persons in the dominant CDU coalition who served to mediate between the rival city and county factions (see Chapter 6). Access to persons with such clout would certainly be a "big help" on any controversy. Recall also that honorable brokerage was activated on the two issues, the city hall and the pop festival, most involved in structuring the interface (compare Table 11.7 in Chapter 11 to Table 12.4).

Turning to a consideration of popular political participation in the community, none of the correlations involving percentage nonvoters achieve statistical significance. There is good reason to believe, however, that the correlations were artificially depressed by the inclusion of the student group in the analysis. Since a very large proportion of the members of this group were too young to vote in the city election of 1969, we must base our estimate of the percentage of nonvoters on a very few cases. When this group is dropped from the analysis, the correlation with subgroup influence would be .93 ($p < .01$). The *rho* for public mobilizer would also be substantially higher, although not quite achieving statistical significance.

It is especially noteworthy that favorable access to public mobilizers seems to "lead" to generalized community satisfaction, while favorable access to influence over subgroups appears to provoke electoral participation. If we can, for the moment, accept this pattern as really descriptive of the state of affairs in this community (and not a statistical artifact), we believe it is plausible to argue that access to public mobilizers signifies access to the very integrative core of the community decision-making system and results in or reflects high levels of diffuse community satisfaction. Access to subgroup leaders, on the other hand, is a much more political, conflict-grounded means of achieving a group's goals and is channeled through electoral participation. In highly differentiated systems, general or diffuse satisfaction with the social system and political nonalienation are by no means necessarily correlated with one another (cf. Gamson, 1968).

CONCLUDING REMARKS

Many valid theoretical and methodological criticisms can be leveled against the very intricate analysis of the preceding pages. In our effort to take very seriously the "community power" literature's stress on the importance of studying the potentially divergent orientations of the elite decision-making system and its "subject" population, we may not have always successfully avoided falling into the trap of reifying our analytic metaphor, the community–elite interface structure. On the other hand, by pushing the metaphor as far as we could, we believe that it has helped to clarify some very important theoretical issues. It is, however, important to remind ourselves that our analytic procedures may be especially conducive to finding an order or structure when there may, in fact, not be one at all or when it might be of quite a different sort. Given sufficient ingenuity and massaging of the data, we can almost guarantee that these procedures will produce a structural representation of a data matrix—regardless of the meaningfulness or justifiability of using the original data set to provide even ordinal estimates of the proximities among a set of points. Our only real precaution against a completely arbitrary or artificial solution is a careful examination of the set of substantive assumptions that guided the construction and manipulation of the original data. Given the long chain of inferences involved, however, there are still many points at which we might have made an empirically problematic assumption that effectively generated the conclusions.

In other words, we have essentially invented (manufactured) a new dependent variable, the interface distances in a joint space of individuals and population groups, that has few known statistical or substantive properties simply because of its novelty. We have then assumed that it adequately represents, at least for a single point in time, a meaningful hypothetical construct that pulls together the essentials of a rather vague and ill-defined set of images about complex and highly differentiated systems of control (that is, systems involving simultaneous asymmetric influence transactions across a highly differentiated set of participants, no major subset of whom will necessarily be involved or activated across a set of diverse controversial events demanding binding collective decisions). Finally, we have proceeded to "explain" this new dependent variable's variability according to alternative models of the mechanisms one might postulate to be involved in forming the given structural constellation. A particularly troublesome theoretical element in all this is our explicit recognition that the formation of this hypothetical construct is essentially of a process or time-dependent nature, yet we have only cross-sectional or static data on hand to be analyzed.

It is principally for these reasons that we stress the tentative and speculative character of the entire analysis. The data in no way can be regarded as a fair test of our speculations since they often provided the stimulus for further conceptual refinement or distinction. The empirical data have been used in creative interaction with our theoretical presuppositions to generate a more elaborated theoretical model. Of course, we do not for a moment believe that the analysis is an exercise in pure artifact generation. The results obtained in the case study simply accord much too closely with what we know about the relationships between the community subgroups and specific elite members, based on many different sources of evidence ranging from participant observation of the community for 4 or 5 years to a systematic review of the local newspaper, to be so easily dismissed. It remains, however, for future research to apply the same procedures and assumptions to new data sets to demonstrate whether or not the approach is generalizable.

13

Prospects and Conclusion

In this final chapter, we shall not try to summarize the contents of the preceding chapters nor to provide a thoroughgoing critique of what we have done. In fact, we have already done this, at least in part, in the critical summaries of the key arguments at the ends of various chapters. Our intent here, on the contrary, is to be even more speculative than we have been. In drawing some lessons from what we have learned in our illustrative case study, we shall formulate some general propositions to guide us in extending our theoretical and empirical approach to other research contexts. We may even be able to discern the rudiments of a theory of social system differentiation and integration.

The bulk of this book has been devoted to specific theoretical questions about differentiation and integration in community social systems and the empirical procedures we adopted to answer them in a particular case study. This analysis should provide a useful context for our speculative discussion, giving it some empirical substance. Because we are now reaching for generality of formulation, however, there is no meaningful sense in which the case study can help us test the validity of these general propositions because they refer to variable features of system differentiation and integration that characterize different social systems and not to a single instance.

Before turning to these propositions, it may first be useful to recall

Figure 1.1, which provided a theoretical overview of the model of community decision-making systems that has directed our efforts. We, of course, have been highly selective regarding the parts of this model to which we gave special attention. As we noted in the first chapter, Clark (1968a) has already provided a useful compendium of empirical propositions, resting on comparative research, that relate various community and extracommunity characteristics to selected features of community decision-making subsystems and their outputs. We have little to add to such discussions because we looked at only one community whose context and characteristics were already fixed before the analysis began.

In contrast to much current work, our focus throughout has been on an intensive analysis of the population and the elite subsystems of a community and their interrelationships—our so-called "black box"—in order to specify some of the mechanisms or processes whereby "inputs" derived from the differentiation of claims arising from the population and its elite are translated into decision outcomes. Now we want to propose some propositions that will also require comparative research on many such "black boxes." The propositions are grouped into three sets, relating to comparative structural analyses of the population subsystem, the elite subsystem, and the interrelations between the two subsystems, respectively. They are not intended to exhaust all the pertinent generalizations one could devise, but merely to suggest the sorts of propositions our approach can generate.

The propositions are of different logical statuses. Some are intended to be empirical hypotheses testable in future research, while others are really nothing more than useful empirical guidelines to assist the investigator in analyzing specific cases or tautologies that clarify certain theoretical linkages. The logical status of any given proposition will be apparent from its discussion context. All the propositions presuppose a "social choice" model of integration in which there is assumed to be a substantial likelihood that the differentiated interests of rank-and-file participants (or subunits) will somehow be taken into account when binding decisions relevant to the social system as a whole are made (see Chapter 1, pp. 9–11).

SOME PROPOSITIONS RELATING TO THE POPULATION SUBSYSTEM

The following postulates and propositions primarily refer to social structures based on bonds of intimate relationships, such as marriage, friendship, and informal social intercourse, among population subgroups defined as internally homogeneous with respect to persons occupying similar social positions either in the division of labor and/or other bases of social solidarity, including, particularly, membership in various status groups (Weber's *Stände*). In general, we expect that:

Proposition I: Structural differentiation of a population's intimate relations will tend to be multidimensional in form (that is, there will usually be several principal axes of differentiation). Moreover, these several axes of differentiation will tend to be the axes of cleavage with respect to the differentiation of demands for collective action of the system as a whole.

Our reasoning here rests on our postulated distance-generation mechanism underlying social structures based on intimate bonds; it holds that such bonds tend to form only between positions whose incumbents share a variety of important attitudinal and behavioral similarities (cf. Laumann, 1973). Correlatively, the farther apart two positions are in a social structure, the more likely that their incumbents will hold views and preferences that are at least dissimilar, if not actually in conflict. By definition, the social links between such positions will be weak, or even nonexistent, further reducing the capacity of these groups to form coalitions in defense of their common interests (if, indeed, any should exist).

As collary propositions to Proposition I, we argue, first, that:

Proposition Ia: One of the axes of structural differentiation will usually map the differential material rewards and/or prestige or honor accorded different social positions.

In communities and societies, this axis has usually been called the class structure (cf. Giddens, 1973). In addition, we propose that:

Proposition Ib: Another axis of differentiation will usually be associated with the nature of different ascriptive solidarities in the population.

These ascriptive solidarities can derive from many different sources, depending on the compositional history of a given population subsystem, whose population elements have been recruited from more or less homogeneous ascriptive sources, be they generational, ethnic, religious, racial, or nativity based. The empirical task is, of course, to measure the presence and relative importance of these axes as bases of differentiation in the population and their implications for demands on the collective decision-making system.

But what about the limiting case of undifferentiated population sub-systems in terms of these axes? We assert that:

Proposition II: The less differentiated the social positions in a population subsystem are (i.e., the more homogeneous the elements in the population subsystem are with respect to the division of labor and ascriptive solidarities), the more will idiosyncratic personal ties among its members determine the coalitional and factional structure of the population subsystem (cf. Barnes, 1954; Kapferer, 1969; Mitchell, 1969a).

Such homogeneous population subsystems are usually quite small in population size as well. Moreover, their integrative problems tend to be relatively simple to resolve as there is such a limited basis for systematic and long-lasting differences among the population elements.

The limiting case of a homogeneous population subsystem naturally leads us to speculate about its obverse:

Proposition III: The more differentiated the population subsystem, the more differentiated the claims or demands it will make on the integrative subsystem and the more functionally and structurally differentiated the integrative subsystem is likely to be in order to generate collective binding decisions for the system as a whole.

This proposition, of course, has a long and honorable history in sociological theory; one can at least trace it back to Emile Durkheim's (1933) classic discussion of the division of labor (cf. Parsons, 1937; Clark, 1968a).

We shall conclude this section with four empirical generalizations that deserve research attention:

Proposition IV: The more self-selective a population subgroup is with respect to the formation of intimate ties, the more isolated and peripheral it will be from other population groups (that is, it lacks intimate ties with others) and the more likely it will be to possess and express distinctive value profiles (that is, the more likely it is to form a subcommunity with distinctive claims on the larger system).

Proposition V: The maximum potential for conflict among population subgroups with respect to collective decision making occurs when most component subgroups have strong tendencies toward self-selection and avoidance of intimate ties with out-group members—a form of structural crystallization (see Chapter 1) or social segmentation (e.g., Lijphardt, 1968). In other words, they all are located at considerable distances from one another on the periphery of the social space without having any mediating groups in the center who have ties with them. Conflict will tend to be highly expressive, episodic, and non-negotiable.

Proposition VI: Structures that have large numbers of centrally located subgroups (that is, they maintain links with many other groups and lack strong self-selective tendencies) will have, as a consequence, many potential mediating links joining them to more peripherally located groups. Conflict will, therefore, tend to be instrumental, continuingly adjustive, and bargaining oriented.

Proposition VII: The structure of value differentiation among population subgroups will tend to mirror the social structural differentiation among these groups, but not necessarily perfectly or without consequential inconsistencies.

This last proposition requires some elaboration. Groups may be quite liberal on some value orientations and conservative on others, given the domain of relevant social values for that social system. These profiles of value commitments provide multiple bases of mutual attraction and repulsion among groups that differ among themselves with respect to how they assess the relative importance of different values. As issues dividing the community arise, activating one or another value dimension and thus making it more salient than before, groups change in their relative attractiveness to one another. That is, a group may be attractive to a particular group because of shared orientations on certain issues; this same group may become highly unattractive when an issue arises that activates "another side" of that group's concerns that is not mutually shared.

SOME PROPOSITIONS RELATING TO THE
ELITE (INTEGRATIVE) SUBSYSTEM

Turning to selected propositions concerning the elite subsystem, we find it useful first to propose an orienting proposition:

Proposition VIII: Structural analysis may usefully distinguish between two fundamental types of social relationships: (*1*) expressive relations involving bonds of intimacy and affect (both positive and negative) among incumbents of social positions, and (*2*) instrumental relations involving exchanges between incumbents of positions that are required in order to fulfill their respective functional tasks (e.g., the business–professional relations discussed in Part II or the exchanges of money, goods, and services among business firms). Instrumental relations may involve quite diverse exchange transactions, the most important of which in complex systems involve money, power (orders), information, and personnel (cf. Parsons, 1969).

The distance-generating mechanisms discussed in Postulate II of Chapter 1 refer to principles of systematic bias in channeling the formation of relationships between certain kinds of positions and the avoidance of such relationships between others. Obviously, these principles should differ, depending on which fundamental type of relationship, or its subvarieties, is considered.

We premise the following empirical generalizations on Proposition VIII:

Proposition VIIIa: The bases of differentiation of the network of informal social relations (that is, expressive relations) among elite members will tend to coincide with those observed in the population subsystem's structure of intimate relations.

Since elite members are always also members of specific population subgroups in the community social system, they are likely to share many of the attitudinal and behavioral preferences of their origin groups, especially regarding origin group attitudes toward other groups and to conceptions of group interests. Of course, there is usually considerable heterogeneity of views in a given group so that specific individuals may depart substantially from the modal tendencies of the group. Moreover, elite members may develop distinctive attitudes resulting from their socialization into leadership positions or from the very nature of such roles that may place them in considerable variance with (even opposition to) their putative origin groups (e.g., Stouffer, 1955). (Consider, as an additional example, the changes wrought in people's opinions by being co-opted into the elite or the desire to identify with groups superior in status to one's own group.) Thus, this proposition is by no means necessarily true by definition.

The following propositions relate to the structural differentiation of instrumental relations within elite subsystems:

Proposition VIIIb: The structure of instrumental relations within the elite subsystem will tend to segregate members into institutionally specialized subsectors (e.g., religious, governmental, economic).

This proposition should already be familiar to us as the principle of sectoral differentiation discussed in Part II. A further proposition of considerable importance asserts:

Proposition VIIIc: The more internally differentiated an institutionally specialized subsector is in the elite network of instrumental relations, the more it will be subject to internal disagreements about preferred collective action for the system as a whole—in other words, the subsector itself is confronted with integrative problems in representing its claims on the larger system.

Moreover, we propose that:

Proposition VIIId: The more structurally differentiated the elite subsystem is into institutionally specialized sectors that are only loosely coupled to one another, the more likely it is that integrative functions mediating the different sectors will be performed by full-time incumbents of integrative positions—in other words, integrative functions will be assigned to specialized positions located in the center of the network of institutionally instrumental relations.

Taking into account simultaneously the distinction between expressive and instrumental relations, we may advance two key empirical propositions:

Proposition IXa: The greater is the correspondence between the structure of informal relations among elite members and the structure of their instrumental relations, the greater is the stability of the coalitional structure over time.

Proposition IXb: The weaker is the correspondence between the structure of informal relations among elite members and the structure of their instrumental relations, the more fluid and ad hoc is the coalitional structure likely to be. In other words, the composition of coalitions will rapidly shift as one moves from one issue to another that activates a different constellation of interests.

The rationale for these two propositions is not difficult to find. Personal bonds between individuals tend to be based on much more diffuse, shared understandings and mutual expectations (cf. Laumann, 1973) than instrumental relations that usually rest, at least initially, on more negotiable, limited, and strictly defined agreements (contracts) between the parties. If instrumental relations were to have personal bonds superimposed upon them as well, one would expect the relationships to be resistive to change or breakdown because of their multistranded and more affective character (cf. Mitchell, 1969a).

We are by no means contending, however, that instrumental relations tend to be transitory or ephemeral in character. On the contrary, shared functional interests and responsibilities can easily generate long-term collaboration and cooperation among the relevant actors, *presupposing a community of interest*. Functional differentiation, however, may also generate instrumental relations reflecting stable conflicts of interest. Under such circumstances, instrumental relations (e.g., between labor union leaders and top business managers) are conflicting in their very nature. They are most unlikely to lead to close interpersonal ties. Thus, it is unwarranted to assert the unqualified proposition that, within elite subsystems, the structure of informal social relations and the structure of instrumental relations tend to coverage over time. A version of such a proposition has, in effect, been advanced by Mills (1959), Zeitlin (1974), and Domhoff (1967) in discussing the ways in which the specialized economic, political, and military elites in America tend to become linked socially to a ruling class sharing interpersonal bonds as well as intsrumental ties.

Keller (1963), on the other hand, has argued that the extreme functional specialization of different institutional sectors in highly developed societies effectively precludes the possibility that the elite personnel in one sector will come into contact with elite personnel outside of their sector on a sufficiently sustained basis to permit the development of interpersonal bonds. Moreover, she contends that the interest fragmentation is so complete that elite members typically come into contact in resolving collective disputes as agents of their respective institutional sectors with oppositional interests, again tending to mitigate against their forming positive personal bonds.

To date, evidence mobilized to support either side of the controversy has been unconvincing and contradictory. In our view, the contradictory results can be traced to the selective gathering of data emphasizing more cooperative, as opposed to more conflictive, sorts of instrumental ties and to incomplete enumerations of the relevant population universes and their linkages, owing to the highly biased and selective data sources currently available on the national elite.

We could advance many propositions regarding empirical relationships between different structural arrangements (i.e., different organizing principles) of the elite subsystem and their implications for the performance of integrative functions. Undoubtedly, the reader has already thought of some. The following three propositions merely illustrate some means of generalizing the causal modeling approach proposed in Part II, extending its restrictive cross-structural comparisons within an elite subsystem to permit the consideration of integrative consequences as well:

Proposition Xa: The more homogeneous the persons in the center of the social system's coordinating network (e.g., the community affairs network) are with respect to institutional sector recruitment, value orientations, and social origin groups, the more likely collective decisions are to be nonresponsive and biased with respect to the articulation and aggregation of interest-based demands for collective action from the population subsystem as a whole.

This proposition is by no means self-evident or true by definition. Consider the following two counterexamples.

As our first counterexample, imagine an empirical system in which homogeneously recruited and trained integrative specialists perform a strictly technocratic mediating function for a large number of highly specialized subunits that are in strict competition with one another for scarce resources. This mediating function, in principle, could be executed without regard to the personal and social preferences of the specialist. For instance, bankers are, ideally, supposed to perform such a mediating function for economic actors in a free market economy, according to highly institutionalized rules regulating their behavior as mediators. Much of the debate over the role of the banks in regulating economic activity rests precisely on disagreements regarding the extent to which banks do, in fact, approximate this passive mediating and coordinating role or perform a more active and biased interventionist role (cf. Thompson, 1967; Mace, 1971). The fact that banks are centrally located in the economic system is not really disputed by anyone (cf. Levine, 1972; Zeitlin, 1974). What is very much in dispute, however, is the nature of the role the banks perform as a result of their top leadership personnel being drawn from relatively homogeneous social origins and the putative social biases associated with these origins.

As our second counterexample, consider a democratic political theory that postulates integrative specialists being strictly subservient to their functional role, irrespective of their personal and social characteristics, and that treats the electoral process itself as the key integrative mechanism. Elected public officials, in such a theory, are merely brokers whose task it is to compose differences between contending groups according to the relative electoral strength of the respective groups, subject to the proviso that they also fashion a coalition of groups that will yield an electoral majority. The official's proactive leadership function is thus supposed to be regularly subjected to validation by the electoral process. It is in this sense that his behavior is forced to be unbiased by his personal preferences and strictly responsive to weighing the overall preferences of the population subsystem as a whole.

To continue our presentation of empirical propositions relating different elite structural arrangements and integrative functions, we propose:

Proposition Xb: The more the social origins of elite members and their commitments to different value orientations determine the structure of informal relations among them, and the more these factors jointly determine the structure of their community affairs linkages, the more ideologically rooted are the elite's coalitions and the more likely are disagreements on given issues within the elite to escalate into expressive issues that are recurrent and difficult to resolve.

We would further surmise that ideologically rooted coalitional structures in the elite subsystem are especially likely when the population subsystem itself is structurally crystalized (see Propositions IV and V in the preceding section). Finally, we assert:

Proposition Xc: The more instrumental relations (e.g., professional–business relations) determine the structure of community affairs linkages among elite members and the less the value differentiation among elite members is, the more the elite coalitional strucutre will tend to be broadly consensual and nonideological in character, relatively fluid in the compositional membership of contending coalitions from issue to issue, and oriented toward bargaining and compromise within the elite subsystems itself in resolving specific disputes.

Again we might surmise that such an elite subsystem is especially likely to appear in conjunction with population subsystems having limited structural differentiation (Proposition II) or possessing many centrally located subgroups (Proposition VI).

Both of these propositions also have implications for the relative usefulness of different types of elite influence resources in elite subsystems organized according to different principles. For example, we might expect ideologically organized elite subsystems (see Proposition Xb) to tend to place premiums on the influence resources of "influence over population subgroups" and "popular mobilizer." More consensually and instrumentally constructed elite subsystems (see Proposition Xc), on the other hand, will emphasize the intra-elite influence resources of "good connections" and "honorable brokerage."

Of course, we must always face the fact that the empirical world is usually much more complicated than our theoretical models permit. A given elite subsystem may, thus, be a mixed type in which some parts are organized according to strong value or ideological commitments, while other parts are explicable in terms of more instrumentally and consensually grounded principles of organization. Specifying the conditions under which these different models hold and permitting greater flexibility in representing real-world systems are major tasks for future work.

SOME PROPOSITIONS RELATING TO THE INTERFACE OF POPULATION AND ELITE SUBSYSTEMS

Turning, finally, to propositions about the interface between the population and its integrative subsystem, of the many propositions that could be formulated, we shall consider here only three. Each is intended to exemplify a type of proposition referring to one particular aspect of the structure of the interface. The three aspects of special concern to us include the interface's principles of formation and organization, the conditions for its stability over time, and the nature of the constraints that the interface might impose upon the performance of integrative functions.

The first proposition asserts that:

Proposition XI: In general, expressive issues activating deep-seated value cleavages in the population subsystem will have a greater impact on channeling the structure of the interface between the population and its elite (i.e., the differential attribution of generalized trust and confidence—or popular support—in specific leaders by different population subgroups) than instrumental issues will have.

Developing the rationale for this and related propositions has been the main task of the preceding chapter. Little would be gained by repeating it here. If we hope to avoid the circularity implicit in this proposition, however, we must develop a more satisfactory theory of the types of issues confronting integrative subsystems and how they are resolved. Such a theory must, in turn, be explicitly linked to a theory of structural differentiation. In addition, better empirical procedures must be devised for assessing a given issue's theoretical status. Lacking such developments, we are left in the uncomfortable position of having to assess the character of an issue by evaluating its relative efficacy in predicting population–elite relations. In this case, the proposition, while masquerading as an empirical generalization, is, in reality, only a definition, albeit perhaps a very useful one, of what we mean by expressive and instrumental issues.

With respect to stable and unstable interfaces, we argue that:

Proposition XII: The stability of the interface between a population and its elite is a function of the degree to which all significant (i.e., structurally differentiated and, at least in principle, potentially politically active) population subgroups (or other elements making claims on the system's scarce resources) include elite members who originate from these groups and actively represent their interests.

To the extent that an elite subsystem fails to publicly and visibly represent all relevant subgroups and their respective interests, the excluded subgroups are likely to become dissatisfied and to challenge the legitimacy and acceptability of collective decisions forthcoming from the integrative subsystem. Note here that we speak only of visible representation and do not assume that representatives must actually be effective in modifying collective decisions to make them more acceptable to their constituencies. The common practice of elites to use co-optive tactics whereby representatives of previously excluded interests are brought into some relationship with the elite subsystem, however nominally, is clearly to be expected if we assume that a prime objective of the elite subsystem over time is to maintain the stability of the interface insofar as it is possible.

Finally, regarding constraints imposed by the interface structure on integrative functions, we propose:

Proposition XIII: The degree to which elite members are constrained to behave in accordance with preferences of specific population subgroups is a function of the visibility of their decision-making behavior (political stands) and the ease with which the institutional rules of the game permit these subgroups to register their approval or disapproval of specific elite behavior.

Many different kinds of interface arrangements, in fact, do exist. At the one extreme are those in which there is literally no structural correspondence expected or required between elements in the integrative subsystem and elements in the population subsystem. (Think once again of the idealized model of the banks as technocratic mediators and the highly differentiated economic actors whose behavior is being coordinated.) At the other extreme are those that require a high degree of structural correspondence between the two subsystems. (Think, for example, of an idealized representational model of a democratic polity.)

The character of the interface structure is, thus, really of particular interest only given a normative framework (e.g., democratic political theory) that postulates the need for a responsive interplay between the two subsystems. Lacking such a framework, there is relatively little that can be said in general about how given interface structures will constrain integrative decision-making. In other words, all three propositions make sense only in the context of a discussion of a democratic polity.

SOME CONCLUDING REMARKS

As we warned the reader at the outset, the propositions we have been discussing do not form an exhaustive and systematic summary of the many issues that have attracted our attention in this book, nor do they take us very far toward a theory of social system differentiation and integration, not even one more modestly restricted to community decision-making systems. Their presentation did, we hope, serve to highlight both the more provocative and controversial aspects of our approach to structural analysis and the new directions that might profitably be pursued in future theory-building and research.

Research designed to replicate our study design and to extend it in several important new directions is already well under way in several American communities. Preliminary results are most encouraging. The causal model of an American city's community affairs structure, for example, reveals a number of fascinating similarities to and differences with the one obtained for Altneustadt (see Chapter 8). Specifically, we have found that informal social relations and value differences among elite members play quite contrasting roles in the two communities— but roles that are easily explicable in terms of other features of the two communities.

We have been especially unhappy with our relative neglect of corporate actors, the nature of their exchange relationships, and their role in community decision making (see our all too brief discussion in Chapter 10). This neglect is being partially rectified by our having devised some new procedures for collecting extensive additional data on corporate actors and their interrelationships. Preliminary results again hold out considerable promise for the successful generalization of our network analysis in this direction.

Because we believe our approach can be usefully applied to other types of social systems in addition to community social systems, we have begun field work on a study of the largest professional association of lawyers in a great American metropolis. The association will be treated as a complex organization with a decision-making elite sub-system confronted with a multiplicity of organizational decisions to make in a challenging and variegated internal and external organizational environment. Its associated professional community of practicing lawyers will be treated as equivalent to the population subsystem in a community. While the study is still in the field work stage and no pre-liminary results are available, we can still report satisfaction with the utility of the theoretical and empirical strategy described in this book in guiding the formulation of the data-gathering instruments.

Perhaps the least satisfactory aspect of our work to date has been the relative neglect of process and structural transformations of systems over time. After all, our open-ended model is inherently oriented toward the time-dependent interaction of a large set of variables. The study design for Altneustadt, however, permitted only a static analysis of structure because the data we gathered referred to only one historical point in time. Whatever else we may say about the plausibility of our causal model of structural formation, the process model of resource conversion, or the interactive process model of interface construction, we cannot deny the inherent limitations of our data base in assessing their ade-quacy. Only data gathered on the same system at different points in time can begin to resolve this issue satisfactorily. We are planning sev-eral studies that will attempt to gather relevant data over time on the same system, but the methodological questions encountered thus far are most perplexing and admit of no ready solution. It remains to be seen how successful we shall be.

Whatever the success of these several ventures, much remains to be done in sharpening and refining our methodological apparatus, identi-fying its limits of application, clarifying and improving our theoretical schemata, and applying the approach to diverse empirical systems. Hopefully, we can even begin to make some progress in devising some shortcuts in what is, after all, a rather complex and time-consuming enterprise. Only the accumulation of a number of research studies of specific social systems will permit the exploration of many of the com-parative hypotheses proposed in this chapter. The results reported in this book will hopefully convince some readers of the promise of struc-tural analysis in helping us to answer important questions about differ-entiation and integration that have been troubling all of us for some time.

Appendix A

PART I. STUDY DESIGN AND SAMPLING PROCEDURES FOR THE COMMUNITY SURVEY

Our analysis of the social structure of Altneustadt is based on data drawn from a representative survey of the population eligible to vote, living within Altneustadt's city limits. A sampling universe of 1230 names was drawn by selecting every tenth name from the voter registration list, which is maintained and regularly updated by the city's *Einwohnermeldeamt* (Bureau of Residence Registration) to include people newly arrived in the community. (Everyone 18 years of age or older and holding German citizenship is automatically qualified to vote in Germany. People moving to the city for the first time or changing residences within the city are merely required to report their current address to the *Einwohnermeldeamt*, which automatically adds their names to the voter list with their current addresses.)

In May 1971, interviewers from the *Arbeitsgemeinschaft für System- und Konzeptforschung*, Köln, began field work. Each of the 1230 prospective respondents was sent a letter several days before the interviewer planned to call on him (or her). The letter briefly described the purposes of the study and requested cooperation. If the first attempt to contact the respondent failed, the interviewer was required to try to reach him up to three different times during the day and early evening. Despite strict adherence of the interviewers to these rules, the completion rate was only slightly over 50% after some 5 weeks in the field. To improve the completion rate, we had the interviewers attempt to contact all persons who had either not been successfully contacted before or explicitly refused to be interviewed in September 1971 (after the summer holidays). By this follow-up procedure, we were finally able to get 820 completed interviews. If the number of so-called objective "drop-outs" (that is, people who had died or moved away during the interview period or who had legal residence in Altneustadt but actually lived elsewhere) is subtracted from the original list of names, we obtain a completion rate of 70.5%.

We can partially account for this relatively poor completion rate by the fact that we had set no upper age limit as a criterion for sample inclusion. Normally, persons over 70 years of age are not included in random samples conducted by commercial market and opinion research institutes. Of the original sampling universe, 79 people, or 6.4%, could not be interviewed by reason of excessive old age or physical infirmity. If these people were dropped from our target sample, we would have a completion rate of 75.3%.

Since our theoretical population universe was defined to include only eligible voters residing within Altneustadt's city limits and to exclude residents of several small villages in the surrounding area that belong to the official census statistical unit and those ineligible to vote (for example, foreign workers, the so-called *Gastarbeiter*, and their families), our sample estimates are not strictly comparable to the official census statistics for the area. Despite these discrepancies between our and the census's population universes, we found a comfortingly close similarity between the 1970 census figures on the occupational distribution of Altneustadt and our sample estimates. Only for the "worker" category does our sample appear to underestimate their proportion in the population—the census figure is 35.2% in comparison to our sample estimate of 28.9%. (See Pappi, 1973b: 32–34, for more detailed comparisons and discussion.)

PART II. STUDY DESIGN FOR THE ELITE SURVEY

Obviously there are no hard and fast rules that one can impose to distinguish unambiguously between highly influential actors (individual or corporate) and those low in potential or actual influence. The boundary between these two categories is highly fluid and permeable because the criteria employed in identifying influence on specific decision outcomes are usually poorly specified and, more importantly, depend on people's varying knowledge of the situation and differing subjective evaluations of this knowledge. Moreover, influence is, to an important degree, situationally defined and subject to change as situations change. We can only hope that the procedures employed for identifying the elite population will typically converge on the most influential positions and people with relatively few "errors," that is, not missing highly consequential actors in the elite network. The opposite "errors" of identifying actors as influential when they are not influential by most criteria have, in fact, far less serious implications because one can easily design the subsequent analysis in such a way that it will identify and eliminate such cases, if necessary.

The tremendous advantage of a network approach to studying elite decision-making subsystems is that it has a theoretically justified, self-correcting device for identifying relevant actors. Provided one devises a strategy that guarantees a sufficient number of possible entry points into the diverse, potentially consequential network of actors involved in the full range of matters relevant to community collective decision making, these "access points" can be used, following a snowball procedure, to name the other influential actors, at least for their respective subnetworks. When no additional actors are mentioned with any frequency, one can reasonably assume that one has achieved approximate "closure" for that system, provided, of course, that the respondents are cooperative and do not intend to deceive the investigator.

In an effort to maximize the spread and inclusiveness of our search for potentially relevant actors, we employed Parsons' categorization of the various institutional sectors of a community according to his AGIL paradigm for distinguishing among corporate actors in the economy, the polity, the integrative sector (including voluntary associations, such as political parties, unions, sport clubs, and so on), and the pattern-maintenance sector with its religious, educational, health, and science organizations. As a first approximation, we assumed that elite members typically hold the highest positions of authority in the largest organized collectivities in the respective institutional sectors.

To obtain manageable lists of such collectivities and the incumbents of their top authority positions, we employed the following guidelines, justified more on grounds of expediency than theoretical considerations. For business firms in manufacturing, construction, and wholesale and retail trade, we listed only organizations with 50 or more employees. People who owned firms with numbers of employees below this cut-off point were included in the elite universe only when they headed economic associations, such as the Retail Business Association or the District Handicraft Association. Having obtained a quasi-official and apparently quite comprehensive list of voluntary associations prepared by a city governmental office, we decided to include only persons heading voluntary associations who were visibly active in community affairs as indexed by the frequency of reports about their organizations' activities in the two local newspapers over the preceding 2-year period. The heads of the city and county administrative units, as well as all the elected city and county council members, were all initially included in the list of the elite population. In addition to the heads of organized collectivities, we included self-employed professionals, such as lawyers and *Notars*, assigning them to the appropriate institutional sector on the basis of their primary functional responsibilities.

Since we had included all the members of the city council and those members of the county council who were residents of Altneustadt, the polity sector had the largest number of persons. Many of these council members did not occupy authority positions in other sectors of the community. Even so, the total number of top authority positions identified was, of course, higher than the total number of individuals because a substantial number of people held more than one authority position. For persons holding several authority positions, we attempted to distinguish their primary and secondary institutional sectors on the basis of the relative amounts of time they spent on the various activities related to their several positions.

Two problems remained in evaluating the comprehensiveness and adequacy of our tentative listing of elite members. First, were there influentials who, for whatever reason, did not currently occupy a top authority position as a consequential corporate actor? Second, did our list include people who did not, in fact, have any reputed or actual influence on community affairs? To identify the noninfluentials on the list as well as to ferret out the "missing" influentials, we adopted two procedures. First, we asked selected community informants to evaluate the reputations of the individuals on the list in terms of their influence on community affairs and to add influentials we had missed. Second, we reviewed newspaper coverage of these people's activities over the past several years. Thus, we were able to eliminate some who lacked any reputed influence or newsworthy coverage in the newspapers. Even here, however, our principle was to keep at least a few key people in every institutional sector of the community, even if their visibility in recent community affairs was negligible. We were considerably aided in our search by the fact that one of our research assistants had lived in Altneustadt for 3 years and had closely followed community affairs over the entire period. She was especially useful in identifying well-placed community informants to assist us in the supplementary reputational procedures.

The relative success of our procedures is indicated by the fact that when we finally began interviewing the "target" elite population of 50 people, we identified only one businessman who was mentioned by 5 respondents (see Q29, Appendix C) as deserving to be included in our list of influentials. He was, in fact, subsequently interviewed.[1] Fifteen other people were mentioned only once by the elite respondents. It was evident from a variety of sources that all of them were active on only one issue and could be reasonably left out on the grounds that they were only marginally influential during a particular issue episode and peripherally involved in the community decision-making system, having become completely quiescent in community affairs once "their" issue was resolved.

From the "final" list of 51 elite members, 46 people were interviewed. The interviewing was done by three professional interviewers from the end of March through April, 1971. Since we employed a number of reputational and sociometric questions which asked the respondents to report about the activities and orientations of other persons on the list, we have some information even on those elite members who were not themselves interviewed.

---

[1] Although he was interviewed, we did not add him to the list of influentials that was presented to the respondents to assist them in answering several questions during the interview. In retrospect, we have come to see our failure to add him to this list as a procedural and substantive mistake. He should have been added to the list as soon as several influentials had "agreed" about his importance in community affairs. In replicational studies currently underway in the United States, we have added such persons as soon as two influentials spontaneously mention them.

Appendix B

PART I. INDICATORS OF SOCIAL VALUE ORIENTATIONS

List of Item Components of Value Scales

The following is a list of all the items (and their response distributions) used in constructing the value scales for the cross-section sample. The same item numbers used in Pappi and Laumann (1974: 163–164) have been retained here to facilitate reference to the more extended description of the items and the construction of the value scales presented in that article. (See Chapter 4 also.)

2. How strongly do you interest yourself in politics? Very strongly (8%), strongly (17%), moderately (47%), little (18%), or not at all (10%).

3. Do you believe that industry has, in general, too much political influence in the Bundesrepublik (55%), or that it has just the right amount of influence (35%), or that it has too little political influence (10%)?

4. And how is it with the unions? Do you believe that the unions, in general, have too much political influence in the Bundesrepublik (45%), or that they have just the right amount (41%), or that they have too little political influence (14%)?

5. If the federal government had to decide between reduction of taxes or more money for social services, what should they more likely do in your opinion?

Reduce taxes (30%) or make available more money for social services (61%)? (9% undecided)

6. What about strikes and arguments over wages; are your sympathies in general more on the side of the unions (54%) or on the side of the employers (19%)? (27% undecided)

7. The churches have an important public role in Germany. They must, for example, always be consulted when there is an issue concerning the school system. Do you regard this as right (31%) or do you believe their influence should be curtailed (58%)? (11% undecided)

8. We have written down here a series of possibilities that can be important to a person with respect to his occupational activities. (Hand over card.) If you were to decide on a new job or occupational activity, how important would you consider each of the following characteristics? Please order the characteristics according to their importance to you.[1] Application of own abilities (Average rank, 3.4)

9. Satisfactory chances for promotion (Average rank, 2.8)

10. Good income (Average rank, 4.1)

11. Good relations with colleagues (Average rank, 3.5)

12. Independence in own area of work (Average rank, 3.4)

13. Economic and social security (Average rank, 3.8)

14. Please imagine for a moment two men: The one owns a small business and the other works as an employee in a large office. The employee has a regular income and works 8 hours a day. Then he does not need to think any more about his work and can enjoy his free time. The other must work much longer during the day in his small business than the office worker and does not have so much free time. The small businessman does not have a secure income, but he has the chance to earn more than the office worker. If you had the choice, which work would you choose? Salaried office worker (65%), businessman (32%), undecided (3%)

15. Let's assume for a moment that the income of an auto mechanic in customer service and an office worker are the *same*. Which job would you choose, assuming that you had the necessary training for both jobs? Repairman (28%), office worker (68%), undecided (4%)

16. Some people think that they could not really be satisfied without work and an occupation. Others think that they would get more from life without working. Which opinion is closer to your own? Work makes one satisfied (83%), satisfied without working (15%), undecided (2%)

17. Suppose you had children between 10 and 15 years of age. How important would you regard it that your children climb to a higher social position in the course of their lives than you yourself have done? Very important (27%), important (44%), less important (20%), or not important at all (9%)

18. If one has a high social or economic position in Germany today, it is a rather good sign that one has exhibited special capacities for accomplishments.[2] (75%/4%/21%)

---

[1] The ranks ranged from 1 to 6, with the rank of 6 being the most important characteristic.

[2] The first percentage refers to those who agreed with the item, the second to those who were undecided (including "don't know" and "no answer"), and the third to those who disagreed with the item. The answers for items 18–37 are reported in this

19. The citizen has the right to strike and demonstrate even if he endangers the public order in doing so. (31%/4%/65%)
20. In spite of the commentary in newspapers and on television, national and international events are seldom as interesting as events that occur in the community in which one lives. (47%/5%/48%)
21. One can easily permit youths from around 15 years of age to decide most things for themselves. (61%/4%/35%)
22. The main problem of a democracy is that most people don't really know what is in their own best (well-understood) interests. (70%/6%/24%)
23. The bad thing in today's world is that most people don't believe in anything. (50%/5%/45%)
24. Young people sometimes have rebellious ideas, but, with the years, they ought to get over them. (76%/5%/19%)
25. The rank differences among men are acceptable because they essentially express what one has done with one's chances. (60%/6%/34%)
26. Arguments among the various interest groups in our society and their demands on the government harm the general good. (46%/6%/48%)
27. It is meaningful to select one's acquaintances in terms of whether or not they can be useful to one. (26%/5%/69%)
28. The most important decisions in the life of a family ought to be made by the man as head of the household. (40%/5%/55%)
29. What is missing in the present day is the old kind of friendship that lasted throughout one's life. (67%/5%/28%)
30. Without doubt, many persons who have moved here are capable people, but when someone is to be selected for a responsible position in the community, I favor persons from families who have been here a long time. (30%/5%/65%)
31. Economic profits are, by and large, justly distributed in Germany today. (29%/6%/65%)
32. The task of the political opposition is not to criticize the government but to support it in its work. (66%/7%/27%)
33. When one thinks that present day students will sometime come into responsible positions, one can have fear for the future. (32%/5%/63%)
34. Persons with approximately equal social or economic positions ought to stick to themselves. (26%/5%/70%)
35. I have more respect for someone who has made a name for himself in his own community than for persons who are well-known in their field but have no close connections in their community. (52%/5%/43%)
36. General measures for the community should only be decided when the people have been informed and have been able to express their opinion. (87%/4%/9%)
37. The only possibility in our complex world to learn something essential is to listen to personalities whom one can trust. (61%/5%/34%)
38. In general, how often do you go to church? More than once a week (3%), once a week (25%), less than once a month (12%), several times a year (16%), seldom or never (44%)

---

fashion. Each item had a six-point Likert scale, with three degrees of agreement and three degrees of disagreement. In calculating correlations, the full scale was retained. All Likert-type items were in a self-administered questionnaire answered by the respondent during the course of the interview.

Sources of Items

For each item number listed below, we have indicated the study and the original scale (in brackets), if it was not an individual question, from which the item is drawn. When the reference given is an English text, it means that we have translated the items into German. Items that do not appear in the list are either standard questions of survey research, for example, item 2, or were devised by us.

Item number	Source
3, 6	Laumann, 1966: 165–166, Q. 4 and 6 (economic ideology); item 6 originally part of Centers' (1949: 232, Q. 7) conservatism-radicalism battery of questions.
5	Butler and Stokes, 1969: 468, Q. 28.
7	Klingemann and Pappi, 1970: 133.
8–13	Closed question which covers some of the most frequently mentioned answers to an open-ended question about the "likes" and "dislikes" of one's job; see Gurin *et al.*, 1960, and the discussion of this question by Robinson, 1969.
14, 15	Laumann, 1973: 278, Q. 57–58 (entrepreneurial–bureaucratic orientation).
16	Lenski, 1963: 377–378, Q. 5.
17	Mayntz, 1958: 191.
18, 25, 31, 34	Duke, 1967: 119–124 (index of egalitarian attitudes). Originally developed by Seeman, 1960, as an index of status attitude.
19, 26, 32	Kaase, 1971: 144–145 (Demokratie-Skala).
20, 30, 35	Dye, 1966 (local–cosmopolitan scale). Scale published in Robinson *et al.*, 1968: 397–399.
21, 28	Levinson and Huffman, 1955 (traditional family ideology).
22	McClosky, 1964 (belief in equality scale). Scale published in Robinson *et al.*, 1968: 170–178.
23, 29	McClosky and Schaar, 1965 (anomy scale).
24	Roghman, 1966: 409, item 22; German translation of an *F*-Scale item (Adorno *et al.*, 1950: 248).
37	Roghman, 1966: 405, item 28; German translation of a dogmatism item (Rokeach, 1960: 79).

Construction of Value Scales

All scales were constructed following the rules of Likert scaling. Items varied, however, in the number of response categories permitted. When this occurred for items comprising a scale, we reassigned category numerical values for the items with fewer response categories to correspond to the range of category numerical values used for items with the most response categories. Reflected items are characterized by a minus sign.

The following value scales (with their component items) were constructed:

(1) Economic ideology favoring unions: Items 3, —4, 6, 19.
(2) Preference for work autonomy: Items 8, 12, —14, 15.
(3) Religious traditionalism: Items 7, 23, 29, 38.
(4) Justification for social inequalities: Items 25, 31, 34.
(5) Upward mobility orientation: Items 5, 10, 17, 18, 27.
(6) Localism: Items 20, 30, 35, 37.
(7) Family traditionalism: Items —21, 24, 28, 33.

PART II. INDEX OF COMMUNITY SATISFACTION

Answers to the following questions were used to construct an index of community satisfaction for respondents in the cross-section survey.

1. How do you like living here in Altneustadt? (Read through list.)
    (4) like it very much (36%),
    (3) like it (34%),
    (2) like it as much as somewhere else (18%), or
    (1) not so much (11%)?

2. If you had to move away from Altneustadt for some reason, how strongly would you miss it? (Read through list.)
    (4) very strongly (19%),
    (3) strongly (27%),
    (2) little (30%), or
    (1) not at all (20%)?

3. Does it happen now and again that you wish you didn't live in Altneustadt? (Read through list.)
    (1) often (8%),
    (2) sometimes (23%),
    (3) seldom (19%), or
    (4) never (48%)?

To determine the index score for each respondent, we summed the appropriate category numerical value (in parentheses) for each of the 3 questions and subtracted 2. Thus, the index values range from 1 to 10, from lowest to highest level of community satisfaction. The percentages do not sum to 100% because we treated "don't know" responses as missing data in the index construction (listwise deletion). The correlation of this index with the actual intention to move away from Altneustadt is $r = -.85$.

PART III. COMMUNITY PREFERENCES ON
FOUR CONTROVERSIES IN ALTNEUSTADT
(See Pappi and Laumann, 1974: 178.)

In the following, we have singled out some local political issues that have played a certain role in Altneustadt in recent years.

1. There was, for example, the discussion about the secular terminal school and the confessional school (i.e., religiously organized school). What was your attitude on this issue? At the time, were you for the establishment of the secular terminal school, or were you for the continuation of the confessional terminal school, or were you uninterested in the whole question?

For secular terminal school	68%
For confessional terminal school	10
For another solution	1
Not interested	14
Don't know any more	2
Did not live in city at the time	5
	100%

($N = 820$)

2. Then there was a discussion about the construction of the city hall. Were you, at that time, for or against the construction of this city hall, or were you not interested in the issue?

For construction of present city hall	66%
Against construction	12
Not interested	16
Don't know any more	2
Did not live in city at the time	5
	100%

($N = 820$)

3. Consider the following issue: Suppose that a business firm in the electrical industry, which employed about 600 workers, was considering locating in Altneustadt. Would you be for or against such an industrial relocation, or would you not be interested in the issue?

For relocation	82%
Against it	6
Not interested	11
Don't know	2
	100%

($N = 820$)

4. Perhaps you still remember the pop festival which took place in Aachen last year. Imagine, for a moment, that a similar festival was to take place in Altneustadt this summer in the fields of Brückenkopf. What would be your position? Would you be for the pop festival, would you be against the pop festival, or would you not be interested in this issue?

For it	33%
Against it	33
Not interested	31
Don't know	3
	100%

($N = 820$)

Appendix C*

PART I. INTERVIEW SCHEDULE FOR COMMUNITY ELITE SURVEY

As we have already told you, we want to talk with you about Altneustadt. Since a comparable investigation concerning community problems is also to be carried out in the United States, we cannot conduct a completely free conversation but must use a fixed questionnaire. In this manner, the comparability of answers will be guaranteed.

Q1. How much do you like living here in Altneustadt? (Give categories)
   like it very much
   like it
   as well as any other place, or
   not so much

Q2. How long have you lived in Altneustadt?
   since birth
   came later to live   When? _____ (Ask for number of years)

Q3. If you had to move away from Altneustadt for some reason, how strongly would you miss Altneustadt? (Give categories)
   very strongly

* Interview Schedule for Community Elite Survey, University of Cologne (Zentralarchiv für empirische Sozialforschung, Altneustadt Project).

strongly
little, or
not at all

Q4. We have written down on this little card various things that are promoted in varying degrees in most cities. (Hand over set of cards to put in rank order.) One cannot, of course, attain everything at the same time. Look through the list please and order them according to their importance, that is, the importance that you allot to each problem.

E Safeguarding good conditions for local industry and business in order to guarantee economic growth.

F Promotion of public housing—for the creation of good living conditions for the working classes.

G Maintenance and extension of Altneustadt as an attractive place to live— with good housing possibilities, leisure time facilities, and recreational opportunities.

H Avoidance of detrimental conflicts between various population groups.

I Preservation of the cultural heritage and traditional values.

K Promotion of active participation of the citizens in community affairs.

L Insuring an efficient, just and economical community administration.

Q5. We have just said that most communities have to deal with such questions. Depending on how these tasks and problems are solved in individual communities, one can distinguish in general three different community types.

First, there are those communities in which *considerable conflicts between the same leaders or population groups* appear again and again in the handling of community affairs and public measures so that the same persons or groups are always found together in a coalition.

In the *second* type of community, there is certainly also controversy about various problems, but there are *constantly changing coalitions* between various groups or persons so that the coalitions are different depending on the problem being considered.

Then there are the *third type* of communities in which relatively little argument about public measures takes place because there is a *relatively high consensus* among the various leaders and groups about what needs to be done.

In general, how would you characterize the situation in Altneustadt during the past 4 or 5 years? Does it fit closer to the first, the second, or the third description?

first description
second description
third description
other   What? (Please note)

Q5a. If the respondent does not accept one of the three types but *uses a mixed type,* probe:

Which of the two (three) descriptions still fits most closely the relationships in Altneustadt? (Make a cross here if this follow-up question is used.)

If mixed type of 1 and 2 is used, ask both of the following questions (5b and 5c):

Q5b. If the first description was chosen, then ask: Could you please tell us those persons or groups that are more or less regularly joined together in the same coalition?

Q5c. If the second description was chosen, then ask: Could you please illustrate this situation with an example that shows how particular persons or groups are in one case opponents and in another allies?

AGAIN TO ALL:

Q6. Why do you think that such a situation exists in Altneustadt?

Q7. Which of the three situations described is ideal for a community?
> first
> second
> third
> other   Which? (Please note)

Q8. And why do you think so?

Q9. In the following we have selected some community decisions (issues) that played a certain role in Altneustadt in recent years. Let's first talk about the question of the secular terminal school (fifth to ninth grades inclusive) discussed a few years ago.

Q9a. Have you participated in any way in the decision process concerning the establishment of the secular terminal school, that is, did you make an attempt to influence this decision?
> yes
> no

Q9b. What was your original attitude? Were you for the establishment of the secular terminal school or against it, that is, for the maintenance of the confessional school?
> for it
> against it

Q9c. Could you tell me which persons and groups were most strongly in favor of the secular terminal school? (For persons named who are not on the list, please ask for the exact position of the person: name, occupation, group membership [identify by number on the list] and position in the group, old/new resident.) (Please make a cross if persons or groups are named first.)

Probe: Are there still other persons or groups who supported the secular terminal school? (If at first only persons were named, ask for additional persons and then ask about groups. Do the corresponding thing if groups were named first.)

> Persons   Groups

Q9d. Do you remember which persons and groups were against the establishment of the secular terminal school, that is, were for the continuance of the confessional school?

> Persons   Groups

Probe: Were there still other persons or groups?

> Persons   Groups

Q9e. How strong would you say the conflict in this issue was? (Give categories.)
        very strong
        strong
        not so strong

Q10a. (And if you now think of the *construction of the city hall:*) Have you participated in any way in the decision process concerning the construction of the city hall in Altneustadt, that is, did you make an attempt to influence the decision?
        yes
        no

Q10b. What was your original attitude (opinion)? At that time, were you for or against the construction of the city hall?
        for it
        against it

Q10c. Could you tell me which persons and groups stood most strongly *for* the decision in favor of the city hall?
                  Persons   Groups
Probe: Were there other persons and groups for it?

                  Persons   Groups

Q10d. Do you remember which persons and groups were against the construction of the city hall?
                  Persons   Groups
Probe: Were there other persons and groups against it?

                  Persons   Groups

Q10e. Was a conflict in this issue visible to the outside, that is, to the public at large?
        yes
        no (Proceed to Question 10g)

Q10f. How strong would you say the conflict was? (Give categories)
        very strong
        strong, or
        not so strong

Q10g. Was there a nonpublic conflict in this issue?
        yes
        no (Proceed to Question 11)

Q10h. How strong was it? (Give categories)
        very strong
        strong, or
        not so strong

In the next questions, we would like to talk about the community annexations.

Q11. In the recently published official opinion from Düsseldorf, the *community annexations* of the city of Altneustadt are proposed in which the following communities and community sections of the district of Altneustadt will be incorporated into the city of Altneustadt. (List of communities to be incorporated)

Q11a. Have you yourself participated in any way in the decision whether these communities ought to come into Altneustadt or not?

        yes

        no (Proceed to Question 11c)

Q11b. If yes: Could you tell us whether you were originally for or against the incorporation of these places?

        for it

        against it

Q11c. If no: Despite this, could you tell us whether you are for or against the incorporation of these communities?

        for

        against

Q11d. Do you know which persons and groups have stood most strongly for the incorporation of these communities?

                    Persons   Groups

probe: Were there other persons and groups for it?

                    Persons   Groups

Q11e. Which persons and groups were against the incorporation of these specified places?

                    Persons   Groups

Probe: Were there other persons and groups against the incorporation of these places?

                    Persons   Groups

Q11f. How strong would you say the conflict was or still is inside of Altneustadt on this issue?

        very strong

        strong

        not so strong

Up to now, we have talked about actual decisions. Now we would like to direct your attention to two hypothetical cases which, nevertheless, lie within the realm of possibility.

Q12. Let us suppose first that an enterprise in the *electrical industry* with 500 to 700 employees showed an interest in *settling in Altneustadt*. The enterprise would have a large demand for skilled workers and would want to establish its own apprentice program.

Q12a. Which persons and groups would, in your opinion, welcome and support this sort of industrial settlement?

                    Persons   Groups

Probe: Would there be other persons and groups for it?

      Persons   Groups

Q12b. Which persons and groups would probably be reserved or negative about such an industrial settlement?

      Persons   Groups

Probe: Would there be other persons and groups against it?

      Persons   Groups

Q12c. Do you think there would be a public or non-public conflict over this issue?
   public
   nonpublic

Q12d. How strong do you think the conflict would be in this issue?
   very strong
   strong
   not so strong

Q12e. Who, in your opinion, would be successful, the supporters or the opponents?
   supporters
   opponents

Q12f. What would be your own opinion on this issue? Would you welcome or reject the industrial settlement?
   welcome
   reject

Q12g. Why would you welcome or reject such an industrial settlement?

Q13. Perhaps you still remember the pop festival which took place last year in a nearby large city. Imagine for a moment that a similar festival were to be put on this summer in the fields of Brückenkopf. The promoter has already asked the city for a permit and the newspaper has been informed about the intended meeting.

Q13a. In your opinion which persons and groups would welcome and support the festival?

      Persons   Groups

Probe: Would there be other persons and groups for it?

      Persons   Groups

Q13b. Which persons and groups would probably try to prevent the festival?

      Persons   Groups

Probe: Would there be other persons and groups against it?

      Persons   Groups

Q13c. In this issue would there be a public or nonpublic conflict?
   public
   nonpublic

Q13d. How strong would you say the conflict would be? (Give alternatives)
   very strong
   strong
   not so strong

Q13e. Who, in your opinion, would win, the supporters or the opponents?
> supporters
> opponents

Q13f. What would be your personal opinion, would you welcome or oppose the festival?
> welcome
> oppose

Q13g. Why would you welcome (or oppose) such a pop festival?

Q14. We have now talked about the community school, the construction of the city hall, community reorganization, a new industrial settlement, and the pop festival. If you think of how the individual issues were decided or would be decided, with which of the five issues could one best see who has, in general, the greatest influence in Altneustadt?
> community school
> construction of the city hall
> community reorganization
> industrial settlement
> pop festival

Q15. Now think of the various groups in Altneustadt that have common interests in one or another issue. Which groups would you distinguish in Altneustadt? By "groups" we mean formal organizations, such as business firms, organizations, and voluntary associations, as well as looser, unorganized population categories, which share particular characteristics and think of themselves as a group.

Q16. Here we have tried to put together as complete a list of various groups as possible. (Hand over group list.) We have numbered the groups for the sake of simplicity. In answers, please just give us the corresponding number. Could you first name those groups that are generally very influential in Altneustadt? (If doubtful which groups, always let him name the more important.)

Q17. Which is the most influential group of those you have named?

Q18. Which group is in second place?

Q19. Which three groups would you place in the third position?

Q20. In your opinion, which five groups have, in general, little influence in Altneustadt?

Q21. In the leadership of the CDU, decisions about community affairs are frequently made. To which three groups do you believe the CDU ascribes special weight in such cases?

Q22. Could you please rank the three groups according to the importance that is attributed to them in the CDU? (in your opinion)
> 1.
> 2.
> 3.

Q23. When you think of decisions in the SPD (German Social Democratic Party), which three groups are attributed special importance by the SPD?
1.
2.
3.

Q24. Would you please once again rank the three groups according to the importance that, in your opinion, the SPD attributes to them?
1.
2.
3.

Til now, we have talked predominantly about groups in Altneustadt. We would now like to learn something from you about persons who have a certain significance for Altneustadt in one or another sector. Here we have put together a list of persons—the names arranged in alphabetical order. We are assuming that these persons have influence in various fields. (Hand over the person list.) Once again, I will ask you to give in your answers the corresponding numbers.

Q25. Which persons on this list would you say are *now*, in general, very influential in Altneustadt? Please give the corresponding number.

Q26. Who is the most influential of those whom you have named? (If the respondent says that more than one is in first place, after one probe do not force any rank order.)

Q27. Who is in second place?

Q28. Which three persons would you put in third place?

Q29. Do you know any other persons who are generally influential in Altneustadt but are not included in our list? Who are they? (Obtain the exact position of these persons.)
Name   Position   Association

Q30. Are there persons on this list of whom one can say that their influence was very great 5 or 10 years ago but has declined since then? Who are they?

Q31. What about questions that concern Altneustadt but must be decided officially by the state government in the capital city? Which five persons would you say are very influential in such decisions?

Q32. Would you please rank order these five persons according to their influence as you see it?
1.
2.
3.
4.
5.

Q33. Would you please indicate the three persons from the list with whom you most frequently meet socially (privately)?
   1.
   2.
   3.

Q34. If no one or fewer than three persons are named: Could you please name the three persons with whom you are most likely to meet socially?

Q35. When you think of your best friends in Altneustadt and the surrounding area, would you include the aforementioned persons?
   yes all three
        two of them
        one of them
   no

Q36. With which enterprises or organizations do you have frequent business or professional relationships? You can use our list of groups for your answer.

Q37. Could you now indicate the three persons from our list with whom you have the closest business or professional contact?

Q38. Could you please indicate the three persons with whom you most frequently discuss community affairs?

Q39. If no one or fewer than three persons are named: Could you tell me the three persons with whom you are most likely to discuss problems of Altneustadt?
   1.
   2.
   3.

Q40. Usually, persons are regarded as significant and influential in a community because of certain personal characteristics or resources. We have written down here some such possibilities. (Hand over the list.) One can, for example, be influential on the basis of an official position in the city administration or as an elected public official, which corresponds to our first point, or because one has at his disposal economic resources, such as money, land, or jobs. This would correspond to our points 2 and 3, which we have differentiated according to the fluidity of the resource, that is, between money on the one hand and land and jobs on the other. Then there are experts in specific fields who are influential because of their expertise—that is our point 4—or persons who can accomplish a great deal through their good connections with other influential people in and outside of the city—that is our point 5. One can also be influential in a community because one is known as someone who makes good suggestions and is a good speaker who can mobilize the people for these proposals. This is our point 6. Our point 7 describes the honorable broker, and point 8 describes the representative of specific subgroups of the population.

Q40a. Could you please indicate, for the persons on our list whom you believe yourself capable of exactly judging, the most important characteristics or resources that this person possesses? If several possibilities are relevant for a person, please give me the characteristic or resource that you regard as the most important. (Enter characteristics/resources on own list of persons)

(1) Official decision-making authority as elected public official or occupant of a high position in the public service.
(2) Power of disposal over fluid capital, possible giver of credit.
(3) Power of disposal over less fluid economic resources, such as land or jobs.
(4) Special expert knowledge of certain limited fields of community interest.
(5) Good connections with influential persons in and outside of Altneustadt.
(6) General respect as someone who can mobilize the public for good proposals in the interest of the city as a whole.
(7) Honorable broker who can mediate in a nonpartisan way points at issue.
(8) Influence in certain subgroups of the population, such as voters of a particular party, members of a voluntary association, and so on.
(9) Other (please get exact particulars).

Q40b. Would you now please indicate the most important characteristic or resource that is most relevant for you?

Q41. If we now consider how goals are defined, that is, in our case, how one forms the conviction about what must be done in a community, one can identify various possibilities. We have written down on this card two such possibilities (hand over the card) and, in order to make clear the essential differences between them, they are perhaps more strongly emphasized than one could observe in practice. Thus, it might be that neither A nor B exactly describes how particular persons define goals.

—A has developed a systematic conception of goals that he believes is the only correct one for the interests of the community in the long term. A accepts other conceptions only if they coincide with his own view, independently of the concrete chances of implementing them.

—B believes that there cannot be a single correct goal for the community but that there are many legitimate goals. B chooses a program that can be achieved practically yielding advances for particular sectors without neglecting other sectors too much.

Q41a. Which two persons on our list would you say correspond most closely to person A?
Number   Number

Q41b. Which two persons correspond most closely to person B?
Number   Number

Q41c. How would you classify yourself?
closer to A
closer to B

Q42. In the preceding question we broached the problem of how one decides for or against particular proposals. Now we would like to discuss how one tries to realize one's goals concretely. We have again written down two contrasting methods. (Hand over card)

—A meets informally with his friends and acquaintances in order to enlist their support for a particular measure or goal. When A wants to implement something, he prefers to turn to persons whom he already knows and does not like to present his suggestion in public meetings, where there is always the danger of a public controversy.

—B also likes to turn to his friends and acquaintances to discuss particular objectives. If B wants, however, to implement something, he likes to bring his concern before the public, for example, by presenting a position in the newspaper or speaking in public gatherings even if there is the danger of public controversy.

Q42a. Which two persons on our list would you say are closest to A in the manner in which they try to enact something?

Number   Number

Q42b. Which two persons correspond more closely to person B?

Number   Number

Q42c. How would you classify yourself?
      closer to A
      closer to B

Q43. When it is a matter of new suggestions and proposals for the community, there are persons who frequently suggest such proposals and goals for discussion while others are known more as good critics of proposals that have already been made.

Q43a. Could you name two persons on our list who frequently propose new measures and objectives?

Number   Number

Q43b. Which two persons are known more as good critics of suggestions that have already been made?

Number   Number

Q43c. How would you classify yourself?
      suggester of new measures
      good critic of already made proposals

Q44. Ought one promote a development in Altneustadt that brings industries and firms from various sectors to Altneustadt so that the composition of the population becomes more heterogeneous, or ought one consolidate existing industries and organizations so that Altneustadt, by and large, retains its present character?
      new industries from various sectors
      consolidate (extend) existing activities
      other   What?

Q45. If you think of the time that you normally spend on community affairs in a week and bear in mind all discussions in which you talk about issues that relate to the city of Altneustadt as well as meetings and more informal gatherings and other work, how many hours in the week do you normally spend on community affairs?
      number of hours_____

Q46. We have written down here a series of opinions that one sometimes hears.

Go through the statements in order and make a cross, in the appropriate place, indicating whether you agree or disagree. For the strength of your agreement or disagreement we have provided three posibilities: strong, moderate, weak. (Hand over the list of items [See Part II, Appendix C])

In conclusion, we would like to ask you some questions to collect statistical data.

Q47. Where were you born?
     Altneustadt
     Rheinland
     Westfalen
     other parts of West Germany
     East Germany
     former German eastern provinces
     foreign

Q48. When were you born? (year of birth)

Q49. Where have you lived for the longest time?
     Altneustadt
     Rheinland
     Westfalen
     other parts of West Germany
     East Germany
     former German eastern provinces
     foreign

Q50. If not in Altneustadt: Approximately how many inhabitants lived in the place where you lived the longest part of your life?
     number of inhabitants_____
     TO ALL:

Q51. Are you:
     single
     married
     widowed
     divorced, or
     separated?

Q52. If not single: How many children?
     none, etc.

Q53. Ages of children:

Q54. Could you tell us from which region your wife comes?
     Altneustadt area
     Rheinland
     Westfalen
     other parts of West Germany
     other formerly German sections
     foreign

TO ALL:

Q55. Do your parents originate from Altneustadt or its surrounding area?
yes
no

Q56. Do most of your relatives live in Altneustadt or its surroundings?
yes
no

Q57. What is your principal occupation at the present time? (Please get exact particulars.)
If retired: What was your last principal occupation?

Q58. Are you self-employed or are you employed by a firm or public authority?
self-employed
firm or public authority (Proceed to Question 63)

Q59. If self-employed: Are you the owner of
a manufacturing enterprise
a retail enterprise, or
an artisan trade?

Q60. Do you own one or several enterprises?
one
several

Q61. To which sector does it belong?

Q62. Do you employ other persons?
yes   How many?
no

Q63. If not self-employed: Where are you employed?

Q64. Could you tell us your exact status in your occupation?

In the case of officials: Which title or service grade do you have?

In the case of salaried employees: Exact grade of service, such as authorized clerk, cashier.

In the case of workers: for example, skilled worker.

In the case of artisans: for example, master, journeyman.

Q65. Are you the supervisor of other persons?
yes
no

Q66. If yes: How many people do you supervise?

Q67. What level of education have you completed?

1. Primary and junior high school (from 7 to 9 years, terminal school)
without completing vocational certification (as butcher, carpenter, bank clerk, auto mechanic)
with completing vocational certification

2. Intermediate school—high school without university entry certification—several years of technical school
>commercial school (usually 10 or 11 years school)
>high school through ninth grade
>high school through tenth grade with school certificate
>high school beyond tenth grade without certificate
>higher technical school with certificate (*Polytecknikum*)
>13 years of school (graduate engineers)

3. Completion of university entrance certificate (examination: *Arbitur*)

4. University
>university without diploma
>university with diploma

Q68. What was the principal occupation of your father? (Obtain exact particulars)

Q69. To which religious community do you belong?
>Catholic
>Evangelical–Protestant
>other religions
>none

Q70. We have here a list of organizations and voluntary associations in Altneustadt. (Hand over list of organizations) Would you please first indicate with a cross those organizations and voluntary associations of which you are a member?

Q71. If no memberships, probe: Are there other organizations or voluntary associations of which you are a member? (Note organizations)

TO ALL MEMBERS:

Q72. Are you at this time
>holder of an executive position
>active member, that is, do you participate frequently in events or meetings of the organization, or
>are you only a passive or paying member?

Q73. Do you have presently an office or an honorary office, are you a member of a committee, or do you have otherwise an official position in the city or county of Altneustadt?

Q74. Do you have, at this time, an office, honorary office, or otherwise an official position outside of the county or above the county level?

Q75. How about boards of directors or similar nonpolitical offices and honorary offices?

Q76. If not a party member: Do you regard yourself in general as a supporter of a particular party?
>yes
>no

Q77. If yes: Which party?
>CDU
>SPD

FDP

other   Which?

Q78. If no: Which party do you normally vote for in federal elections?

CDU

SPD

FDP

other   Which?

TO ALL:

Q79. And which party did you vote for in the last election for city council?

CDU

SPD

FDP

other   Which?

PART II. ITEM LIST FOR COMMUNITY ELITE SURVEY

Please indicate for each of the following propositions whether you agree or disagree and how strongly. Do this by making a cross in *one* of the six little boxes under each statement.

S 1. If one has a high social or economic position in Germany today, it is a rather good sign that one has exhibited special capabilities for accomplishments.

	Agree			Disagree	
Strongly	Moderately	Weakly	Strongly	Moderately	Weakly

S 2. The citizen has the right to strike and demonstrate even if he endangers the public order in doing so.

	Agree			Disagree	
Strongly	Moderately	Weakly	Strongly	Moderately	Weakly

S 3. In spite of the commentary in newspapers and on television, national and international events are seldom as interesting as events that occur in the community in which one lives.

	Agree			Disagree	
Strongly	Moderately	Weakly	Strongly	Moderately	Weakly

S 4. One can easily permit youths from around 15 years on to decide most things for themselves.

	Agree			Disagree	
Strongly	Moderately	Weakly	Strongly	Moderately	Weakly

S 5. The main problem of a democracy is that most people don't really know what is in their own best interests.

	Agree			Disagree	
Strongly	Moderately	Weakly	Strongly	Moderately	Weakly

S 6. The bad thing in today's world is that most people don't believe in anything.

	Agree			Disagree	
Strongly	Moderately	Weakly	Strongly	Moderately	Weakly

S 7. Young people sometimes have rebellious ideas, but, with the years, they ought to get over them.

Agree			Disagree		
Strongly	Moderately	Weakly	Strongly	Moderately	Weakly

S 8. The rank differences among men are acceptable because they essentially express what one has done with the chances one has had.

Agree			Disagree		
Strongly	Moderately	Weakly	Strongly	Moderately	Weakly

S 9. Arguments among the various interest groups in our society and their demands on the government harm the general good.

Agree			Disagree		
Strongly	Moderately	Weakly	Strongly	Moderately	Weakly

S10. Present day youth are no worse than the youth of earlier times.

Agree			Disagree		
Strongly	Moderately	Weakly	Strongly	Moderately	Weakly

S11. The most important decisions in the life of a family ought to be made by the man as head of the household.

Agree			Disagree		
Strongly	Moderately	Weakly	Strongly	Moderately	Weakly

S12. What is missing in the present day is the old kind of friendship that lasted throughout one's life.

Agree			Disagree		
Strongly	Moderately	Weakly	Strongly	Moderately	Weakly

S13. Undoubtedly many persons who moved here are capable people, but when someone is to be selected for a responsible position in the community, I favor persons from families who have been here a long time.

Agree			Disagree		
Strongly	Moderately	Weakly	Strongly	Moderately	Weakly

S14. Economic profits are, by and large, justly distributed in Germany today.

Agree			Disagree		
Strongly	Moderately	Weakly	Strongly	Moderately	Weakly

S15. Most voters don't have enough judgmental capacity to make up their minds sensibly among the candidates for public office.

Agree			Disagree		
Strongly	Moderately	Weakly	Strongly	Moderately	Weakly

S16. The differences in prestige among the various occupations should be reduced.

Agree			Disagree		
Strongly	Moderately	Weakly	Strongly	Moderately	Weakly

S17. When one thinks that present day students will at some time come into responsible positions, one has fear for the future.

Agree			Disagree		
Strongly	Moderately	Weakly	Strongly	Moderately	Weakly

S18. Persons with approximately equal social or economic positions ought to stick to themselves.

<table>
<tr><td></td><td colspan="3">Agree</td><td colspan="3">Disagree</td></tr>
<tr><td>Strongly</td><td>Moderately</td><td>Weakly</td><td>Strongly</td><td>Moderately</td><td>Weakly</td></tr>
</table>

S19. The opposition's criticism of the government should not be permitted to be politically motivated but should be an expression of responsibilty for the collective good.

<table>
<tr><td></td><td colspan="3">Agree</td><td colspan="3">Disagree</td></tr>
<tr><td>Strongly</td><td>Moderately</td><td>Weakly</td><td>Strongly</td><td>Moderately</td><td>Weakly</td></tr>
</table>

S20. A housewife should not expect her husband to help her in the household when he comes home from a hard day's work.

<table>
<tr><td></td><td colspan="3">Agree</td><td colspan="3">Disagree</td></tr>
<tr><td>Strongly</td><td>Moderately</td><td>Weakly</td><td>Strongly</td><td>Moderately</td><td>Weakly</td></tr>
</table>

S21. I have more respect for someone who has made a name for himself in the community than for persons who are very well-known in their field but have no tie to the community in which they live.

<table>
<tr><td></td><td colspan="3">Agree</td><td colspan="3">Disagree</td></tr>
<tr><td>Strongly</td><td>Moderately</td><td>Weakly</td><td>Strongly</td><td>Moderately</td><td>Weakly</td></tr>
</table>

S22. General measures for the community should be decided only when the people have been informed and have been able to express their opinion.

<table>
<tr><td></td><td colspan="3">Agree</td><td colspan="3">Disagree</td></tr>
<tr><td>Strongly</td><td>Moderately</td><td>Weakly</td><td>Strongly</td><td>Moderately</td><td>Weakly</td></tr>
</table>

S23. Most men in low positions are quite satisfied because they know that they do not want to take on the responsibility that a higher position entails.

<table>
<tr><td></td><td colspan="3">Agree</td><td colspan="3">Disagree</td></tr>
<tr><td>Strongly</td><td>Moderately</td><td>Weakly</td><td>Strongly</td><td>Moderately</td><td>Weakly</td></tr>
</table>

S24. One can easily exaggerate the idea of co-determination; there are problems that cannot be co-decided by employees.

<table>
<tr><td></td><td colspan="3">Agree</td><td colspan="3">Disagree</td></tr>
<tr><td>Strongly</td><td>Moderately</td><td>Weakly</td><td>Strongly</td><td>Moderately</td><td>Weakly</td></tr>
</table>

References and Selected Bibliography

Adams, Bert N.
  1967   "Interaction theory and the social networks." *Sociometery* **30**: 64–78.
Adorno, Theodor W., Else Frenkel-Brunswik, Daniel J. Levinson, and R. Nevitt Sanford
  1950   *The Authoritarian Personality*. New York: Norton.
Agger, Robert E., Daniel Goldrich, and Bert E. Swanson
  1964   *The Rulers and the Ruled: Political Power and Importance in American Communities*. New York: John Wiley.
Aiken, Michael
  1970   "The distribution of community power: Structural and social consequences." Pp. 487-525 in Michael Aiken and Paul Mott (Eds.), *The Structure of Community Power*. New York: Random House.
Aiken, Michael, and Robert R. Alford
  1970   "Comparative urban research and community decision-making." *New Atlantis* **1** (Winter): 85–110.
Aiken, Michael, and Paul Mott, Eds.
  1970   *The Structure of Community Power*. New York: Random House.
Alba, Richard D.
  1973   "A graph theoretic definition of a sociometric clique." *Journal of Mathematical Sociology* **3**:113–126.
  1975   "Defining proximity in social networks: A reanalysis of the Laumann-Pappi data." Unpublished manuscript. Bureau of Applied Social Research, Columbia University.

Alba, Richard D., and Charles Kadushin
    1970   "The construction of sociograms by computer methods." New York: Bureau of Applied Social Research, Columbia University.
    n.d.   "A note on the application of multidimensional scaling to the problem of sociometric clique identification." Columbia University.

Allport, Gordon W., Philip E. Vernon, and Gardner Lindzey
    1960   *Study of Values*. Boston: Houghton Mifflin.

Almond, Gabriel, and James S. Coleman
    1960   *The Politics of the Developing Areas*. Princeton, N.J.: Princeton University Press.

Almond, Gabriel A., and Sidney Verba
    1963   *The Civil Culture: Political Attitudes and Democracy in Five Nations*. Princeton, N.J.: Princeton University Press.

Aron, Raymond
    1950   "Social structure and the ruling class." *British Journal of Sociology* 1: 1–17, 126–144.

Arrow, Kenneth J.
    1963   *Social Choice and Individual Values*. 2d ed. New York: John Wiley.

Bachrach, Peter, and Morton S. Baratz
    1962   "Two faces of power." *American Political Science Review* 56: 947–952.
    1963   "Decisions and non-decisions: An analytical framework." *American Political Science Review* 57: 632–642.

Bailey, Kenneth D.
    1974   "Cluster analysis." Pp. 59-128 in David R. Heise (Ed.), *Sociological Methodology 1975*. San Francisco: Jossey-Bass.

Bales, Robert F.
    1958   "Task roles and social roles in problem solving groups." Pp. 437–447 in Eleanor E. Maccoby, T. M. Newcomb, and E. L. Hartley, Eds., *Readings in Social Psychology*. 3d ed. New York: Holt.

Banfield, Edward C.
    1961   *Political Influence*. New York: Free Press.
    1965   *Big City Politics*. New York: Random House.

Banfield, Edward C., and James Q. Wilson
    1963   *City Politics*. New York: Vintage Books.

Barnard, Chester I.
    1938   *The Functions of the Executive*. Cambridge, Mass.: Harvard University Press.

Barnes, J. A.
    1954   "Class and committees in a Norwegian Island Parish." *Human Relations* 7: 39–58.
    1966   "Graph theory and social network: A technical comment on connectedness and connectivity." *Sociology* 3: 215-232.
    1969   "Networks and political process." In J. C. Mitchell (Ed.), *Social Networks in Urban Situations*.
    1972   "Social networks." Addison-Wesley Module in Anthropology.

Bavelas, A.
    1950   "Communication patterns in task-oriented groups." *Journal of Acoustical Society in America* 22: 725–730.

Berry, Brian J. L.
    1972   "Latent structure of the American urban system, with international comparisons." Pp. 11–60 in Brian J. L. Berry (Ed.), *City Classification Handbook: Methods and Applications*. New York: Wiley Interscience.

Beshers, James M., and Edward O. Laumann
  1967   "Social distance: A network approach." *American Sociological Review*
         32: 225–236.

Black, Max
  1961   *The Social Theories of Talcott Parsons.* Englewood Cliffs, N.J.: Prentice-
         Hall.

Blau, Peter M.
  1964   *Exchange and Power in Social Life.* New York: John Wiley.
  1974   "Parameters of social structure." *American Sociological Review* **39**: 615–
         635.
  1975   *Approaches to the Study of Social Structure.* New York: Free Press.

Blau, Peter M., and Otis Dudley Duncan
  1967   *The American Occupational Structure.* New York: John Wiley.

Boissevain, J., and J. Clyde Mitchell, Eds.
  1973   *Network Analysis: Studies in Human Interaction.* The Hague: Mouton.

Bonacich, Phillip
  1972a   "Technique for analyzing overlapping memberships." In Herbert L.
         Costner (Ed.), *Sociological Methodology 1972.* San Francisco: Jossey-
         Bass.
  1972b   "Factoring and weighting approaches to status scores and clique identifi-
         cation." *Journal of Mathematical Sociology* **2**: 113–20.

Bonjean, Charles M.
  1971   "The community as a research site and object of inquiry." Pp. 5–15 in
         Charles M. Bonjean, Terry N. Clark, and Robert L. Lineberry
         (Eds.), *Community Politics: A Behavioral Approach.* New York:
         Free Press.

Bonjean, Charles M., Terry N. Clark, and Robert L. Lineberry
  1971   *Community Politics: A Behavioral Approach.* New York: Free Press.

Boorman, S. A., R. L. Breiger, and P. Arabie
  1974   "An algorithm for blocking relational data, with applications to social
         network analysis and comparison with multidimensional scaling." Un-
         published paper. Institute for Mathematical Studies in the Social Sci-
         ences, Stanford University.

Borgatta, Edgar F., Arthur S. Couch, and Robert F. Bales
  1954   "Some findings relevant to the great man theory of leadership." *American
         Sociological Review* **19**: 755–759.

Bott, Elizabeth
  1957   *Family and Social Network: Roles, Norms and External Relationships
         in Ordinary Urban Families.* London: Tavistock Publications.

Brams, S.
  1966   "Transaction flows in the international system." *American Political
         Science Review* **60**: 880–898.
  1968   "Measuring the concentration of power in political systems." *American
         Political Science Review* **62**: 461–475.

Breiger, Ronald L.
  1974   "The duality of persons and groups." Social Forces **53**.

Buckley, Walter
  1967   *Sociology and Modern Systems Theory.* Englewood Cliffs, N.J.: Pren-
         tice-Hall.

Butler, David, and Donald Stokes
  1969   *Political Change in Britain.* London and New York: Macmillan and St.
         Martin's Press.

Campbell, Angus, Philip E. Converse, Warren E. Miller, and Donald E. Stokes
    1960   *The American Voter.* New York: John Wiley.
Carr-Saunders, A. M., and P. A. Wilson
    1944   "Professions." Pp. 476–480 in *Encyclopedia of the Social Sciences.* Vol. XXII. New York: Macmillan.
Cartwright, Dorwin
    1965   "Influence, leadership, control." Pp. 1–47 in James G. March (Ed.), *Handbook of Organizations.* Chicago: Rand McNally.
Centers, Richard
    1949   *The Psychology of Social Classes: A Study of Class Consciousness.* Princeton, N.J.: Princeton University Press.
Chapman, Gerald W.
    1967   *Edmund Burke: The Practical Imagination.* Cambridge, Mass.: Harvard University Press.
Clark, Terry N.
    1968a   *Community Structure and Decision-Making: Comparative Analyses.* San Francisco: Chandler.
    1968b   "Who governs, where, when and with what effects?" Pp. 15–23 in Terry N. Clark (Ed.), *Community Structure and Decision-Making: Comparative Analyses.* San Francisco: Chandler.
    1968c   "The concept of power." Pp. 45–81 in Terry N. Clark (Ed.), *Community Structure and Decision-Making: Comparative Analyses.* San Francisco: Chandler.
    1968d   "Community structure and decision-making." Pp. 91–126 in Terry N. Clark (Ed.), *Community Structure and Decision Making: Comparative Analyses.* San Francisco: Chandler.
    1968e   "Community structure, decision-making, budget expenditures, and urban renewal in 51 American communities." *American Sociological Review* 33: 576–593.
    1973   *Community Power and Policy Outputs: A Review of Urban Research.* Beverly Hills and London: Sage Publications.
Cnudde, Charles F., and Deane E. Neubauer
    1969   *Empirical Democratic Theory.* Chicago: Markham.
Cnudde, Charles F., and Donald J. McCrone
    1966   "The linkage between constituency attitudes and Congressional voting behavior: A causal model." *American Political Science Review* 60: 66–72.
Coleman, James S.
    1964   *Introduction to Mathematical Sociology.* New York: Free Press.
    1973   "Loss of power." *American Sociological Review* 38: 1–17.
Coleman, James S., Elihu Katz, and Herbert Manzel
    1966   *Medical Innovation: A Diffusion Study.* Indianapolis: Bobbs-Merrill.
Coleman, James S., and Duncan McRae, Jr.
    1960   "Electronic processing of sociometric data for groups up to 1,000 in size." *American Sociological Review* 25: 722–727.
Converse, Philip
    1964   "The nature of belief systems in mass publics." Pp. 206–261 in David E. Apter (Ed.), *Ideology and Discontent.* New York: Free Press.
Crane, Diana
    1969   "Social Structure in a group of scientists: A test of the 'invisible college' hypothesis." *American Sociological Review* 34: 335–352.

Craven, Paul, and Barry Wellman
    1973   "The network city." *Sociological Inquiry* 43 (3–4): 57–88.
Curtis, Richard
    1963   "Differential association and the stratification of the urban community." *Social Forces* 42: 68–77.
Cutler, Stephen J.
    1973   "Voluntary association membership and the theory of mass society." Pp. 133–59 in E. O. Laumann (Ed.), *Bonds of Pluralism. The Form and Substance of Urban Social Networks.* New York: Wiley Interscience.
Dahl, Robert A.
    1956   *A Preface to Democratic Theory.* Chicago: University of Chicago Press.
    1961   *Who Governs? Democracy and Power in an American City.* New Haven, Conn.: Yale University Press.
Dahrendorf, Ralf
    1959   *Class and Class Conflict in Industrial Society.* Stanford: Stanford University Press.
    1961   "Struktur und Funktion. Talcott Parsons und die Entwicklung der soziologischen Theorie." Pp. 49–84 in Ralf Dahrendorf (Ed.), *Gesellschaft und Freiheit. Zur soziologischen Analyse der Gegenwart.* München: R. Piper Verlag.
    1965   *Gesellschaft und Demokratie in Deutschland.* München: R. Piper.
    1967   *Society and Democracy in Germany.* New York: Doubleday.
    1968   "On the origin of inequality among men." *Essays in the Theory of Society.* Stanford: Stanford University Press.
D'Antonio, William V., and William H. Form
    1965   *Influentials in Two Border Cities: A Study in Community Decision Making.* Notre Dame: University of Notre Dame Press.
D'Antonio, William V., William H. Form, Charles P. Loomis, and Eugene C. Erickson
    1961   "Institutional and occupational representations in eleven community systems." *American Sociological Review* 26: 440–446.
Danzger, M. Herbert
    1964   "Community power structure: Problems and Continuities." *American Sociological Review* 29: 707–719.
Danzig, C. B.
    1960   "On the shortest route through a network." *Management Science* 6: 187–190.
Davis, Allison, Burleigh B. Gardner, and Mary R. Gardner
    1941   *Deep South: A Social Anthropological Study of Caste and Class.* Chicago: University of Chicago Press.
Davis, James A.
    1963   "Structural balance, mechanical solidarity and interpersonal relations." *American Journal of Sociology* 68: 444–462.
    1967   "Clustering and structural balance in graphs." *Human Relations* 20: 181–187.
    1970   "Clustering and hierarchy in interpersonal relation: Testing two graph theoretical models on 742 sociometrices." *American Sociological Review* 35: 843–851.
Davis, James A. and Samuel Leinhardt
    1967   "The structure of positive interpersonal relations in small groups." In J. Berger (Ed.), *Sociological Theories in Progress.* Boston: Houghton Mifflin.

Davis, Kingsley
  1948   *Human Society.* New York: Macmillan.
Davis, Kingsley, and Wilbert E. Moore
  1945   "Some principles of stratification." *American Sociological Review* **10**: 242–249.
Djilas, Milovan
  1957   *The New Class. An analysis of the Communist System.* New York: Praeger.
Dobzhansky, Theodosius
  1962   *Mankind Evolving.* New Haven, Conn.: Yale University Press.
Domhoff, G. William
  1967   *Who Rules America?* Englewood Cliffs, N. J.: Prentice-Hall.
Downes, Bryan T.
  1968   "Suburban differentiation and municipal policy choices: A comparative analysis of suburban political systems." Pp. 243–267 in Terry N. Clark, *Community Structure and Decision-Making: Comparative Analyses.* San Francisco: Chandler.
Duke, James T.
  1967   "Egalitarianism and future leaders in Jamaica." Pp. 115–139 in Wendell Bell (Ed.), *The Democratic Revolution in the West Indies.* Cambridge, Mass.: Schenkman Publishing.
Duncan, Otis Dudley
  1966   "Path analysis: Sociological examples." *American Journal of Sociology* **72**: 1–16.
Duncan, Otis Dudley, and J. W. Artis
  1951   "Some problems of stratification research." *Rural Sociology* **16**: 17–29.
Duncan, Otis Dudley, Ray P. Cuzzort, and Beverly Duncan
  1961   *Statistical Geography: Problems in Analyzing Areal Data.* Glencoe, Ill.: Free Press.
Duncan, Otis Dudley, and Beverly Duncan
  1955   "A methodological analysis of segregation indexes." *American Sociological Review* **20**: 210–217.
Duncan, Otis Dudley, David L. Featherman, and Beverly Duncan
  1972   *Socioeconomic Background and Achievement.* New York: Seminar Press.
Duncan, Otis Dudley, A. O. Haller, and A. Portes
  1968   "Peer influences on aspirations: A reinterpretation." *American Journal of Sociology* **74**: 119–137.
Durkheim, Emile
  1933   *The Division of Labor in Society.* (Translated by George Simpson.) Glencoe, Ill.: Free Press.
Dye, T. R.
  1966   "The local-cosmopolitan dimensions and the study of urban politics." *Social Forces* **41**: 239–246. Scale reported on pp. 397–399 in John P. Robinson, Jerrold G. Rusk, Kendra B. Head, *Measures of Political Attitudes.* Ann Arbor: Survey Research Center, 1968.
Ekeh, Peter P.
  1974   *Social Exchange Theory.* Cambridge: Harvard University Press.
Ellis, Robert A.
  1957   "Social stratification and social relations: An empirical test of the disjunctiveness of social classes." *American Sociological Review* **22**: 570–578.
Emerson, Richard
  1962   "Power-dependence relations." *American Sociological Review* **27**: 31–41.

Epstein, A. L.
    1969   "The network of urban social organization: Gossip, norms and social network." Pp. 77–127 in J. Clyde Mitchell (Ed.), *Social Networks in Urban Situations*. Manchester, Eng.: Manchester University Press.
Etzioni, Amitai
    1961   *A Comparative Analysis of Complex Organizations*. New York: Free Press.
Farace, V.
    1972   "Analysis of human communication networks in large social systems." Unpublished paper. Department of Communication, Michigan State University.
Fararo, T. J., and Morris H. Sunshine
    1964   *A Study of a Biased Friendship Net*. Syracuse University, Youth Development Center.
Festinger, Leon
    1949   "The analysis of sociograms using matrix algebra." *Human Relations* **2**: 153-158. [Reprinted in J. L. Moreno (Ed.), *The Sociometry Reader*. Glencoe: Free Press, 1960.]
Flament, Claude
    1963   *Applications of Graph Theory to Group Structure*. Englewood Cliffs, N.J.: Prentice-Hall.
Frank, Ove.
    1971   *Statistical Inference in Graphs*. Stockholm: FOA Repro.
Freeman, Linton C.
    1968   *Patterns of Local Community Leadership*. Indianapolis: Bobbs-Merrill.
Freeman, Linton C., and others
    1963   "Locating leaders in local communities: A comparison of some alternative approaches." *American Sociological Review* **28**: 791-793.
French, J. R. P., and B. Raven
    1959   "The bases of social power." Pp. 150–167 in D. Cartwright (Ed.), *Studies in Social Power*. Ann Arbor: University of Michigan Institute for Social Research.
Freyhold, Michaela von
    1971   *Autoritarismus und politische Apathie*. Frankfurt am Main: Europäische Verlagsanstalt.
Galbraith, John
    1952   *American Capitalism: The Concept of Countervailing Power*. Boston: Houghton Mifflin.
Gamson, William A.
    1966a   "Rancorous conflict in community politics." *American Sociological Review* **31**: 71–81.
    1966b   "Reputation and resources in community politics." *American Journal of Sociology* **72**: 121–131.
    1968   *Power and Discontent*. Homewood, Ill.: Dorsey Press.
Giddens, Anthony
    1973   *The Class Structure of the Advanced Societies*. New York: Harper Torchbooks.
Gilbert, Claire W.
    1968   "Community power and decision making: A quantitative examination of previous research." Pp. 139–156 in Terry N. Clark (Ed.), *Community Structure and Decision-Making: Comparative Analyses*. San Francisco: Chandler.

Glanzer, Murray, and Robert Glaser
  1959 "Techniques for the study of group structure and behavior: 1. Analysis of structure." *Psychological Bulletin* **56**: 317–332.
Gleason, Terry C.
  1969 "D.I.P. A Directed Graph Processor." Mimeo. Institute for Social Research, University of Michigan, Ann Arbor.
Goldberg, Arthur
  1966 "Discerning a causal pattern among data on voting behavior." *American Political Science Review* **60**: 913-922.
Goldberger, Arthur S.
  1970 "On Boudon's method of linear causal analysis." *American Sociological Review* **35**: 97–101.
Gouldner, Alvin W.
  1959 "Reciprocity and autonomy in functional theory." Pp. 241–270 in Llewellyn Gross (Ed.), *Symposium on Sociological Theory*. Evanston, Ill.: Row, Peterson.
  1970 *The Coming Crisis of Western Sociology*. New York: Basic Books.
Granovetter, Mark
  1973 "The strength of weak ties." *American Journal of Sociology* **78**: 1360–1380.
  1974 *Getting a Job: A Study of Contacts and Careers*. Cambridge, Mass.: Harvard University Press.
Guetzkow, Harold
  1965 "Communications in organizations." Pp. 534–537 in James G. March (Ed.), *Handbook of Organizations*. Chicago: Rand McNally.
Gurin, Gerald, Joseph Veroff, and Sheila Feld
  1960 *Americans View Their Mental Health*. New York: Basic Books.
Guttman, Louis
  1959 "Introduction to facet design and analysis." Pp. 130–132 in *Proceedings of the 15th International Congress of Psychology*. Brussels.
  1968 "A general nonmetric technique for finding the smallest coordinate space for a configuration of points." *Psychometrika* **33**: 469-506.
Habermas, Jürgen
  1973 *Legitimationsprobleme im Spätkapitalismus*. Frankfurt am Main: Suhrkamp.
Habermas, Jürgen, and Niklas Luhmann
  1971 *Theorie der Gesellschaft oder Sozialtechnologie*. Frankfurt am Main: Suhrkamp.
Hallinan, M.
  1974 "A structural model of sentiment relations." *American Journal of Sociology* **80**: 364–378.
Harary, F., and Harold Miller
  1970 "On the measure of connectedness in a social group." *General Systems* **15**: 67–69.
Harary, Frank, Robert L. Norman, and Dorwin Cartwright
  1965 *Structural Models: An Introduction to the Theory of Directed Graphs*. New York: John Wiley.
Hatt, Paul K.
  1950 "Occupation and stratification." *American Journal of Sociology* **55**: 533–543.
Hauser, Robert M.
  1970 "Educational stratification in the United States." Pp. 102–130 in Edward

O. Laumann (Ed.), *Social Stratification: Research and Theory for the 1970s.* Indianapolis: Bobbs-Merrill.

Hawley, Amos H.
1963 "Community power and urban renewal success." *American Journal of Sociology* **68**: 422–431.

Heider, F.
1958 *The Psychology of Interpersonal Relations.* New York: John Wiley.

Hirsch-Weber, Wolfgang
1969 *Politik als Interessenkonflikt.* Stuttgart: Enke.

Hodge, Robert W., and Paul M. Siegel
1968 "The measurement of social class." Pp. 316–325 in David L. Sills (Ed.), *International Encyclopedia of the Social Sciences.* Vol. 15.

Holland, Paul and Samuel Leinhardt
1970 "A method for detecting structure in sociometric data." *American Journal of Sociology* **76**: 492–513.
1971 "Transitivity in structural models of small groups." *Comparative Group Studies* **2**: 107–124.
1973 "The structural implications of measurement error in sociometry." *Journal of Mathematical Sociology* **3**: 85–111.
1974 "The statistical analysis of local structure in social networks." Working paper No. 44. National Bureau of Economic Research.

Homans, George C.
1950 *The Human Group.* New York: Harcourt.
1961 *Social Behavior: Its Elementary Forms.* New York: Harcourt.

Hook, Sidney
1943 *The Hero in History: A Study in Limitation and Possibility.* Boston: Beacon Press.

Hubbell, Charles H.
1965 "An input–output approach to clique identification." *Sociometry* **28**: 377–399.

Hunter, Floyd
1953 *Community Power Structure.* Durham, N.C.: University of North Carolina Press.

International Labor Office
1969 *International Standard Classification of Occupations.* Geneva, Switzerland.

Izard, C. E.
1960 "Personality similarity and friendship." *Journal of Abnormal and Social Psychology* **61**: 47–51.

Jackson, Elton F., and Richard F. Curtis
1972 "Effects of vertical mobility and status inconsistency: a body of negative evidence." *American Sociological Review* **37**: 701–713.

Johnston, J.
1972 *Econometric Methods.* New York: McGraw-Hill.

Johnson, Stephen C.
1967 "Hierarchical clustering schemes." *Psychometrika* **32**: 241–254.

Kaase, Max
1971 "Demokratische Einstellungen in der Bundesrepublik Deutschland." Pp. 119–326 in Rudolf Wildenmann (Ed.), *Sozialwissenschaftliches Jahrbuch für Politik.* Vol. 2. München und Wien: Olzog.
1972 "Political ideology, dissatisfaction and protest." Unpublished manuscript. Institut für Sozialwissenschaften an der Universität Mannheim.

Kadushin, Charles
   1966   "The friends and supporters of psychotherapy: On social circles in urban life." *American Sociological Review* 31: 786–802.
   1968   "Power, influence, and social circles: A new methodology for studying opinion makers." *American Sociological Review* 33: 685–689.
   1970   "Sociometry and macro-sociology." Paper presented at the 1970 meetings of the International Sociological Association, Varna, Bulgaria.

Kadushin, Charles, and R. Rose
   1974   "Recent developments in comparative political sociology: Determinants of electorial behavior and the structure of elite networks." In N. S. Archer (Ed.), *Current Research in Sociology.* The Hague: Mouton.

Kapferer, B.
   1969   "Norms and the manipulation of relationships in a work context." Pp. 181–244 in J. Clyde Mitchell (Ed.), *Social Networks in Urban Situations.* Manchester, Eng.: Manchester University Press.

Katz, Daniel, and Robert L. Kahn
   1966   *The Social Psychology of Organizations.* New York: John Wiley.

Kaufman, Herbert, and Victor Jones
   1954   "The mystery of power." *Public Administrative Review* 14: 205–212.

Keller, Suzanne
   1963   *Beyond the Ruling Class: Strategic Elites in Modern Society.* New York: Random House.

King, Morton B., Jr.
   1961   "Socioeconomic status and sociometric choice." *Social Forces* 39: 199–206.

Klingemann, Hans D., and Franz Urban Pappi
   1970   "Die Wählerbewegungen bei der Bundestagswahl am 28. September 1969." *Politische Vierteljahresschrift* 11: 111–138.

Klovdahl, Alden Stephen
   1972   "Structure and performance of service systems." Unpublished Ph.D. Dissertation. University of Michigan.

Kluckhohn, Clyde
   1951   "Values and value orientations in the theory of action." In Talcott Parsons and Edward A. Shils (Eds.), *Toward a General Theory of Action.* Cambridge, Mass.: Harvard University Press.
   1962   "Values and value-orientations in the theory of action: An exploration in definition and classification." Pp. 338–433 in Talcott Parsons and Edward A. Shils (Eds.), *Toward a General Theory of Action.* Cambridge, Mass.: Harvard University Press.

Kluckhohn, Florence R., and Fred L. Strodtbeck
   1961   *Variations in Value Orientations.* Evanston, Ill., and Elmsford, N.Y.: Row, Peterson.

Kluczka, Georg
   1970   *Nordrhein-Westfalen in seiner Gliederung nach zentralörtlichen Bereichen.* Düsseldorf: Schriftenreihe des Ministerprasidenten des Landes Nordrhein-Westfalen Vol. 27.

Knoke, David
   1972   "A causal model for the political party preferences of American men." *American Sociological Review* 37: 679–689.

Kohn, Melvin L.
   1969   *Class and Conformity: A Study in Values.* Homewood, Ill.: Dorsey Press.

Kornhauser, William
  1959   *The Politics of Mass Society.* New York: Free Press.
Kruskal, J. B.
  1964   "Multidimensional scaling by optimizing goodness of fit to a nonmetric hypothesis." *Psychometrika* **29**: 1–27.
Land, K. C.
  1969   "Principles of path analysis." Pp. 3–37 in Edgar F. Borgatta (Ed.), *Sociological Methodology 1969.* San Francisco: Jossey-Bass.
Laumann, Edward O.
  1966   *Prestige and Association in an Urban Community.* Indianapolis: Bobbs-Merrill.
  1969   "The social structure of religious and ethnoreligious groups in a metropolitan community." *American Sociological Review* **34**: 182–197.
  1973   *Bonds of Pluralism. The Form and Substance of Urban Social Networks.* New York: Wiley Interscience.
Laumann, Edward O., and James S. House
  1970   "Living room styles and social attributes: The patterning of material artifacts in a modern urban community." Pp. 189–203 in Edward O. Laumann, Paul Siegel, and Robert W. Hodge (Eds.), *The Logic of Social Hierarchies.* Chicago: Markham.
Laumann, Edward O., and Franz U. Pappi
  1973   "New directions in the study of community elites." *American Sociological Review* **38**: 212–230.
Laumann, Edward O., and David R. Segal
  1971   "Status inconsistency and ethno-religious group membership as determinants of social participation and political attitudes." *American Journal of Sociology* **77**: 36–61.
Laumann, Edward O., and Richard Senter
  1976   "Subjective social distance, occupational stratification, and forms of status and class consciousness: A cross national replication and extension." *American Journal of Sociology* **82**.
Laumann, Edward O., Lois Verbrugge, and Franz U. Pappi
  1974   "A causal modelling approach to the study of a community elite's influence structure." *American Sociological Review* **39**: 162–174.
Lawrence, Paul, and Jay Lorsch
  1967   *Organization and Environment.* Boston: Graduate School of Business Administration, Harvard University.
Lazarsfeld, Paul F., Bernard Berelson, and Hazel Gaudet
  1944   *The People's Choice.* New York: Columbia University Press.
Lazarsfeld, Paul F., and Robert K. Merton
  1954   "Friendship as a social process: A substantive and methodological analysis." Pp. 18–66 in M. Berger, T. Abel, and C. Page (Eds.), *Freedom and Control in Modern Society.* Princeton, N.J.: Van Nostrand-Reinhold.
Lenski, Gerhard
  1963   *The Religious Factor.* Garden City, N.Y.: Doubleday (Anchor Books).
  1966   *Power and Privilege: A Theory of Social Stratification.* New York: McGraw-Hill.
Levine, J. H.
  1972   "The sphere of influence." *American Sociological Review* **37**: 14–27.
Levinson, D., and P. Huffman
  1955   "Traditional family ideology and its relation to personality." *Journal of Personality* **23**: 251–273. Pp. 295–300 in John P. Robinson and Philip H.

Shaver (Eds.), *Measures of Social Psychological Attitudes.* Ann Arbor: Survey Research Center, 1969.

Levi-Strauss, Claude
1963   "Social structure," "Postscript to Chapter XV." Pp. 277–345 in *Structural Anthropology.* (Translated from the French by Claire Jacobson and Brooke Grundfest Schoepf.) New York: Basic Books.

Lieberson, Stanley, and James F. O'Connor
1972   "Leadership and organizational performance: A study of large corporations." *American Sociological Review* **37**: 117–130.

Lijphart, Arend
1968   *The Politics of Accommodation: Pluralism and Democracy in the Netherlands.* Berkeley, Cal.: University of California Press.

Lingoes, James C.
1965a   "An IBM 7090 program for Guttman-Lingoes smallest space analysis—I." *Behavioral Science* **10**: 183–184.
1965b   "An IBM 7090 program for Guttman-Lingoes smallest space analysis—II." *Behavioral Science* **10**: 487.
1966   "An IBM 7090 program for Guttman-Lingoes multidimensional scalogram analysis—I." *Behavioral Science* **11**: 76–78.
1967   "An IBM 7090 program for Guttman-Lingoes multidimensional scalogram analysis—II." *Behavioral Science* **12**: 268–270.
1968   "An IBM 7090 program for Guttman-Lingoes multidimensional scalogram analysis—III." *Behavioral Science* **13**: 512–513.
1969   "A general nonparametric model for representing objects and attributes in a joint metric space." In J. C. Gardin (Ed.), *Les compte-rendus de colloque international sur l'emploi des calculateurs en archeologie: Problemes semilogiques et mathematiques.* Marseilles: Centre National de la Recherche Scientifique.
1972   "A survey of the Guttman-Lingoes nonmetric series." Pp. 52–71 In R. N. Shepard, A. K. Romney, and S. B. Nerlove (Eds.), *Multidimensional Scaling: Theory and Applications in the Behavioral Sciences.* New York: Seminar Press.
1973   *The Guttman-Lingoes Nonmetric Program Series.* Ann Arbor: Mathesis Press.

Lindzey, Gardner, and D. Byrne
1968   "Measurement of social choice and interpersonal attractiveness." Pp. 452–525 in G. Lindzey and E. Aronson (Eds.), *The Handbook of Social Psychology.* Vol. II. Reading, Mass.: Addison-Wesley.

Lipset, Seymour M.
1959   "Some social requisites of democracy: Economic development and political legitimacy." *American Political Science Review* **53**: 69–105.
1960   *Political Man.* New York: Doubleday.
1963a   *The First New Nation.* New York: Basic Books.
1963b   "The sources of the 'Radical Right'," Three decades of the Radical Right: Coughlinites, McCarthyites, and Birchers." Pp. 259–377 in Daniel Bell (Ed.), *The Radical Right.* Garden City, N.Y.: Doubleday.

Lipset, Seymour M., Martin A. Trow, and James S. Coleman
1956   *Union Democracy.* New York: Free Press of Glencoe.

Litwak, E., and L. F. Hylton
1962   "Interorganizational analysis: A hypothesis on co-ordinating agencies." *Administrative Science Quarterly* **63**: 395–415.

Loomis, Charles, and J. Allen Beegle
 1950   *Rural Social Systems.* Englewood Cliffs, N.J.: Prentice-Hall.
Lorraine, Francois, and Harrison C. White
 1971   "Structural equivalence of individuals in social networks." *Journal of Mathematical Sociology* **1**: 49–80.
Luce, Duncan R.
 1950   "Connectivity and generalized cliques in sociometric group structure." *Psychometrika* **15**: 169–190.
Luce, Duncan R., and Albert D. Perry
 1949   "A method of matrix analysis of group structure." *Psychometrika* **14**: 94–116.
Lynd, Robert S., and Helen Merrell Lynd
 1937   *Middletown in Transition: A Study of Cultural Conflicts.* New York: Harcourt.
McClosky, Herbert
 1964   "Consensus and ideology in American politics." *American Political Science Review* **58**: 361–382.
McClosky, Herbert, and John H. Schaar
 1965   "Psychological dimensions of anomy." *American Sociological Review* **30**: 14–40.
McFarland, A. S.
 1969   *Power and Leadership in Pluralistic Systems.* Stanford: Stanford University Press.
McFarland, David, and Daniel Brown
 1973   "Social distance as a metric: A systematic introduction to smallest space analysis." Pp. 213–253 in E. O. Laumann (Ed.), *Bonds of Pluralism. The Form and Substance of Urban Social Networks.* New York: John Wiley.
Mace, Myles L.
 1971   *Directors: Myth and Reality.* Boston: Division of Research, Graduate School of Business Administration, Harvard University.
March, James G.
 1955   "An introduction to the theory and measurement of influence." *American Political Science Review* **49**: 431–451.
 1965   *Handbook of Organizations.* Chicago: Rand McNally.
 1966   "The power of power." Pp. 39–70 in David Easton (Ed.), *Varieties of Political Theory.* Englewood Cliffs, N.J.: Prentice-Hall.
March, James G., and Herbert A. Simon
 1958   *Organizations.* New York: Wiley Interscience.
Mason, R., and A. N. Halter
 1971   "The application of a system of simultaneous equations to an innovation diffusion model." Pp. 200–218 in Hubert M. Blalock, Jr. (Ed.), *Causal Models in the Social Sciences.* Chicago: Aldine.
Mayhew, Bruce H., Jr., L. N. Gray, and J. T. Richardson
 1969   "Behavioral measurement of operating power structures: Characteristics of asymmetrical interaction." *Sociometry* **32**: 474–489.
Mayhew, Leon
 1971   *Society. Institutions and Activity.* Glenview, Ill.: Scott, Foresman.
Mayntz, Renate
 1958   *Soziale Schichtung und sozialer Wandel in einer Industriegemeinde.* Stuttgart: Enke.

Merelman, Richard M.
    1968   "On the neo-elitist critique of community power." *American Political Science Review* **62**: 451–460.
Merton, Robert K.
    1957   "Manifest and latent functions." Pp. 19–84 in *Social Theory and Social Structure*. Revised and enlarged edition. Glencoe, Ill.: Free Press.
Michels, Robert
    1925   *Zur Soziologie des Parteiwessens in der modernen Demokratie*. Stuttgart: Alfred Kroner Verlag.
    1959   *Political Parties. A Sociological Study of the Oligarchical Tendencies of Modern Democracy*. (Translated by Eden and Cedar Paul.) New York: Dover Publications.
Milgram, Stanley
    1967   "The small-world problem." *Psychology Today* **1** (May): 62–67.
Miller, Daniel R., and Guy E. Swanson
    1958   *The Changing American Parent*. New York: John Wiley.
    1960   *Inner Conflict and Defense*. New York: Henry Holt.
Miller, Delbert C.
    1970   *International Community Power Structures: Comparative Studies in Four World Cities*. Bloomington: Indiana University Press.
Miller, Warren E., and Donald E. Stokes
    1961   "Constituency influence in Congress." *American Political Science Review* **57**: 45–56.
Mills, C. Wright
    1959   *The Power Elite*. New York: Oxford University Press.
Mitchell, J. Clyde, Ed.
    1969a   *Social Networks in Urban Situations*. Manchester, Eng.: Manchester University Press.
    1969b   "The concept and use of social networks." In J. C. Mitchell (Ed.), *Social Networks in Urban Situations*. Manchester, Eng.: Manchester University Press.
    1969c   "Bibliography." In J. C. Mitchell (Ed.), *Social Networks in Urban Situations*. Manchester, Eng.: Manchester University Press.
    1969d   "Norms, networks and institutions." Paper presented to Seminar on Networks Approaches, September 22–26, University of Leiden.
    1974   "Social networks." *Annual Review of Anthropology* **3**: 279-299.
Moreno, Jacob L.
    1953   *Who Shall Survive? Foundations of Sociometry, Group Psychotherapy and Sociodrama*. New York: Beacon House.
Morris, Richard T., and Raymond J. Murphy
    1959   "The situs dimension in occupational structure." *American Sociological Review* **24**: 231–239.
Mortimer, Jeylan
    1972   "Family background and college influences upon occupational value orientations and the career decision." Unpublished Ph.D. dissertation. University of Michigan.
Nadel, S. F.
    1957   *The Theory of Social Structure*. London: Cohen and West.
Narr, Wolf-Dieter, and Frieder Naschold
    1971   *Theorie der Demokratie*. Stuttgart: Kohlhammer.

Nellessen-Schumacher, Traute
1969   *Sozialstruktur und Ausbildung der deutschen Katholiken.* Weinheim:
       Julius Beltz Verlag.
Neuendorff, Hartmut
1973   *Der Begriff des Interesses: Eine Studie zu den Gesellschaftstheorien von
       Hobbes, Smith und Marx.* Frankfurt am Main: Suhrkamp.
Newcomb, Theodore
1961   *The Acquaintance Process.* New York: Holt.
Nuttall, Ronald L., Erwin Scheuch, and Chad Gordon
1968   "The structure of influence." Pp. 349–380 in T. N. Clark (Ed.), *Com-
       munity Structure and Decision-Making: Comparative Analyses.* San
       Francisco: Chandler.
O'Connor, Len
1975   *Clout.* Chicago: Regnery.
Offe, Claus
1972   *Strukturprobleme des kapitalistischen Staates.* Frankfurt am Main:
       Suhrkamp.
Olsen, Marvin E., and Judy Corder Tully
1972   "Socioeconomic–ethnic status inconsistency and preference for political
       change." *American Sociological Review* 37: 560–574.
Olson, Mancur
1965   *The Logic of Collective Action.* Cambridge: Harvard University Press.
Ossowski, Stanislaw
1963   *Class Structure in the Social Consciousness.* London: Routledge and
       Kegan Paul.
Pappi, Franz U.
1973a "Parteiensystem und Sozialstruktur in der Bundesrepublik." *Politische
       Vierteljahresschrift* 14: 191–213.
1973b "Sozialstruktur und soziale Schichtung in einer Kleinstadt mit hetero-
       gener Bevölkerung." *Kolner Zeitschrift fur Soziologie und Sozialpsychol-
       ogie* 25: 23–74.
Pappi, Franz U.
1974   "Soziale Schichten als Interaktionsgruppen. Zur Messung eines deskrip-
       tiven Schichtbegriffs." In M. Rainer Lepsius (Ed.), Verhandlungen des
       17. Deutschen Soziologentages. Stuttgart: Enke. In press.
Pappi, Franz U., and Edward O. Laumann
1974   "Gesellschaftliche Wertorientierungen und politisches Verhalten." *Zeit-
       schrift fur Soziologie* 3: 157–188.
Pappi, Franz U., and Edward O. Laumann
1975   "Erwiderung auf Bertrams Kritik von 'Gesellschaftliche Wertorienter-
       ungen und politisches Verhalten.'" *Zeitschrift für Soziologie* 74.
Parsons, Talcott
1937   *The Structure of Social Action.* New York: Free Press of Glencoe.
1951   *The Social System.* Glencoe, Ill.: Free Press.
1956   "Suggestions for a sociological approach to the theory of organizations."
       Administrative Science Quarterly 1: 63–85, 225–239.
1960   *Structure and Process in Modern Societies.* New York: Free Press.
1961   "An outline of the social system." Pp. 30–79 in Talcott Parsons, Edward
       Shils, Kasper D. Naegele, and Jesse R. Pitts (Eds.), *Theories of Society.*
       Vol. I. New York: Free Press.

1966   *Societies: Evolutionary and Comparative Perspectives.* Englewood Cliffs, N.J.: Prentice-Hall.

1968a   "On the concept of value commitments." *Sociological Inquiry* **38**: 135–160.

1968b   "Professions." Pp. 536–547 in *International Encyclopedia of the Social Sciences.* Vol. 12. New York: Macmillan and the Free Press.

1969   "On the concept of influence," "On the concept of political power," and "On the concept of value commitments." In Talcott Parsons, *Politics and Social Structure.* New York: Free Press.

Parsons, Talcott, and Edward A. Shils
1951   *Toward a General Theory of Action.* Cambridge, Mass.: Harvard University Press.

Parsons, Talcott, Edward Shils, Kaspar D. Naegele, and Jesse R. Pitts
1961   *Theories of Society: Foundations of Modern Sociological Theory.* New York: Free Press.

Parsons, Talcott, and Neil J. Smelser
1956   *Economy and Society.* London: Routledge and Kegan Paul.

Parthasarathy, K.
1964   "Enumeration of paths in digraphs." *Psychometrika* **29**: 153–165.

Perrow, Charles
1970   *Organizational Analysis: A Sociological View.* Belmont, California: Wadsworth.

Perrucci, Robert, and Marc Pilisuk
1970   "Leaders and ruling elites: The interorganizational bases of community power." *American Sociological Review* **35**: 1040–1057.

Polsby, Nelson W.
1963   *Community Power and Political Theory.* New Haven: Yale University Press.

Presthus, Robert
1964   *Men at the Top: A Study in Community Power.* New York: Oxford University Press.

Proctor, C. H.
1969   "Analyzing pair data and point data on social relationships, attitudes and background characteristics of Costa Rican Census Bureau employees." Social Statistics Section, Proceedings of the American Statistical Association, 457–465.

Rae, Douglas W., and Michael Taylor
1970   *The Analysis of Political Cleavages.* New Haven and London: Yale University Press.

Rapoport, Anatol, and William Horvath
1961   "A study of a large sociogram." *Behavioral Science* **6**: 279–291.

Reiss, Albert J., Jr.
1961   *Occupations and Social Status.* New York: Free Press of Glencoe.

Reuband, Karl Heinz
1974   "Differentielle Assoziation und sociale Schichtung." Doctoral Dissertation. Universität Hamburg.

Richards, W.
1974   "Network analyses in large communication systems: Techniques and methods—tools." Unpublished paper. Institute for Communication Research, Stanford University.

Riecken, Henry W., and George C. Homans
    1954   "Psychological aspects of social structure." Pp. 786–832 in G. Lindzey (Ed.), *Handbook of Social Psychology.* Vol. II. Reading, Mass.: Addison-Wesley.

Robinson, John P.
    1969   "Occupational norms and differences in job satisfaction: a summary of survey research evidence." S. 25–78 in John P. Robinson, Robert Athanasiou, Kendra B. Head, *Measures of Occupational Attitudes and Occupational Characteristics.* Ann Arbor: Survey Research Center.

Robinson, John P., Jerrold G. Rusk, Kendra B. Head, Eds.
    1968   *Measures of Political Attitudes.* Ann Arbor: Survey Research Center.

Rogers, Mary F.
    1974   "Instrumental and infra-resources: The bases of power." *American Journal of Sociology* **79**: 1418–1433.

Roghmann, Klaus
    1966   *Dogmatismus und Autoritarismus.* Meisenheim am Glan: Anton Hain.

Rokeach, Milton
    1960   *The Open and the Closed Mind.* New York: Basic Books.
    1969   *Beliefs, Attitudes, and Values: A Theory of Organization and Change.* San Francisco: Jossey-Bass.
    1971   "The measurement of values and value systems." Pp. 21–39 in Gilbert Abcarian and John W. Soule (Eds.), *Social Psychology and Political Behavior.* Columbus, O.: Charles E. Merrill.
    1973   *The Nature of Human Values.* New York: Free Press.

Rose, Arnold M.
    1967   *The Power Structure: Political Process in American Society.* London: Oxford University Press.

Rosen, Richard, and Peter Abrams
    1970   "CHAIN: A sociometric linkage program." New York: Bureau of Applied Social Research, Columbia University.

Rosenthal, Donald B., and Robert L. Crain
    1966   "Structure and values in local political systems: The case of fluoridation decisions." *Journal of Politics* **28**: 169–196.

Roskam, E., and J. C. Lingoes
    1970   "MINISSA-I: A FORTRAN IV (G) program for the smallest space analysis of square symmetric matrices." *Behavioral Science* **15**: 204–220.
    1971   "A mathematical and empirical study of two multidimensional scaling algorithms." *Michigan Mathematical Psychology Program* **1**: 1–169.

Rossi, Peter H.
    1960   "Power and community structure." *Midwest Journal of Political Science* **4**: 390–401.

Rueschemeyer, Dietrich
    1973   *Lawyers and Their Society: A Comparative Study of the Legal Profession in Germany and in the United States.* Cambridge: Harvard University Press.

Russett, Bruce M.
    1968   "Probabilism and the number of units affected: Measuring influence concentration." *American Political Science Review* **62**: 461–475.

Schelling, Thomas
    1956   "An essay on bargaining." *American Economics Review,* Pp. 281–306.

1960   *The Strategy of Conflict.* Cambridge: Harvard University Press.
Scheuch, Erwin K.
1966   "Cross-national comparisons using aggregate data: Some substantive and methodological problems." Pp. 131–167 in Richard L. Merritt and Stein Rokkan (Eds.), *Comparing Nations: The Use of Aggregate Data in Cross-National Research.* New Haven, Conn.: Yale University Press.
Scott, William A.
1968   "Attitude measurement." Pp. 204–273 in Gardner Lindzey and Elliot Aronson (Eds.), *The Handbook of Social Psychology.* Vol. 2. Reading, Mass.: Addison-Wesley.
Sears, David O.
1969   "Political behavior." Pp. 315–458 in Gardner Lindzey and Elliot Aronson (Eds.), *The Handbook of Sociol Psychology.* Vol. 5. Reading, Mass.: Addison-Wesley.
Seeman, Melvin
1960   *Social Status and Leadership: The Case of the School Executive.* Columbus, O.: Bureau of Educational Research and Service, Ohio State University.
Segal, David R., and Thomas S. Smith
1970   "Congressional responsibility and the organization of constituency attitudes." *Social Science Quarterly* 51: 743–749.
Sheingold, Carl A.
1973   "Social networks and voting: The resurrection of a research agenda." *American Sociological Review* 38: 712–720.
Shepard, Roger N., A. Kimball Romney, and Sara Beth Nerlove
1972   *Multidimensional Scaling. Theory and Applications in the Behavioral Sciences.* Vol. 1. New York: Seminar Press.
Siegel, Paul M.
1971   *Prestige and the American Occupational Structure.* Unpublished doctoral dissertation. University of Chicago.
Siegel, Paul M., and Robert W. Hodge
1968   "A causal approach to the study of measurement error." Pp. 28–59 in Hubert M. Blalock, Jr., and Ann B. Blalock (Eds.), *Methodology in Social Research.* New York: McGraw-Hill.
Simmel, Georg
1950   *The Sociology of Georg Simmel.* (Edited by Kurt Wolff.) Glencoe, Ill.: Free Press.
Spilerman, Seymour
1966   "Structural analysis and the generation of sociograms." *Behavioral Science* 11: 786–797.
Stewart, Douglas, and William Love
1968   "A general canonical correlation index." *Psychological Bulletin* 70: 160–163.
Stinchcombe, Arthur L.
1968   *Constructing Social Theories.* New York: Harcourt.
Stouffer, Samuel A.
1955   *Communism, Conformity, and Civil Liberties.* New York: Doubleday.
Suttles, Gerald D.
1972   *The Social Construction of Communities.* Chicago: University of Chicago Press.

Sztompka, Piotr
    1974   *System and Function: Toward a Theory of Society.* New York: Academic Press.
Tatsuoka, Maurice M.
    1971   *Multivariate Analysis: Techniques for Educational and Psychological Research.* New York: John Wiley.
Theil, Henri
    1970   "Social mobility and social distance: A Markov chain approach." Chapter 5 in *Statistical Decomposition Analysis in the Social and Administrative Sciences.* University of Chicago, Department of Economics, Graduate School of Business.
Thompson, J. D.
    1967   *Organizations in Action.* New York: McGraw-Hill.
Travers, Jeffrey, and Stanley Milgrim
    1969   "An experimental study of the small-world problem." *Sociometry* **32**: 425–443.
Treiman, Donald J.
    in press   *Occupational Prestige in Comparative Perspective.* New York: Academic Press.
Turk, Herman
    1970   "Interorganizational networks in urban society: Initial perspectives and comparative research." *American Sociological Review* **35**: 1–18.
    1973   *Interorganizational Activation in Urban Communities. Deductions from the Concept of System.* ASA Rose Monograph Series. Washington, D.C.: American Sociological Association.
Verba, Sidney, and Norman H. Nie
    1972   *Participation in America: Political Democracy and Social Equality.* New York: Harper and Row.
Verbrugge, Lois Marie
    1974   "Adult friendship contact: Time constraints and status-homogeneity effects, Detroit and Jülich, West Germany." Unpublished doctoral dissertation. University of Michigan.
Vidich, Arthur J., and Joseph Bensman
    1960   *Small Town in Mass Society.* Garden City, N.Y.: Doubleday.
Walton, John
    1966a   "Substance and artifact: The current status on research of community power structure." *American Journal of Sociology* **71**: 403–308.
    1966b   "Discipline, method and community power: A note on the sociology of knowledge." *American Sociological Review* **31**: 684–689.
    1970   "A systematic survey of community power research." Pp. 443–464 in Michael Aiken and Paul Mott (Eds.), *The Structure of Community Power.* New York: Random House.
Warner, W. Lloyd, *et al.*
    1960   *Social Class in America.* New York: Harper Torchbooks.
    1963   *Yankee City.* One volume, abridged ed. New Haven: Yale University Press.
Weber, Max
    1922   Grundriss der Sozialokonomie. III. *Abteilung. Wirtschaft und Gesellschaft.*Tubingen: Verlag Von J. C. B. Mohr (Paul Siebeck).
    1947   *The Theory of Social and Economic Organization* (Translated by

A. M. Henderson and T. Parsons; edited by T. Parsons. New York: Free Press of Glencoe.

1953 "Class, status, and power." Pp. 63–75 in Reinhard Bendix and Seymour M. Lipset (Eds.), *Class Status, and Power*. Glencoe, Ill.: Free Press.

Weiss, Robert S., and Eugene Jacobson

1955 "A method for the analysis of the structure of complex organizations." *American Sociological Review* **28**: 661–668. [Reprinted in A. Etzioni, *Complex Organizations: A Sociological Reader*, 1961.]

Wellman, Barry, and Marilyn Whitaker

1971 "Community–network–communication, An annotated bibliography." Center for Urban and Community Studies, University of Toronto.

White, Harrison C.

1970 *Chains of Opportunity: System Models of Mobility in Organizations.* Cambridge, Mass.: Harvard University Press.

White, Harrison C., and Ronald L. Breiger

1974 "Multiple networks in small populations: I. Block Models." Unpublished manuscript. Department of Sociology, Harvard University.

White, Harrison C., Ronald L. Breiger, and Scott A. Boorman

in press "Multiple networks in small populations—I. Blockmodels." *American Journal of Sociology.*

in press "Multiple networks in small populations—II. Equations." *American Journal of Sociology.*

Wolfe, Alain S.

1970 "On structural comparisons of networks." *Canadian Review of Sociology and Anthropology* **7**: 226–244.

Wolfinger, Raymond E.

1960 "Reputation and reality in the study of 'community power'." *American Sociological Review* **25**: 636–644.

1971 "Nondecisions and the study of local politics." *American Political Science Review* **65**: 1063–1080.

Wonnacott, R. J., and T. H. Wonnacott

1970 *Econometrics.* New York: John Wiley.

Wright, D., and Mary S. Evitts

1961 "Direct factor analysis in sociometry." *Sociometry* **24**: 82–98.

Wrong, Dennis

1961 "The oversocialized conception of man in modern sociology." *American Sociological Review* **26**: 183–193.

Zeitlin, M.

1974 "Corporate ownership and control: The large corporation and the capitalist class." *American Journal of Sociology* **70**: 1073–1119.

Ziegler, Rolf

1968 *Komunikationsstruktur und Leistung sozialer Systeme.* Kölner Beiträge zur Sozialforschung und Angewandten Soziologie. Vol. 6. Meisenheim am Glan, West Germany: Verlag Anton Hain.

1973 "Typologien und Klassifikationen." Pp. 11–47 in Günter Albrecht, Hansjürgen Daheim, and Fritz Sack (Eds.), *Soziologie*. Festschrift für Rene König zum 65. Geburtstag. Opladen: Westdeutscher Verlag.

Author Index

Subject Index

QUANTITATIVE STUDIES IN SOCIAL RELATIONS

Consulting Editor: Peter H. Rossi

UNIVERSITY OF MASSACHUSETTS
AMHERST, MASSACHUSETTS